COND[...] TO

The Plight of the Unwanted Child

For Ms. Shirley Lukka
with best wishes

Waldo Zimmerman

Nov, 27, 1981

WALDO ZIMMERMANN

ISBN 0-9605680-1-8
Library of Congress Catalog Number 81-52472

Dedicated to America's liberated Catholics and to
millions of other compassionate Americans who want
to reduce the need for abortion.

No Compassion, Please!

President Reagan, Senators Helms and East, Congressman Hyde and similar easy-bleeders are paranoid about "protecting the fetus," but once the babies are born their compassion seems to evaporate and they show little or no concern for the children whose lives they have saved. Where were these rabid anti-abortionists when the United Nations was trying to stop greedy, multi-national corporations from forcing their feeding formulas on destitute mothers of the Third World? By pressuring them to forego natural, wholesome breast-feeding these jackals not only intensify the stark poverty of their victims but endanger the lives of their children as well, fully aware that lack of pure water and refrigeration make use of their formulas dangerous in such localities. Backed by the "compassionate" Reagan and his cohorts, the United States was the only country in the world to stand up for the "right" of these ruthless corporations to continue this lethal practice.

CONTENTS

Foreword vii

PART ONE

Introduction 1

  1. The Strange Case of Dr. Jekyll and Congressman Hyde 7

  2. The Supreme Court Turns Back the Clock............................23

  3. The Hierarchy's "Secret Weapon".......................................28

  4. Contraception: Logical Alternative to Abortion..................40

  5. Weep for the Unwanted Child—At Birth!............................58

  6. Abortion as the Last Resort...68

  7. Anything But the Truth..87

PART TWO

  8. Liberated Women vs. Male Chauvinist Prigs....................103

  9. Pope Paul's Flight From Reality.......................................116

  10. Revolt of the Angels...124

  11. An Orchid for President Kennedy....................................132

PART THREE

  12. When Is a "Myth" not a Myth?...151

  13. Worldwide Need for Population Control...........................157

  14. We Are All in the Same Boat...172

  15. "We Breed—You Feed!"..186

Appendix 204

References 207

Index 221

v

Publisher's Note
regarding
The Global 2000 Report

In his Environmental Message to Congress on May 23, 1977, President Carter directed the Council on Environmental Quality and the Department of State, working with other fedéral agencies, to study the "probable changes in world population, natural resources, and environment through the end of the century."

The results of this three-year study, entitled *The Global 2000 Report,* were announced just as *Condemned To Live* was going to press. Obviously we, as publishers, were somewhat disturbed at first, wondering if this extensive study by the Council of Environmental Quality, the State Department and eleven federal agencies, with all the federal and state governments' vast reservoir of information at their disposal, might show some variations or discrepancies that would challenge the author's monumental documentation. A careful study of *The Global 2000 Report* proved that our fears were groundless.

Nothing could show the extent and soundness of the author's research more conclusively than this federal report. Virtually all the facts, figures and references cited by the author in this book tally with those of the three-year federal survey, as do most of the observations and recommendations for solving, at least to some extent, what is unquestionably the most serious problem ever to confront the human race.

Further comparisons of the author's research and conclusions with this Global Study would lead us too far afield. For those who wish to make their own comparisons, the *Global 2000 Report* is now available in most public libraries, or may be purchased from the Government Printing Office, Washington, D. C.

FOREWORD

In the 1977 Congressional debate over the Hyde Amendment to ban Medicaid funding of abortions for indigent women, Massachusett's Senator Edward Brooke said that in his eleven years in Congress, he had never encountered a more divisive issue.

As everyone knows, the controversy over abortion has polarized not only members of Congress and religious denominations, but the entire nation. It is an ethical issue, an emotional issue, a religious issue. It is doubtful that any conflict in our nation's history—certainly none since Vietnam—has enflamed the passions of all persuasions to such a degree. In today's highly charged atmosphere it is hard for anyone—opponent or advocate—to maintain an objective position. At the moment it looks as if this controversy will be as futile, as long-continued as the Western world's tragic involvement in that devastating, no-win war in Vietnam.

As the late Dr. Alan Guttmacher, founder of the Alan Guttmacher Institute, observed, perhaps the most distressing thing about this controversy is that advocates and opponents seek the same goal— *the complete elimination of abortion.* Anti-abortionists would do this by restrictive laws. Pro-choice advocates contend that such laws have never worked in the past and merely drive the distressed victims into the lair of criminal abortionists; that the logical, indeed, only acceptable alternative is to eliminate the *need* for abortion by making contraceptive information and effective methods of birth control freely available to all, young and old.

Without any doubt such a step would go a long way toward reaching the common goal. Of course, no matter how careful a woman might be, no matter which method she might employ, there are bound to be failures from time to time. In such cases, instead of forcing a woman to bear a child she doesn't want—for the sake of the child, even more than that of the incipient mother— advocates feel that it should be every woman's right to choose abortion as the last resort; *that it is grossly unfair to deny this right to indigent women, the very ones who need such help the most.*

As an obstetrician and gynecologist, naturally I examined with a cautious eye every part of this book that deals with contraception or abortion. I found the author's treatment to be ethically sound, scientifically correct, and thoroughly in line with approved medical practice.

I am impressed with the author's comprehensive research, especially his authoritative handling of divisive religious issues, where he relies mainly on Roman Catholic authorities, as well as questions of law, where his legal training enables him to speak with authority. In short, I consider this analytical monograph an important contribution toward the solution of the world population explosion, perhaps the most baffling problem ever to confront the human race.

Phil C. Schreier, M. D.
Professor Emeritus of Obstetrics and Gynecology
University of Tennessee, Memphis, Tennessee

INTRODUCTION

Students of history know that the fiercest, most savage wars of the Christian era have all been *religious* wars. Even though a growing percentage of the Protestant-Fundamentalist world is joining the anti-abortionists, there is no denying that the Roman Catholic hierarchy is the epicenter of the movement to "cry havoc and let slip the dogs of war."

Whether they are right or wrong, no one can charge the anti-abortionists with a lack of sincerity. But, as everyone knows, sincerity and fanaticism often go hand in hand. Pope Innocent III was utterly sincere when he lit the fires of the Inquisition that incinerated countless thousands who didn't hew to the orthodox line. In the same spirit, opponents of abortion are utterly sincere when they break the law, vandalize, bomb and set fire to birth control and abortion clinics and when they infiltrate such clinics, threaten, terrorize and attack their clients, employees and supporters, as described in recent news dispatches and news-magazines. [1]

In the years since Vatican II there has been a gratifying *rapprochement* between the Roman Catholic Church and the non-Catholic world; in fact, the ecumenical movement made more progress in those few years than in all the centuries since the Reformation. Now, as a recent study in *TIME* Magazine shows, the great majority of Protestants, and a vast segment of the

1

Catholic world, fear this rapidly growing bond of unity is being jeopardized by the "lunatic fringe" of the opponents and the intransigence of the Roman Catholic hierarchy in their attempt to foist their views of abortion on those who don't share their beliefs.[2] Lined up against the hierarchy in this war are the majority of the Catholic laity, some of the clergy, and the editors of Catholicism's leading magazines.[3]

Right here is where the Roman Catholic church is confronted with one of the most divisive dilemmas in its two thousand year history. As Catholic doctrine has held from the start, the *raisin d'etre* of the ancient church is to pave the way and transport to heaven as many souls as possible: "the more children produced on earth, the greater the population of heaven."

In pursuing this objective, the Vatican was thoroughly consistent in its unyielding stand against birth control: for the individual, for the family, for the entire world—a position announced unequivocally by Pope Pius XI in his encyclical, *Casti Connubii* (December 31, 1930).

But time moves on. Mental attitudes change, if doctrines do not. In a concession to modern conditions—financial, emotional, physical problems—Pope Pius XII opened the door a little with his approval of the rhythm method. As students of the problem know, however, the Vatican and the hierarchy are unalterably opposed to other, more reliable methods, which they call "artificial" and consider a breach of the "natural law." They also oppose sex education for the young, despite the fact that one million teenagers—including 30,000 girls under 15—are getting pregnant every year.[4]

Whether it be due to ineffective measures of contraception, or to open defiance of their church's teaching, it is ironic that a disproportionate number of Catholic girls and women are now having abortions. Authority for this statement is Dr. Samuel J. Barr, nationally known obstetrician and gynecologist. Dr. Barr has long been the Director of a clinic in central Florida which handles an average of 4,000 abortions a year, so he should know whereof he speaks. Though the Catholic population of his operating radius is only about 22 percent, he says that 38 percent of all patients seen in his clinic give their religion as Catholic.[5]

In *A Woman's Choice*, perhaps the most definitive and pragmatic book on abortion ever written, Dr. Barr says Catholic parents and grandparents are upset over the Supreme Court's legalization of abortion—until their teenage daughter or grand-daughter turns up pregnant; then they head for his clinic as fast as non-Catholic parents. "We also have a steady trickle of 'Right-to-Life' parents, as the problem touches them directly," he

2

adds.[6]

Will the Vatican eventually lift the ban on "artificial" contraception and thus materially reduce unwanted pregnancies that plague the whole world? Or will it maintain the *status quo* and go on crusading against its own folly? Will it continue to ignore the greatest problem mankind has ever faced: *the world population explosion*?

Will the Vatican continue to compound the plight of the unwanted child in an overpopulated world; a world the unwanted child never asked to enter, a world in which, if the myoptic anti-abortionists have their way, millions of such unfortunate children will be condemned to live?

Time alone will tell; but day by day legalized abortion is gaining acceptance throughout the world. In 1976 more than two-thirds of the world's population were living in countries where abortion is legal, compared with little over one-third in 1971. This is a gain of about 60 percent in five years.[7]

Perhaps the most revolutionary change of all occurred in Italy, the cradle of Catholicism. Early in the 1970's that country's Supreme Court nullified as unconstitutional all laws banning contraception. In the spring of 1978 the Italian parliament bowed to the demands of their Catholic constituents, ignored the protests of the Vatican, and not only legalized abortion but *subsidized it as well*!

To those who make an objective analysis of the situation, it is clear there is a strong punitive element in the adamant position of the anti-abortionists, a throwback to the teachings of the early Church Fathers as expressed by St. Augustine: "Apart from child-bearing the marriage chamber is a brothel . . . husbands are shameful lovers, wives are harlots."[8]

One needn't go back to the *early* church fathers to find such dementia. Some of our *modern* church fathers are every bit as irrational. In a Washington conference of about fifty leaders from various anti-abortion organizations held in the year of our Lord 1980, K. D. Whithead, vice president of *Catholics United for the Faith*, castigated contraception as "a form of moral insanity."

Commenting on scores of polls showing that more than 80 percent of the American public consider abortion to be a matter for a woman's choice, Paul Weyrich, director of the *Committee for the Survival of a Free Congress*, told his conferees: "It doesn't matter what the majority of the American people think on a poll. What matters is the perception members of Congress have about your issue and their future."[9]

In *The Bible and Liturgy Sunday Bulletin* of March 27, 1977, Father Paul Marx, O.S.B., wrote: " . . . 'contraception' often

3

turns out to be 'silent' (early) abortion induced by the pill or the I.U.D."

One might dismiss this statement as the prattling of a naive, celibate priest, but in his February 1977 testimony before Congress on Extension of the Health Service Act, Robert G. Marshall, Legislative Counsel for the nationally powerful *U. S. Coalition for Life*, said in all seriousness: "We are opposed to the continued funding of the so-called 'family planning services and population research act' . . . both the I.U.D. and one mode of action of the current pill are abortifacients."

In the light of the world population glut—with something like three billion of this planet's four billion inhabitants hungry, on the verge of starvation, or actually *starving*—such reactionary ideas seem incredible to the modern mind; but it is our tendency to laugh at such patent nonsense that makes our world population problem so horrendous.

In this gullible world we must never underestimate the power of fanaticism. Blind to all viewpoints but its own, fanaticism, like a tornado, concentrates its catastrophic force in a single, narrow path and, like a tornado, *carries death and destruction in its wake.*

In the early thirteenth century when, "to stamp out heresy," Pope Innocent III ordered a crusade against Languedoc in southern France—incomparably the most enlightened and powerful principality in Christian Europe—who would have believed that fanaticism could conquer such a fortress? Yet in less than a decade that powerful country was laid waste from border to border and the majority of its inhabitants—men, women and children—brutally slaughtered.

In 1973, when the Supreme Court put an end to our nightmare of illegal, death-dealing abortions, who would have believed that in little over three years a well-organized group of fanatics, Catholic and Protestant, could stampede Congress into enactment of the vicious Hyde Amendment—*and that the Supreme Court would knuckle under?* Who would have believed that in a few more years this same group of fanatics could browbeat nineteen of our state legislatures into calling for a Constitutional Convention to outlaw abortion completely—a Convention that could easily wreck our form of government and make a shambles of religious freedom?

Who would have believed that in this "enlightened" age a handful of avaricious evangelists could take over the airwaves and talk millions of their semi-literate followers into defying the Constitution by making their ideas of religion a qualification for public office, thus threatening to turn our democracy into a medieval theocracy; or a modern theocracy such as Iran suffers today? [10]

4

When these incredible fanatics were bombing and burning abortion clinics all over the country, threatening to kill their operators and patients or kidnap their children, who would believe that law-enforcement officers wouldn't lift a finger to stop the vandals? Who would believe that, in the few cases where the police did their duty, judges would dismiss the criminals without a word of reproof?

Don't laugh when fanatical groups like the *U. S. Coalition for Life, Catholics United for the Faith*, or Congressman Dornan's cohorts seek to outlaw birth control. Only a few decades ago contraception was a dirty word, contraceptives were barred from interstate commerce by the Comstock Law, and the practice was outlawed by every denomination of orthodox Christianity, Protestant as well as Catholic.

Don't laugh at the fanatics who are working night and day to condemn millions of unwanted children to a life of misery in an overpopulated world.

It hardly seems possible in this "enlightened" age; but unless we keep our guard up we may well be plagued by much more oppressive laws than the Hyde Amendment.

In this gullible world it behooves everyone who values individual liberty to stand up and be counted. *The lifestyle you save may be your own!*

5

PART ONE

The trouble with "Right-to-Lifers" is that they have little or no imagination. Guided by celibate men, few of them have ever learned the granite-hard facts of life. If these do-gooders could only envision themselves as the miserable victim of an unwanted pregnancy and reflect, "There but for the grace of God go I," they would realize that, abhorrent as it may be, abortion is a thousand times more humane than forcing a hapless child or woman to give birth to a baby that too often nobody wants —neither the mandatory mother nor a hostile, overcrowded world.

1

The Strange Case of Dr. Jekyll and Congressman Hyde

You would have to go back more than a hundred years to the Dred Scott-Missouri Compromise ruling of 1857 to find a decision of the Supreme Court that has stirred up as much controversy nationwide as their 1973 edict legalizing abortion in certain situations. Two score and nine months after the Dred Scott decision this nation embarked on a Civil War the likes of which we had never known before. Now this nation—conceived in liberty and theoretically dedicated to the proposition that all men and all women are created equal—is engaged in an uncivil war testing whether that nation, or any nation so conceived and so dedicated, can long endure.

The Court's agonizing decision brought a sigh of relief to that segment of the American public, male and female, which felt that child-bearing should be a matter of *choice*, not *chance*. They thought their long fight was over; that now they could take time to relax, rejoice, and lick their wounds. That segment of the public dedicated to the Dreaconian Code, mostly male, breathed fire instead of relief, and set about, come what may, to put women in their place—at the bottom of the heap. Their recourse, as the *Chicago Tribune* recommended in the Dred Scott controversy, would be through the ballot box.

As might be expected, the Supreme Court's 1973 ruling brought agonized cries from the American Catholic hierarchy. Patrick Cardinal Boyle called the decision "a catastrophe for America" and declared the Court's ruling did not make abortion morally permissible. "In fact," he said, "it remains a hideous and heinous crime."[1]

Terence Cardinal Cooke pointed out that "judicial decisions are not necessarily sound moral decisions" and added, "I hope and pray that our citizens will do all in their power to reverse this injustice to the unborn." John Cardinal Krol called the Court's ruling a "monstrous injustice," adding, "One trusts in the decency and good sense of the American people not to let an illogical court decision dictate to them on the subject of morality and human life."[2]

No one who understands the background and training of these "Princes of the Church" and other members of the hierarchy will judge these men too harshly. Their religious training is still permeated with the medieval concept that the good things of this world are for the rich, the good things of the next world for the downtrodden poor. A life brimful of misery, pain, humiliation, and frustration is a bed of roses compared with the pangs of an eternal hell that awaits us if we don't shape up. Furthermore, they are men and they are celibates. So far as the records show none of them has ever been caught with his finances down, his health on the ragged edge, struggling with the problem of trying to feed, clothe, and educate seven children, with an eighth—possibly twins—on the way. So to them abortion is nothing more than an academic question that calls for an academic answer.

Liberationists who for years had been working for the repeal of restrictive abortion laws were ecstatic over the Supreme Court's 1973 decision, thought they had won the war; but soon they were wondering if it wasn't just a skirmish. Within a few weeks anti-abortionists were attacking in force, frantically stepping up their opposition. Something like 200 restrictive bills were introduced in the legislatures of more than forty states. Newspapers were flooded with anti-abortion "Letters-to-the-Editor." Anti-abortion groups were addressing service clubs all over the land. On January 22, 1974 marking the first anniversary of the Supreme Court's decision, more than 6,000 anti-abortionists demonstrated on Washington's Capitol Hill and hundreds of newspapers published "mourning boxes" like this one, reproduced from the *Santa Barbara News Press* of January 22, 1974:

On Capitol Hill senators and congressmen were falling all
over themselves to see who could be the first to introduce a
Constitutional amendment that would put the Supreme Court in its
place. Among the first, introduced by Maryland's Congressman
Lawrence Hogan, was this typical example:

Neither the United States, nor any State shall deprive
any human being, from the moment of conception, of
life without due process of law; nor deny any human
being, from the moment of conception . . . the equal
protection of the law.

Since a Constitutional amendment must be approved by a
two-thirds majority of Congress and ratified by three-fourths of the
states, most of these lawmakers realized their proposals had little
chance for adoption, but they concluded that "thar's votes in them
thar bills," so who could fault them for trying?

These opportunists soon found, however, that they had
overestimated their support. Among the many who got fooled was
the Honorable Lawrence Hogan himself, along with two other
vociferous leaders of the anti-abortion crusade: Harold V.
Froehlich (R. Wisc.) and Angelo D. Roncallo (R. N.Y.). All three
were defeated in the 1974 congressional election. Much to their
surprise, the seventy-nine members of the House who had
consistently cast their votes against legalized abortion during the

following session suffered in disproportionate numbers at the polls: nineteen, or nearly twenty-five percent, were defeated. On the other hand, of the thirty-eight congressmen who supported the Supreme Court's decision, all of the thirty-seven who chose to run again were reelected.

Similarly, in gubernatorial campaigns where abortion was a significant issue, candidates favoring "abortion on request" fared very well. This was evidenced by the successful races of Congressman Hugh L. Carey (D. N.Y.), State Representative Richard D. Lamm (D. Colo.), Governor Milton J. Shapp (D. Pa.), and State Senator Robert F. Bennett (R. Kan.).

Under the controversial Supreme Court ruling, virtually all the new abortion bills passed by state legislatures were patently unconstitutional and the Supreme Court acted promptly to implement its decision. While most of the restrictive state laws and the proposed Constitutional amendments proved to be "dry runs," many states passed valid "conscience laws," providing that surgeons in public hospitals who were personally opposed to abortion could not be forced to perform such operations. It was a different story, however, in those situations where administrators of public hospitals tried to bar the use of their facilities for legal abortions. In a clearly related line of cases, federal courts throughout the country held that a public hospital which permits the use of its facilities for the performance of medical procedures which are of the same general type as abortions cannot deny its facilities for "nontherapeutic" abortions. The Supreme Court in the case of *City of Virginia vs Nyberg* let stand such a ruling by a federal court of appeals. In a more recent case, however, the Supreme Court, apparently influenced by the opposition, reversed itself on this point.

Catholic Hierarchy Declares a "Holy War"

While the crusade to nullify legal abortion started within hours after the Supreme Court's decision was announced, it didn't really catch fire until the latter part of 1975, when the Roman Catholic hierarchy implemented a hellbent plan for pro-life activities and created "citizen lobbies" in most congressional districts for the purpose of passing a Constitutional amendment that would outlaw *all* abortions. With a formidable structure that reached into virtually every community, the hierarchy developed an anti-abortion grass roots lobby that was able to generate enough mail to make Congress look on abortion as a political issue, rather than a question of health and human rights as it really is.

In an extraordinary thirteen-page *Pastoral Plan for Pro-Life Activities*, addressed to all "Church-sponsored or identifiable Catholic national, regional, diocesan and parochial organizations and agencies," the National Council of Catholic Bishops (NCCB), which claims to represent forty-eight million American Catholics, set forth a "comprehensive pro-life legislative program" to be organized and implemented at the state, diocesan, and individual parish level.

As approved overwhelmingly at the General Meeting of the NCCB and its twin corporation, the United States Catholic Conference (USCC) November 20, 1975, the Pastoral Plan calls for a four-fold legislative agenda:

1. Passage of a Constitutional amendment providing protection for the unborn child to the maximum extent possible.
2. Passage of federal and state laws and adoption of administrative policies that will restrict the practice of abortion as much as possible.
3. Continual research into and "refinement" and precise interpretation of *Roe* and *Doe* (the abortion cases decided by the Supreme Court in 1973) as well as subsequent court decisions.
4. Support for legislation that provides alternatives for abortion.

All three of America's leading Catholic publications voiced strong opposition to the hierarchy's plan. In a lengthy editorial of December 27, 1975, the Jesuit journal *America* stated that "the stance taken by the bishops is not tenable. Even if IRS accepts it, the public will reject it." *America* found it "regretable that there is no explicit recognition by the bishops that many Catholics have persistent doubts about the correctness and wisdom of the hierarchy's stand."

Shortly before the plan was officially announced, the independent, highly respected *National Catholic Reporter* said editorially:

> If the bishops have created a Catholic party, and only time will tell, they have unleashed a fearsome thing. The Catholic Church—and its bishops—will have moved into the upper reaches on national politics as an

11

identifiable political lobby/party of massive proportions. Such proportions, given the 48 million Catholic population in this country, could yet rival or counterbalance the largest political parties or lobbies in this country: the Republican party, the Democratic party, and the AFL-CIO . . . The National Conference of Catholic Bishops may have signaled a major change in the makeup of U.S. policies.[3]

The scholarly, liberal Catholic magazine *The Commonweal* summarized many of the objections in a twenty-three-inch editorial on January 2, 1976, when it observed that "the bishops have shown their indifference to the ecumenical dimensions of this issue, raised questions about the separation of church and state law and—overestimating their influence with their constituents—have promised a vote they can't deliver."

As plainly stated in the legislative agenda of the Pastoral Plan, the chief focus of the hierarchy's plan is on the passage of a Constitutional Amendment to bar legal abortion. The plan states, "This effort at persuasion is part of the democratic process, and is carried on most effectively in the congressional district or state from which the representative is elected . . . Thus it is absolutely necessary to have in each congressional district an identifiable, tightly knit and well-organized pro-life unit. *This unit can be described as a public interest group or a citizens' lobby.* No matter what it is called: (a) its task is essentially political, that is, *to organize people* to help persuade the elected representatives; and (b) . . . it is focused on passing a Constitutional amendment."

It comes as no surprise that the Roman Catholic hierarchy is the chief source of funds for the campaign to deny women freedom of conscience on abortion. The National Committee for a Human Life Amendment, a committee operated by the bishops, raised $906,404 between January 1976 and March 1977. Of this sum, $459,403 came in the form of donations ranging from $500 to $20,000 from 120 separate Catholic dioceses around the country. These donations are in addition to other diocesan, parish, and Catholic press efforts to overturn the Supreme Court's 1973 ruling. In addition, the Knights of Columbus in July of 1977 made its third $50,000 contribution to the U.S. Catholic Bishops' anti-abortion lobby group.

It is interesting to note that American Catholics are far from solidly behind their church's hierarchy. Opinion polls show that a majority of Catholics oppose an anti-abortion Constitutional

12

amendment. Indeed, the National Assembly of Women Religious, an organization of Catholic nuns meeting in New Orleans in August 1977, voted more than 3 to 1 to support the action taken by Vermont Human Resources secretary, Sister Elizabeth Candon, to continue funding abortions for indigent women. [4]

A 1977 *New York Times*-CBS poll showed that 69 percent of the Catholic and 76 percent of the Protestant respondents agreed that "the right of a woman to have an abortion should be left entirely up to the woman and her doctor." A Gallup poll taken the same year showed that only 19 percent of Catholic respondents felt that abortion should be illegal under all circumstances.

An ABC News-Harris survey, released in March 1979, reported that a substantial 60 to 37 percent majority of Americans support the U.S. Supreme Court's decision legalizing abortions during the first three months of pregnancy. *This figure, reports this survey, is up from a closer 53 to 40 percent majority who held the same view back in 1977.* This survey also showed the following results:

By 73 to 25 percent, a majority nationwide feel that "any woman who is three months or less pregnant should have the right to decide, with her doctor's advice, whether or not she wants to have an abortion." It is clear that a vast majority think the decision on an abortion should be a matter between a pregnant woman and her doctor.

By 61 to 32 percent, a majority of Americans agree with the argument that "most unwanted children end up being subjected to child abuse, and it is a mistake to force unwanted children to be born."

By 49 to 45 percent, a plurality of the public rejected the highly emotional argument of "right-to-life" people that "to perform an abortion is equivalent to murder, because a fetus's life has been eliminated."

By 55 to 37 percent, a majority disagree with the claim that "the life of a baby is just as important as the life of a mother, so abortions should be banned."

All responsible polls taken since the 1973 Supreme Court decision show that the general public is getting better informed every year about the complex problems of abortion and consequently an increasing number of Americans favor a woman's right to choose. The reason the anti-abortionists have been making such political gains of late is that they are better organized than the pro-choice advocates and are more apt to vote for or against a candidate because of his position on abortion, regardless of any other issues.

13

Hyde Amendment to the Rescue

While it may take years to tell how the hierarchy's "Holy War" will come out, no one can deny that it captured Congress, and thus produced the Hyde Amendment which has polarized this nation into a civil war that will be fought with ballots.

The seemingly endless fight in Congress over the Hyde Amendment is so confusing and so complicated that it is hardly feasible to give more than a few highlights of that bitter conflict.

When the Labor/HEW appropriation bill for fiscal year 1976-77 was before the House, Representative Henry Hyde (R. Ill.) offered the following amendment: "None of the funds appropriated under this Act shall be used to pay for abortions or to promote or encourage abortions."

Congressman Hyde, who is a devout Catholic, tried to discount the religious angle. He said, "The old argument that we who oppose abortion are trying to impose our religious concepts on other people is totally absurd. Theology does not animate me: biology does."

No one who is familiar with the situation will take Brother Hyde's statement at face value. It is obvious that he and his colleagues were following the blueprint for political action prepared by the Roman hierarchy's *Pastoral Plan for Pro-Life Activities*, announced only a few months previously.

Colleagues paint Congressman Hyde in glowing terms: a fine character, a genial, friendly, compassionate man—in short, a virtual prototype of the legendary Dr. Jekyll. It is only when the subject of family planning comes up that he begins to change. At the drop of a word—*abortion*—there is a metamorphosis as strange as that in Stevenson's masterpiece. The genial Dr. Jekyll becomes the monstrous Mr. Hyde. The congressman bares his fangs, throws compassion to the winds, scoffs at the countless lives wrecked by his heartless amendment and condemns thousands of *unwanted* children to a miserable *unwanted* life!

During debate over the Hyde Amendment Robert Dornan (R. Ca.) shocked his listeners when he addressed himself to the black members of Congress saying, "They are kidding themselves if they think this is not an issue that is fed by racism on the pro-abortion side." Fiscal conservatives, Dornan claimed, explained their abortion rights votes with "we have to hold them down."

Louis Stokes (D. Ohio), leader of the Congressional Black

Caucus, replied, "I personally deem it the height of arrogance when one who has neither been black nor poor in America chooses to speak in this body for that segment of society." Previously Stokes had said, "The new Hyde Amendment is tantamount to a constitutional amendment outlawing abortion for the poor."

After a long and bitter debate the majority of the House climbed on the hierarchy's bandwagon and adopted the Hyde restriction by a vote of 201 to 155.

The debate in the Senate was just as bitter. Senator John C. Stennis (D. Miss.) said, "I simply do not believe that this country has the responsibility to use our taxpayers' money to provide citizens, rich or poor, with the means of aborting their unborn simply as a convenience to those responsible for them. Congress has . . . no right to tax the American people to provide such a convenience."

In rebuttal Senator Charles H. Percy (R. Ill.) said, "If we can avoid a $100,000 cost for a $200 investment—and make a humanitarian investment at the same time—what sense does it make to say, 'We can't afford $200 for this expenditure (for an abortion)?'"

No doubt some of the representatives who voted for the Hyde Amendment thought the Senate or the Supreme Court would bail them out, but it was not to be. After the Senate had rejected several proposed amendments, Senator Brooke (R. Mass.) offered the following:

> None of the funds contained in this Act shall be used to perform abortions except where the life of the mother would be endangered if the fetus were carried to term, or where *medically necessary,* or for the treatment of rape or incest victims. This section does not prohibit the use of drugs or devices to prevent implantation of the fertilized ovum.

Again there was considerable debate, with a final vote of 56 to 39 in favor of Brooke's amendment. No one was entirely satisfied with this wording, but the pro-choice advocates were pleased that the Senate had at least been willing to protect the abortion rights of poor women who were seriously ill.

When the conferees from the House and Senate met to iron out the remaining discrepancies in the Hyde Amendment, it looked as if we were in for another Thirty Years War. Each chamber held firm during 20 floor votes in the Senate and 14 in the House, to say nothing of 21 votes in Senate-House Conference Committee sessions. The deadlock continued for five months. Finally on the eve of a vacation break with some of the die-hards already heading for home, the House Republican Whip Robert Michel came up with a compromise that the House accepted by a vote of 181 to 167. The revised amendment was far short of what the Senate had fought for, but in the circumstances felt it had to accept. Referring to the split between the two chambers of Congress, Senator Brooke said, "Not since I've been here in the Senate, and this is the eleventh year, have I seen an issue which has so divided us."

Though the anti-abortionists persist in claiming that religion had nothing to do with their votes, seven of the eleven House members of the Conference Committee were Catholics. Since there was not a single woman on that committee and the eventual agreement was sure to bring a terrific increase in welfare costs, American women are entitled to claim a foul: "taxation without representation."

Who Says "All Women Are Created Equal"?

The compromise contained in the Hyde Amendment prohibited Medicaid funding for abortions except in cases that meet one of these conditions: (1) The life of the woman is in danger; (2) Two doctors determine that she risks "severe and long-lasting physical health danger" from pregnancy; (3) The pregnancy results from rape or incest that was "promptly reported" to a law-enforcement or public health agency.

Operation of the 1976-77 Hyde Amendment was promptly suspended by an injunction issued by Judge John F. Dooling of the Federal Court for the Eastern District of New York, but on June 20, 1977, the Supreme Court handed down three decisions that more or less gave the green light to the Hyde Amendment and severely limited access to safe, legal abortions for the poor. In cases from Pennsylvania and Connecticut, the Court held that neither federal statutes nor the Constitution require that states participating in the Medicaid program fund nontherapeutic abortions. The Supreme Court refused to lift Judge Dooling's injunction, but remanded the case to his court with instructions to reconsider his ruling in the light of their decision in the two cases. A few days later—on August 4—Judge Dooling lifted his injunction and in a matter of hours HEW Secretary Califano ordered federal Medicaid payments for abortion to cease, except in cases where the woman's life would be endangered if the fetus were carried to term, where pregnancy resulted from rape or incest that was "promptly reported" to a law enforcement or public health agency, or where two doctors determined that the woman risked "severe and long-lasting physical health damage" from the pregnancy.

Without the slightest doubt this was a great victory for the anti-abortion forces. If the new measure had been in effect in 1976, it would have ruled out two-thirds of the 260,000 abortions that were financed by the federal-state Medicaid programs, about a fourth of all abortions in the United States that year. But before the smoke of battle had cleared the "antis" were mobilizing their forces for a bill that would end *all* federal funding for abortion, come what may—rape, incest, deformed or retarded babies, or death of the mother. Commenting on this situation, *Time* magazine said:

> Buoyed by last week's victory, the right-to-lifers immediately began planning their congressional strategy for next year.They will press for a ban on all Medicaid abortions, without exception, and ask that these procedures be outlawed at military hospitals. They will also lobby against including abortions in any national health insurance program that Congress may consider in the future.[5]

The Supreme Court Retreats

In a Missouri case, decided at the same time as the Pennsylvania and Connecticut cases mentioned above, the Court found no constitutional basis upon which a state or city hospital could be required to perform abortions. Although the majority of the Court said these rulings were not inconsistent with the 1973 decisions, without any doubt there was a distinct retreat from the Court's original position. As Justice Marshall said in his dissenting opinion, these decisions have "the practical affect of preventing nearly all poor women from obtaining safe and legal abortions."

Both the Pennsylvania and Connecticut decisions left the states free to provide funding for nontherapeutic abortions if the decision to abort was reached "through the normal processes of democracy." While some states still provide such funding, most states do not, and few are likely to do so unless there is a strong showing of support by pro-choice advocates.

In the Missouri case an indigent St. Louis woman was unable to obtain a nontherapeutic abortion because the mayor had prohibited abortions in city hospitals except where the life of the woman was endangered. The Court held that St. Louis may refuse to permit elective abortions in its city-owned public hospitals even if it provides hospital services to women who carry their pregnancies to term, a distinct retreat from its position in the *Nyberg* case mentioned above.

Speaking for himself and Justices Marshall and Blackmun in their dissenting opinion, Justice Brennan—a practicing Catholic —said:

> While it may still be possible for some indigent women to obtain abortions in clinics and private hospitals, it is clear that the city policy is a significant, and in some cases insurmountable, obstacle to indigent pregnant women who cannot pay for abortions in those private facilities.

The implications of this decision are the most far-reaching of the three cases, since municipal officials may now limit or prohibit nontherapeutic abortions in public facilities. *All* women will be affected by this ruling—those who can afford to pay as well as those who can't.

A study by Planned Parenthood showed that in 1976 abortion was used to terminate a fourth of all pregnancies. An estimated 1.1 million abortions were performed in the United States that year, an increase of about 10 percent over the one million figure reported the previous year. Despite the rise in the number of U.S. abortions, the study also showed that from 143,000 to 654,000 women in need of abortions in 1976 were unable to get them. The inaccessibility of services was traced to hospitals which refused to provide them and to the concentration of such services in major metropolitan areas. The researchers found that abortion services were excluded from 70 percent of the nation's non-Catholic hospitals and more than 80 percent of public hospitals. "Hospitals, especially public hospitals, continue to ignore the mandate from the Supreme Court to offer abortions to women who want them," said the report. As we have just seen, however, the Supreme Court reversed itself in the Missouri case just cited, so there is no longer any "mandate" for the Court to enforce. In view of this reversal, it is hard to understand how the Court could say it has not changed its position.

Hyde-Bound House Won't Budge

To detail all the steps following the original Hyde Amendment of

18

1976-77 would be like playing a broken record. In the following year, drunk with power, Hyde and his henchmen tried to force through Congress even stronger restrictives, as predicted in *Time's* editorial following the first enactment of the amendment. They tried to restrict Medicaid funding without any exceptions whatsoever. Confronted by a Senate which said in effect, "Over our dead bodies," they had to settle for the same restrictions as the previous year's. It was the same story for the fiscal year 1978-79.

From an economic standpoint, implementing the Hyde Amendment is patently untenable. HEW estimates that for each indigent woman who is forced to carry her pregnancy to term, the federal, state and local costs of maternity and pediatric care, as well as public assistance, would be about $2200 for the first year of the child's life alone, or a total cost to the government of more than $500 million each year. *This is more than four times as much as the government would pay if it financed abortions for all eligible Medicaid clients who want them.* Indeed, as the *Wall Street Journal* said in a recent article, while Governors Hugh Carey of New York and Jerry Brown of California, as well as other governors, "don't talk openly of dollars-and-cents savings, they are obviously concerned about the potential for increased welfare costs if subsidized abortions should cease."

In this "battle of the ballots" there is no doubt that pro-choice advocates were caught off guard. Lulled to complacency by the Supreme Court's 1973 decision, they slept on their arms. It took a resounding defeat like the Hyde Amendment to bring them back, full force, into the firing line.

The results of the 1978 elections were somewhat mixed, though pro-choice advocates had the edge. They did lose a few, chiefly Senator Brooke, who was not defeated on the abortion issue since his opponent, Paul Tsongas, is also a strong pro-choice supporter. Iowa Senator Dick Clark's defeat was a great loss, but not unexpected in a state with a large Catholic population and a well-organized right-wing effort. Clark's stand on tuition tax credits added to his problems in that year's sweep of liberal Democrats.

Countering these losses were some stunning victories for pro-choice advocates. Of forty-nine candidates supported for the general elections by NARAL-PAC (National Abortion Rights Action League—Political Action Committee) thirty-five, or 71 percent, won their races. The most critical victory was the defeat of a referendum in Oregon which would have prohibited all state-funded abortions. This marked the only time when voters have been asked to decide this issue in a referendum. Another important upset was the defeat of abortion foe Robert Griffin, senator from Michigan, who was ousted by Carl Levin with support from pro-choice activists. Among other key gains was pro-choice candidate Bill Bradley's win over right-wing sponsored Jeffery Bell in New Jersey.

The only two single-issue anti-abortion candidates on the ballot were both soundly defeated. They opposed James Jeffords and Mike McCormack. Among pro-choice winners in gubernatorial races, candidates were involved in four critical and closely fought trials. Colorado's Dick Lamm, who as a state legislator introduced the nation's first law to permit therapeutic abortions, beat challenger Ted Strickland. In Illinois, anti-abortion supporters were unsuccessful in their attempt to defeat the pro-choice incumbent, James Thompson. In the race for the Pennsylvania governor's seat, Richard Thornburgh won over vocal abortion foe Pete Flaherty. Michigan's pro-choice governor, William Milliken, easily defeated anti-abortion candidate William Fitzgerald.

A strong pro-choice leader in the House of Representatives, Ab Mikva, was reelected in Illinois. Both of Alabama's new senators, Howell Heflin and Donald Stewart, supported a woman's right to choose abortion. In the House, abortion rights supporter John Buchanan was reelected over an anti-abortion challenger.

Pro-choice activists in Washington State helped to elect two new congressmen who favor the right to choose. Mike Lowry successfully challenged anti-abortion incumbent John Cunningham. The second district open seat was won by Al Swift, who defeated a well-financed abortion opponent, John Nance Garner.

Two Pennsylvania elections show that Catholic voters also elected candidates with strong pro-choice records. Robert Edgar, a suburban Philadelphia clergyman, will continue to represent his 57 percent Roman Catholic district despite the vocal anti-abortion campaign directed at his leadership on abortion rights. In Pittsburgh, abortion foe Stan Thomas counted on the 42 percent Catholic Fourteenth District to support his challenge to William Moorehead, but was badly defeated.

New York's Geraldine Ferraro, a strong supporter of abortion rights, defeated her anti-abortion opponent, and California's Vic Fazio was elected to an open seat vacated by Robert Leggett. As a state Legislator, Fazio has often taken leadership on abortion rights legislation.

"No pro-choice incumbents were defeated in this election

because of their stand on abortion," said Betsy Chotin, NARAL-PAC director. "The vote shows that the convictions of America's pro-choice majority cut across party lines and extend to every region of the country."

It's too early to say what effect these pro-choice victories will have on state legislators who were pressured into voting Medicare restrictions for abortions and on congressmen when the Hyde Amendment comes up for another go-round; but it's a safe bet that the legislators will think twice before hopping on a bandwagon that is obviously running out of gas.

For those legislators, state and national, who base their decisions on a vote count, there is further reason to "watch their step." Nothing in recent history has aroused the women of this nation to such a high pitch as the ruthless Hyde Amendment. In less than a year after that statute went into effect, the NARAL (National Abortion Rights Action League)—probably the most active and most potent defender of a woman's right to choose—increased its membership almost five-fold. There were similar increases in virtually all such organizations. The ruthless opponents of a woman's choice also brought into the fray such strong national organizations as the League of Woman Voters, the American Civil Liberties Union, the potent National Education Association, the American Medical Association, and the national Council of Churches, to name only a few. More than eighty national organizations that support abortion rights are listed in the notes to Chapter 6.

The Travail of Unwanted Births

A report on a survey of the sociological affects of the Hyde Amendment by The Alan Guttmacher Institute says:

> Many Medicaid-eligible women denied government help in paying for their abortions, and unwilling to face possible death or injury at the hands of illegal abortionists, are carrying their unwanted pregnancies to term. The consequences of such unwanted births for the young mothers, the young fathers, their children and society are deep and long-lasting.
>
> Since most women receiving public assistance by definition do not have husbands living with them, they are likely to give birth out of wedlock or to be forced into marriages that have little chance of long-term survival. (Even their future marriages will be more unstable because of the pressures placed on poor young couples by the needs of the child). They are likely to

21

continue to have more births, more unwanted births and more out-of-wedlock births than other young women. Such births tend to deepen their poverty and lengthen their dependency, especially in the case of the substantial proportion who are teenagers. (One-half of AFDC welfare payments—some $4.7 billion annually—goes to households in which the mother has given birth as a teenager). Many of the teenage mothers will be unable to complete high school. If they have already dropped out because of a previous birth, they will probably never be able to resume their interrupted educations. When they get jobs, the jobs will be less remunerative and less satisfying.

The adverse consequences for the children of such unwanted pregnancies have also been demonstrated. If the mother is a teenager, the baby is more likely to be premature or of low birth weight than are infants born to older mothers. Low birth weight, in turn, is a major cause of infant mortality and of a host of childhood illnesses and birth defects—some of which may involve lifelong mental retardation. Babies born to such teenage mothers are much more likely to be brought up in poverty, to be physically and emotionally abused, to suffer from malnutrition and to have their own educations truncated. They are more likely to spend their formative years without a father in the house, and to show signs of emotional disturbance and learning and behavior problems when they reach school age."

In his dissenting opinion to the regressive decisions of the Supreme Court mentioned above, Justice Marshall warned: "I fear the Court's decisions will be an invitation to public officials already under extraordinary pressure from well-financed and carefully orchestrated lobbying campaigns, to approve more such restrictions."

As we shall see in the following chapters, even before Justice Marshall's dissenting opinion was published, irresponsible fanatics were advocating exactly what Justice Marshall was warning against.

2

The Supreme Court Turns Back the Clock

The United States Supreme Court's edict of 1977, upholding the federal ban on Medicaid funding of abortion, was something of a curbstone opinion. The case was rushed to the Court on a direct appeal from Federal Judge Dooling's order restraining enforcement of the Hyde Amendment. Attorneys for the pro-choice advocates had little time to prepare their case and they lost by a Court divided six to three. Meanwhile the stark injustice of the restrictive amendment had taken its toll and several suits challenging its constitutionality were filed. Chief of these was *McRae vs. Califano,* a class-action suit brought by the Center for Constitutional Rights, the American Civil Liberties Union, and the Planned Parenthood Federation. The case was tried in the Federal Court for the Eastern District of New York, before the same Judge Dooling who granted the injunction against the Hyde Amendment in 1977.

The key plaintiffs were five women whose lives were directly affected by the Hyde Amendment: Cora McRae, 24; Mary Doe, 19, unmarried mother of four children; Jane Doe, 25, suffering from a serious case of phlebitis, faced with the continuation of a life-threatening pregnancy; Sharon Roe, 19 year-old native American Indian, pregnant just four months after the birth of her first child; and Ann Moe, 15, unmarried, with a history of hospitalization for severe mental illness.

Despite their pressing need, these five women were unable to

23

obtain Medicaid-funded abortions. They were the legal representatives of thousands of poor women who lost their already precarious control over their lives as a direct result of the Hyde Amendment.

Following the Supreme Court's 1977 reversal of his decision nullifying the Hyde Amendment, Judge Dooling considered *McRae* on its own merits so as to allow both sides to develop the evidentiary record essential to the Supreme Court appeal he knew would follow whatever decision he reached.

The question of religious involvement was central to this case. Plaintiffs contended that the Hyde Amendment violated the establishment and free exercise of religion clause of the First Amendment; also that it was a violation of equal protection if the federal government denied funding for medically necessary abortions while allowing reimbursement for all other medically necessary services in a program designed to finance necessary medical treatment for low income citizens.

Because the case directly challenged the Hyde Amendment, Judge Dooling realized that it was of landmark importance and pulled out all the stops to give it a thorough trial on its merits. After hearings that produced over 3,000 pages of testimony, Dooling took more than a year to write his meticulously considered opinion, which covered 632 pages. That opinion holding the Hyde Amendment unconstitutional was handed down January 16, 1980, accompanied by an order that Medicaid funding for abortions be resumed within 30 days.

The Supreme Court refused to stay Dooling's order and on February 19, 1980, accepted for review his decision, combining it with *Zabacaz*, a case from Illinois they had already accepted for review. The Court set April 21 as the day for oral arguments, alloting both sides only one half-hour to present their case.

In his January 15 ruling, Judge Dooling held that excluding medically necessary abortions from coverage under the Medicaid program violates the First Amendment right of freedom of conscience and the Fifth Amendment rights of privacy, due process and equal protection; but he rejected the plaintiffs' claim that the Hyde Amendment violates the First Amendment's prohibition against laws constituting an establishment of religion, or interfering with the free exercise of religion.

Obviously the advocates of free choice in abortion were disappointed when the Supreme court on June 30, 1980, in a five to four ruling, reversed the decision arrived at by a brilliant, objective, dedicated judge after a painstaking trial that produced more than

3,000 pages of evidence and a scholarly opinion that took him over a year to write.

In view of the vital importance attached to this case by Judge Dooling and by millions of American citizens, one can't help wondering if the majority of the Court had not already decided the case when they set up *only one day* for its hearing and allotted a total of *one-half hour* for each side to present its case.

The plaintiffs' chief argument was that Title XIX of the Social Security Act (Medicaid) requires participating states to pay for medically necessary abortions. The Court rejected this claim, holding that Title XIX does not require a participating state to pay for those medical services for which federal reimbursement is unavailable. The Court also held that neither the Hyde Amendment nor the Illinois funding restriction violates a woman's constitutional right to abortion. Both leave the woman free to decide whether or not to terminate her pregnancy.

By refusing to fund most abortions while providing coverage of childbirth expenses, the government, in the Court's view, simply makes childbirth the more attractive alternative. The Court held that this incentive system is a valid means of furthering the state's legitimate interest in protecting potential life.

Justice Stewart wrote the majority opinion in which Chief Justice Burger and Justices White, Powell and Rehnquist joined. Justices Brennan, Marshall, Stevens and Blackmun strongly dissented, each filing a separate opinion.

It might be well to point out here that the *right* to abortion remains intact. The Court only held that state and federal governments don't have to pay for them. Local courts may interpret state constitutions to require publicly funded abortions. In such states, court orders may well be effective in restoring funds withdrawn by the legislatures.

In his dissent, Justice Brennan recognized that the Hyde Amendment is more than a mere incentive to carry pregnancy to term. "Both by design and in effect," he wrote, "it serves to coerce indigent pregnant women to bear children that they would not otherwise elect to have. By funding all expenses associated with childbirth and none of the expenses incurred in terminating pregnancy, the government literally makes an offer that the indigent woman cannot afford to refuse. It matters not that in this instance the goverment has used the carrot rather than the stick."

Justice Marshall severely criticized the majority ruling and assessed the devastating impact of these restrictions:

Pregnant women. . . will be restricted to two alternatives. First they may carry the fetus to term, even though that route may result in severe injury or death to the mother, the fetus or both. If that course appears intolerable, they may resort to self-induced abortions or obtain illegal abortions—not because bearing a child would be inconvenient, but because it (an abortion) is necessary to protect their health. The result will be . . . to ensure the destruction of both fetal and maternal life. There is another world "out there," the existence of which the Court . . . either chooses to ignore or fears to recognize. It is only by blinding itself to that other world that the Court can reach the result it announces today.

Foreseeing the far reaching implications of the decision, Justice Blackmun said, "The cancer of poverty will continue to grow and the lot of the poorest among us, once again, and still is not to be bettered."

Cash Buys Right To Abortion

Under the above heading syndicated columnist Roger Simon of the Chicago Sun-Times paid his respects to the Supreme Court in his column of July 3, 1980. In a flashback to his youthful days at a South Side hospital, Simon quotes one of Chicago's most prominent physicians:

One young woman after another dragged herself into the emergency room. These unfortunate young women were called "Saturday Night Specials." They were kids, really. They came in bleeding and infected from back-alley abortionists. Before abortion was legalized all this horror existed. . . Knitting needles, coat hangers, hairpins, drugs—we saw it all. After abortion was legalized such cases dropped off to almost nothing. But now it will start up again. Because of the whim of a legislator. The girls and women will start coming in again as they came before. Many will become sterile. A few will die. It will all happen again. . . The Hyde Amendment is not pro-life. It is anti-poor. [1]

"The majority decision of the Supreme Court is an appalling one," concludes Simon. "What a majority of the Court said is that the Constitution is for sale. Abortion is a right, but only if you've got the money to pay for it. Those with money can have abortions for whatever reason they want. Those without money cannot. In America, the Court ruled, *you can have all the justice that money can buy.*

In upholding the penny-wise Hyde Amendment and pointing out with pontifical solemnity that indigent women have the same abortion rights as the affluent, the myoptic majority was simply affirming an aphorism voiced by Anatole France decades ago. "The Law is strictly impartial; it permits the rich as well as the poor to sleep under bridges."

3

The Hierarchy's "Secret Weapon"

While reluctantly conceding setbacks on two major fronts—divorce and the widespread use of "artificial" contraception by Catholic women—the Catholic hierarchy is taking an unyielding position on abortion, a fight it is determined to win at all costs. The highly emotional abortion issue can be dramatized by means of inflammatory rhetoric, enlarged, blood-curdling illustrations of fetuses, lurid propaganda and hysterical political pressure, so the hierarchy is pulling out all the stops.

Stirred up by directives from the institutional church's commandos, egged on Sunday after Sunday from the pulpit, inflamed by persuasive speakers who leave no adversary unstoned, led to believe that abortion under any circumstances is murder, a vast segment of Roman Catholic conservatives has declared war on all who oppose their views with all the fervor that inspired the hierarchy of the Middle Ages in their ruthless efforts to stamp out heresy. One would have to go back a long way in religious history to find as strong a degree of fanaticism as that which has inspired hundreds of thousands of anti-abortionists to inundate Congress and state legislators with letters, phone calls and personal demonstrations—a battle they have won, at least temporarily.

Describing the situation in Congress during the debate on the Hyde Amendment, *Time* magazine said:

Killer! Killer! In Congress the issue cuts confusingly across ideological lines, making it difficult for many liberals from areas with strong Catholic enclaves to vote for abortion. Whatever his own feelings, any legislator in a swing district hesitates to arouse the anger of such an uncompromising group as the anti-abortionists. Their attack can be so personal that New Jersey Congressman Andy Maguire was actually chased through his office building by lobbyists screaming, "Killer! Killer!" He nevertheless maintained his pro-abortion stand. It takes courage for a Congresswoman like Maryland's Barbara Mikulski, whose Baltimore area is heavily Catholic, to fight the right-to-lifers as resolutely as she has. "I am a professionally trained social worker," she explains. "I know what a coat-hanger abortion is all about."[1]

One of the fanatics' chief targets is the Planned Parenthood Federation, whose main objective is not to promote abortions, but to lessen the need for such a drastic step by sex education and teaching girls and women to use effective means of contraception. Instead of cooperating with Planned Parenthood's efforts to lessen the *need* for abortion, the absolutist groups are constantly striving, by fair means or foul, to discredit the Federation and harass its volunteers, office workers, and officials in every way possible. Time and again the fanatic anti-abortionists have infiltrated various chapters of the Federation and similar organizations, posing as friends and volunteers, in order to familiarize themselves with the routine operations of these groups, to make lists of allies and contributors and thus, with threats of physical harm and boycotts, to cut off moral and financial support. Threats of violence, even death, have become commonplace.

Here are excerpts from a recent Associated Press dispatch headed "Abortion Center Burns."

A Cleveland (Ohio) abortion clinic, vandalized earlier in the week, was gutted by flames Saturday. Fire fighters said a man with a package had walked in, temporarily blinded a receptionist with a liquid chemical, and "apparently set the place on fire . . . "

Last Wednesday, vandals severed electrical cords, broke glass containers and splashed an iodine solution on the walls, carpets and furniture of the Concerned

Women's Clinic on the city's east side. Police were called but declined a request for an investigation.[2]

In a seven-page article headed "Abortion Under Attack," *Newsweek* said:

> In Portland, Ore., two vanloads of parochial school children pulled up to the Lovejoy Specialty Hospital and Surgical Center, which performs 75 percent of Oregon's 12,000 abortions. The students chased women leaving the clinic, shouting, "Murderers, murderers." At the Alaska Hospital and Clinic in Anchorage, four opponents of abortion slipped into the operating room and chained themselves to a bed until police arrived and arrested them. In Ohio, Nebraska and Minnesota, several abortion clinics have been set on fire. And in Phoenix, Dr. Robert Tamis, an Arizona physician who performs abortions, says that abortion opponents have put glue in his office lock, shot at his car, poisoned his dog and harrassed his children.
>
> All across America, abortion is under greater attack than at any time since the Supreme Court legalized it in 1973. To its opponents, abortion is murder, and they have engaged in a crusade to wipe it out. Justifying their actions on moral grounds and backed by the authority and money of the Roman Catholic Church, they are engaging in civil disobedience reminiscent of the anti-war movement and taking their case to legislatures and the courts. And they are making considerable headway.[3]

Shortly before this, the same magazine said:

> In Burlington the Vermont Women's Center was destroyed by fire last year and closed for seven months. The Northwest Women's Center in Columbus, Ohio, has been operating out of a doctor's office since suffering $200,000 in arson damage. Police believe that the attacks were deliberate. In Omaha, on the day a fire-bombing caused $35,000 in damage to the Ladies' Clinic, the *Omaha World-Herald* received an unsigned letter that read, "You'd bomb a concentration camp, why not abortion centers?"[4]

30

One of the worst attacks occurred in Hempsted, Long Island, on February 15, 1979, when the Bill Baird Clinic was burned to the ground by a man recognized by staff members as a regular anti-abortionist demonstrator. Over fifty patients and staff members escaped without serious injury, but the three-story clinic was a total loss.

For a time in northern Virginia, demonstrators found a safe haven for their illegal activities. On October 19, 1977, Judge Lewis Griffith of the General District Court in Fairfax found six demonstrators not guilty of trespassing because he said they had broken the law in the belief that they were saving lives.

Not surprisingly the invaders returned to the clinic and again disrupted activities. Once again they were arrested and once again they came to trial in the same court, but before Judge Mason Grove. On February 10, 1978, Judge Grove proceeded to declare the Virginia statute legalizing first trimester abortions unconstitutional.

Since these judges refused to prosecute such cases, commonwealth Attorney Robert Horan ordered city police to ignore the clinic's calls for help. This was an open invitation for the vandals to run riot through the clinic, which they did, but fortunately a federal district court issued an injunction stopping such disruptions.

For the information of those who find these accounts of harassment and physical violence hard to believe, I quote from an "Open Letter to Pro-Lifers" from Frances Frech, director of the Population Renewal Office, in Kansas City, Missouri. Before listing two pages of ways and means of harassing advocates of contraception and abortion, Ms. Frech advised:

> The fastest way to get some action that will lead to saving unborn lives is to create problems for the world's leading abortion promoters, good old Planned Parenthood. Discredit them—cut off their funding, private and public—try to stir up investigations against them, and we'll make giant strides toward winning.

Among other things, Ms. Frech recommended letters to senators, representatives, HEW Secretary Joseph A. Califano, Jr., and President Carter inquiring why "Planned Parenthood has lots of money for pornographic materials," and suggesting that Planned Parenthood be investigated for their "use of sexually-stimulating films in sex education." ("If you haven't seen them, just say you've heard about them and you think the matter should be looked into".)

Under the heading, "How to Overturn Planned Parenthood's Plans," Ms. Frech recommended that anti-abortion activists work to cut off government funding. ("Point out that teenage pregnancies, abortions and V.D. are all on the rise; therefore, instead of giving more money to Planned Parenthood, officials should be asking why they haven't done a better job.") To get private funding reduced: "if you can find out who the donors to Planned Parenthood are in your area, contact them and find out if they really know what their money is being used for." To disrupt Planned Parenthood's relations with the local schools: "ask. . . if Planned Parenthood presents programs to junior high and senior high school students in your area. If so, start asking questions. Write letters to newspapers 'at every opportunity' opposing Planned Parenthood, especially in regard to services provided for adolescents. Get state legislators working for a 'Minors Protection Act' aimed at keeping agencies such as Planned Parenthood from giving them contraceptives and abortions and to protect them against the use of objectionable sex education materials."[5]

A Look Behind the Scenes

The "secret weapon" in the anti-abortionists' arsenal is the millions of children in Catholic schools, their "shock troops" for staging massive demonstrations and letter-writing campaigns. Every year parochial school children look forward eagerly to January 22, when thousands of them will be treated to a free trip to Washington and other metropolitan centers for demonstrations marking the anniversary of the Supreme Court's 1973 decision on abortion.

The estimate of 60,000 juvenile demonstrators in Washington for the sixth anniversary may have been an exaggeration, but no doubt our pressured congressmen thought even more children were crowding the steps of the Capitol and wandering through the legislative halls. There were as many as a thousand or two—often more—in similar demonstrations throughout the country. In most cases the pro-choice advocates would be holding a counter-demonstration, but as a rule they would be outnumbered at least six or eight to one, often more. Obviously the uninformed public is impressed, gets the impression that opponents of free choice are in the majority. The same conclusion is often drawn by uninformed

32

lawmakers, state and federal. The same imbalance pertains to the mail they get.

Those who keep abreast of the national surveys constantly being made by metropolitan newspapers, magazines and TV chains know that the true situation is almost exactly the reverse: that for every adult who opposes legalized abortion there are three or four who support it. So how do you account for the apparent imbalance? If you happen to be present at one of these demonstrations, or see a photograph of one in a newspsper, magazine or newscast, study the faces in the crowd and you'll have your answer. *For every adult in the group you'll find anywhere from five to ten children.*

Most supporters of a woman's right to choose are busy, have little time for letter-writing and find it difficult to get away from business or family chores to join such demonstrations. Parochial school children, on the other hand, have all the time in the world and a demonstration to them is like a picnic.

Parishioners are "educated" from the pulpit on abortion-related legislation. They are urged to write their legislators, to join demonstrations, to become active in anti-choice organizations. Collections are taken up right along for sending thousands of their "shock troops" to strategic spots for marches and demonstrations. (The January marches on Washington are staged predominantly by elementary and high school students carrying rosaries and miniature statues of the Virgin Mary.) Distributed at the masses are letters and bulletins thoroughly informing parishoners about specific bills, telling them how to compose a letter to congressmen or state legislators and exactly what to write. School children are offered free time and other inducements for writing such letters.

With millions of shock troops and unlimited funds, is it any wonder that the hierarchy has been able to overwhelm Congress and state legislatures with propaganda, and *even to influence the Supreme Court?*

In his revealing book, *A Woman's Choice,* Dr. Samuel J. Barr comments on the hysterical campaigns being waged by the anti-abortionists.

> There is little question that one of the reasons for the current feverish campaigns of anti-abortionists is the press of time. They are compelled to race against a swelling tide of direct public involvement, to suppress understanding, and to hope that compassion doesn't enter the minds and hearts of millions of people who still don't know or who are still not sure. Once that

happens, their appeal for public blindness will be lost forever.[6]

The Political Tide Begins to Turn

During the past few years since the hierarchy's call to action, the anti-abortionists have had things pretty much their own way— the ban on Medicaid funding, resolutions for a Constitutional convention by many state legislatures, restrictive ordinances like those found in Akron—but with the 1978 elections the tide began to turn. Much to their surprise many lawmakers who swallowed the anti-choice propaganda found themselves on the losing side. In seven cases out of ten where abortion was the decisive issue, those who voted pro-choice were reelected. No doubt the votes of some of the losers were based on their convictions, but the great majority voted the way they did because they thought it expedient to climb aboard the anti-abortion bandwagon. They learned the hard way what the polls would have told them if they had only listened: *approximately three out of four American voters—male and female, Catholic and non-Catholic—are in favor of a woman's right to choose!*

Many lawmakers have come to realize that the bark of the anti-abortionists is worse than their bite. Many are getting fed up with the never-ending pressure put on them by the pro-life zealots. In the *Newsweek* story mentioned above, a California legislator is quoted as saying, "We're tired of being inundated by pulpit-initiated letter campaigns. We're tired of having pickled fetuses shoved under our noses before every vote."

Another reason why lawmakers are beginning to resist these "feverish campaigns" is that they have come to realize those zealots are not only demanding a complete ban on abortion without any exceptions whatsoever, but are even trying to outlaw contraception. Overt and covert attacks on Planned Parenthood by anti-choice forces in Congress signaled a new phase in their drive to eliminate reproductive freedom in America.

When the major funding bill for family planning programs was being considered in the closing hours of the Ninety-fifth Congress, an effort was made to eliminate federal funds for any family planning programs that provided counseling or referral for abortion.

Right-wing Representative Robert Dornan (R. Ca.) offered several amendments. One would have required parental notification before a minor could be provided with birth control information or devices; another would permit family planning funds to be used to support "alternatives to abortion" groups; still another would have required physicians to report pregnancies among unwed teenagers to police for prosecution under the criminal fornication state laws applicable in the jurisdiction.

Dornan's efforts failed and the bill was passed overwhelmingly by a vote of 343 to 27, but no doubt this was the opening round in a war on reproductive freedom in general and specifically on Planned Parenthood which receives 40 percent of its funding, nationwide, under this bill.

As this is written nineteen states have passed resolutions calling for a Constitutional Convention to outlaw abortion completely—slightly more than half the number required to call such a Convention. These states are: Alabama, Arkansas, Delaware, Idaho, Indiana, Kentucky, Louisiana, Massachusetts, Mississippi, Missouri, Nebraska, Nevada, New Jersey, Oklahoma, Rhode Island, Pennsylvania, South Dakota, Tennessee, and Utah.

In May of 1978 such a resolution was defeated in Florida chiefly through the testimony of Sister Mary Theresa Glenn, who told the Committee that the Catholic Church was divided on the issue of a Constitutional Convention and asked that the move be defeated.

Although Constitutional amendments barring abortions have been consistently voted down in Congress, Senators Jesse Helms (R. NC) and Edward Zorinsky (D. NE) are still trying. They recently sponsored an amendment that would not allow abortions under any circumstances whatsoever. Eight members of the House led by—who else?—Henry Hyde (R. IL) have sponsored similar "no exception" amendments.

Few of those who are so avid for a Constitutional Convention to ban abortion realize to what an extent such a Convention would jeopardize our entire system of government. Almost all lawyers and historians who have studied the question have held that no one can predict with any certainty that if a convention were held on any particular subject, it might not decide to change the Constitution in other substantial respects as well. If delegates were so inclined, they might put an end to separation of church and state, reject the guarantee of free speech and a free press, and repeal the prohibition against unreasonable searches and seizures—in a word, wreck the entire Bill of Rights, the bulwark of freedom which has made the United States unique among nations in the history of the world.

Because of the great risks involved, many legislators and

many Americans who would like to overturn the Supreme Court's 1973 legalization of abortion are taking a second look at the Constitutional Convention approach. The more thoughtful ones also realize that if such a drastic amendment were adopted it would surely mean a return to something like a million illegal, *perilous* abortions every year.

Frightful Cost of the Hyde Amendment

Few of the representatives and senators who voted so glibly for the Hyde Amendment had any real understanding of its frightful cost, not only in *billions of additional welfare dollars* but, even more poignantly, in the human lives and suffering, mental and physical, their action entailed. In a report on the Hyde Amendment, released more than a year before the Supreme Court's ruling of June 30, 1980, the Alan Guttmacher Institute said:

> If the Hyde Amendment and its 39 state counterparts are upheld by the Supreme Court, an estimated 340,000 of the nation's poorest women will be denied effective access to safe, legal abortions. Because of their poverty, those with unwanted pregnancies will be forced to give birth, to use family welfare allotments intended for food, rent and clothing to pay for legal abortions, or turn to clandestine, charnel-house abortionists. In the year-and-a-half since the restrictive policies went into effect, federal Medicaid payments for abortion have been reduced by 99 percent.

The Alan Guttmacher Institute's 48-page report, entitled *Abortions and the Poor: Private Morality, Public Responsibility,* was the first national survey of the effects of the Hyde Amendment on the lives of women on welfare who wish to terminate unwanted pregnancies, as well as the effects on society as a whole. In a concluding essay, William G. Milliken, Governor of Michigan, explained why he twice vetoed restrictive, Hyde-type legislation in his state: "To tell the poor pregnant woman that she has a legal right to an abortion, but that she must pay for it herself is to tell her that her real choices are an unwanted birth, a hazardous self-abortion, cheap quackery, or depriving her existing children of food and clothing so she can make the abortion payment."

Here are some of the highlights of the Alan Guttmacher Institute report:

There are 4.6 million U.S. women of reproductive age eligible for Medicaid. Of these, 2.6 million are at risk each year of incurring an unwanted pregnancy, and about 427,000 actually have unwanted pregnancies that they wish to terminate by abortion.

Nine out of ten of these Medicaid-eligible women are welfare recipients of AFDC (Aid to Families with Dependent Children). Eighty percent are mothers of young babies. Most are young, white, with some high school education.

Poor women used contraception, and the most effective methods, at almost the same level as more affluent women, nevertheless the Medicaid-eligible abortion rate was three times higher than the non-Medicaid rate. This is because poor women have more unwanted pregnancies than other women both because they want fewer children than more affluent women and because they have greater difficulty in using contraceptives effectively.

The Guttmacher Institute report estimates that in Fiscal Year 1977, before the Hyde Amendment cutoff, some 133,000 welfare recipients were unable to obtain Medicaid payments for the abortions they wanted because of unavailability or inaccessibility of abortion services, or restrictive state policies. Now that the Hyde Amendment has been upheld by the Supreme Court the annual unmet need for publicly funded services among Medicaid-eligible women will increase by more than two-and-a-half times—to about 339,000 of the 437,000 in need. Thus the unmet need for publicly funded abortion services among the Medicaid-eligible can be expected to rise from 31 to 79 percent.

Although Medicaid-eligible women represented fewer than one in ten of all women of reproductive age in Fiscal Year 1977, they constituted nearly one in four of the 579,000 women estimated to have been unable to obtain the abortions they wanted during the year. The unmet need for abortions was also disproportionately high among rural, nonwhite and teenage women, all of whom were disadvantaged by the concentration of abortion facilities in relatively few urban locations in each state.

Blacks Are Hardest Hit

On June 17, 1977, speaking on behalf of the Black Caucus of the House, Congressman Parren J. Mitchell, said:

The members of the Congressional Black Caucus are in strong opposition to the so-called Hyde Amendment. There is simply no denying that the effect of the Hyde Amendment would be to exclude only those of limited financial means from access to legal abortions . . . When the government sets up a comprehensive program of medical aid to the indigent but excludes from that program funds for medical aid for abortions, it is obviously imposing a burden on the right to have an abortion. And, as we know, black women are disproportionately represented among the poor and are relatively more likely to need the assistance of Medicaid to obtain the same abortion that their wealthier sisters will be able to obtain in any case.

In dissenting from the June 20, 1977, Supreme Court decisions which made the Hyde Amendment possible, Thurgood Marshall, the nation's first black Supreme Court Justice, declared that "the enactments challenged here (denying Medicaid payments for abortion) brutally coerce poor women to bear children whom society will scorn for every day of their lives," and that "the effect of the challenged regulations will fall with greater disparity upon women of minority races."

Costs To Society

The costs to the individuals extend to the taxpayers—most immediately through the very high medical and welfare costs arising from the failure to offer indigent women the opportunity to obtain the abortions they seek.

HEW's former health financing chief, Robert A. Drezon, reported that each unwanted birth to the woman receiving welfare assistance costs the federal government about $1,000 a year for welfare payments and $100 in Medicaid funds.

Based on this very conservative estimate, if one-third of the 205,000 women who got Medicaid abortions in cutoff states in Fiscal Year 1977, but are no longer eligible, were to carry their pregnancies to term, the *first-year* cost to the federal government would be about $75.2 million.

Another equally conservative estimate of first-year federal *and* state costs for medical services, public assistance and selected social services is $2,330 per woman. The estimated first-year public costs for the same number of women would be nearly $160 million.

Note that these short-term, first-year expenditures do not reflect the astronomical social welfare and medical care expenditures that will be needed to support most of these women and children for many years to come.

Burdensome as these financial outlays are, society pays even more dearly in the contributions lost through interrupted educations, blighted marriages and careers, and the increased poverty and illness of the individual parents and children affected.

In view of this situation one may well ask, *Where is the compassion, where is the humanity that would wreck the lives of countless women and their families? Where is the tenderness that would condemn millions of miserable, unwanted children to live!*

4

Contraception: Logical Alternative to Abortion

While no student of the abortion controversy can help but admire the dedication and ingenuity of the anti-abortion crusaders, at the same time no one could ever accuse them of being objective or truly compassionate. Shutting their eyes to the countless complications that result from denying a woman an abortion that is indicated—physical and mental distress, ruined marriages, disrupted family life, the plight of the unwanted child or the unwed mother, illegal abortions at the risk of life and health, child neglect and abuse—the anti-abortionists chant only one note: "Murder, murder, murder!" Illogically they equate the newly conceived embryo with a viable child; put no limit on sentimentality or their hysterical appeal to the great mass of uninformed people who are not equipped by background or educaton to analyze and appraise the countless factors in such a complex situation. Furthermore, these self-styled "right-to-lifers" never seem to realize that their opposition to sex education for the young, to contraception and world population control are the chief contributing factors to the rapidly increasing *need* for abortion in this imperfect world.

Some years ago when Pope Paul, with his encyclical *Humanae Vitae*, confirmed his ban on the pill and other "artificial" methods of birth control, the American bishops, cognizant of the situation in this country, tried to soften the blow, and many government and private agencies went ahead with campaigns to limit population. But in a quiet counterattack, Paul tried to marshal Catholic forces against all official programs, national or international, that sponsored "artificial" contraception.

An article in *Time* titled "The Rhythm Lobby" told about Pope Paul's covert attack. In a fifteen-page confidential document issued through his secretary of state, Cardinal Villot, and sent to all papal nuncios and apostolic delegates and the Vatican's permanent observers at the UN, Paul stressed the secrecy of the new lobby effort and was sharply critical of the UN for supporting population control programs in the Third World.

In his instructions, Cardinal Villot said that world governments must be persuaded to take positions that "favor Catholic morality;" that papal diplomats should press bishops in each country to build up relations with local representatives of international organizations, key men who are able to influence the secretariats to which they report. Such relations, said Villot, will facilitate the choice of delegates to international conferences "who possess Catholic convictions." Predominantly Catholic countries should be pressured further, said the Cardinal, "to give their delegates unequivocal instructions, and if necessary suggest that those delegates make contacts with representatives of the Holy See."[1]

In spite of the Vatican's efforts to soft-pedal their "rhythm lobby," it is well known that it is the institutional church's intransigent opposition to reliable methods of birth control that is chiefly responsible for a big percentage of the millions of abortions performed each year throughout the world, legal as well as illegal. The number of abortions in Catholic-dominated countries is much greater than in other lands. If the church would only reverse its stand and *actively promote effective contraceptive measures instead of banning them*, the number of abortions would be drastically reduced throughout the world. As we shall see in just a moment, this was proved by actual experience in Corpus Christi, Texas, a Catholic stronghold, as well as in a Florida clinic.

In a *Reader's Digest* article some time ago, the late Dr. Alan F. Guttmacher explained how "years of exposure to the raw edges of human existence" convinced him that legalized abortion is an essential and humane medical service:

> The ironic fact is that those who oppose and those who favor legalized abortion share a common goal — the elimination of *all* abortion. The difference is that while

41

the anti-abortionists believe this can be accomplished by tough, punitive statutes, the abortion-law reformers point to evidence showing that these laws have never worked in the past and never will. In the years preceding liberation of abortion laws in this country, for example, a conservative estimate is that at least one million illegal operations were being performed annually. Those who favor liberalization want to substitute safe abortion laws for the dangerous, clandestine variety, until contraception is so widely practiced that unwanted pregnancy—and therefore the need for abortion—disappears.[2]

As Father John A. O'Brien says in *Family Planning in an Exploding Population,* "Not permitted by the Church to use the simple, cheap, and effective methods of contraception developed by medical science, millions of these (Catholic) women are turning in their desperation to the sad and tragic expedient of abortion."[3]

In France informed observers say there are about as many abortions as births, even though the restrictive law, repealed in November 1974, was very severe.[4] In Italy the proportion is about the same, though in time we may expect a reduction there, since the laws against contraception have been invalidated by Italy's highest court.[5] (In the spring of 1978 the Italian parliament, over the heated objections of the Vatican, legalized abortion.)

When Dr. Luigi Marchi, a family-planning pioneer, was asked what brought about his legal victory after a fifteen-year fight, he said, "Italians have had time to think about this problem and accept new concepts." And Italians, he said, had already tacitly accepted abortion as one form of birth control — a proportion estimated at one abortion for every birth in Italy. "Abortions have prevented a serious population explosion," he says, "but their danger, inconvenience, and even sharper clash with Catholic belief is one reason why contraception is gaining support."

Brazil, more than 90 percent Catholic, with less than half the United State's population, has about the same number of illegal abortions this country had before the change in our abortion laws— estimated at 1,200,000 a year. Chile, with a population just under ten million, has from 125,000 to 150,000 abortions a year—all illegal.6

In their book *Population—Resources—Environment,* eminent biologists Paul and Anne Ehrlich say, "Illegal abortion is rampant in Latin America. . . Bungled abortions are estimated to account for more than 40 percent of hospital admissions in Santiago, Chile. In that country an estimated one-third of all pregnancies end in abortion. For South America as a whole, some authorities believe that one-fourth of all pregnancies end in abortion. Other estimates are that abortions out number pregnancies brought to term. [7]

As everyone knows, Latin America is predominantly Catholic and Catholic influence has made contraceptives difficult to obtain in many places there. As a result, the highest rate of illegitimacy in the world is on that continent, where common-law unions are prevalent. In eight Latin American countries, more than half of all births are illegitimate. [8] Incidentally, Latin America has one of the highest birth rates of all the world, 2.73 percent.

Though abortion among Catholics is more prevalent in foreign countries dominated by the Roman church, let no one think that American Catholics are far behind their non-Catholic sisters in taking advantage of this "last resort," as noted heretofore. Further proof comes from Lawrence Lader. In his book *Abortion*, Lader lists four studies which prove that Catholics comprise over 20 percent of all abortion patients—"almost equal to the Catholic ratio of about 25 percent of the total populaiton." [9] Lader also reports that in two Buffalo hospitals the abortion rate for Catholics ranged from 24 to 38 percent of all such operations. [10]

In the same book Lader tells how a birth control program among the poor in a great Catholic stronghold, Corpus Christi, Texas, achieved a drastic cut in abortions. As they did everywhere else, the Catholic bishops strongly opposed family planning among the poor in that city, claiming that "government birth control aid constitutes discrimination against the poor, since they will feel coerced to adopt control."

After trying unsuccessfully for a long time, the local Planned Parenthood Center finally got enough federal money to set up four one-day-a-week birth control centers in the most depressed neighborhoods, "where the average resident of twenty-six has five children, a third-grade education, and an income of about $35 a week." Among such patients, mainly of Spanish descent, the birth control clinic produced significant results. Births were reduced 28 percent over a period of four years. Illegal abortions, previously estimated at 1,000 a year for the county, performed mainly by unskilled midwives, were cut 41 percent in the same period. "The clinic's physicians are convinced that women who formerly depended on abortion are now being reached by a contraceptive education for the first time. The Corpus Christi clinic offers added proof to Dr. Koya's experience in Japan that an intensive contraceptive campaign quickly lowers the abortion rate."[11]

Catholic Theologians Favor Contraception

While the American Catholic hierarchy lined up 100 percent with Pope Paul in his ban on "artificial" contraception, it is interesting to note that in a four-year study commissioned by the prestigious Catholic Theological Society of America, a group of influential Roman Catholic theologians took sharp issue with the Vatican and the hierarchy on contraception, sterilization, and other aspects of sexuality.

In releasing the 242-page report of this study, published by Paulist Press under the title *Human Sexuality, New Directions in American Catholic Thought,* the press statement of the five authors noted:

> The circumstances which occasioned the study can only be described as a massive breakdown of Catholic adherence to traditional Church teachings on sexuality.
>
> Recent findings of social research indicate (that) 85 percent of U.S. Catholics reject the Church's official teaching on birth control.
>
> Some two-thirds of American Catholic women are practicing some form of birth control officially disapproved by the Church . . .
>
> According to a sociological study among Catholic priests commissioned by the National Conference of Catholic Bishops, only a minority of priests in America still support the Church's official teaching on birth control.

In regard to procreation, the report said:

> The attitude . . . of "leaving it all in the hands of God and accepting whatever He sends" is both simplistic and morally irresponsible. Responsible parenthood demands readiness to acknowledge that there are situations and conditions where it would be irresponsible and hence immoral to beget children . . .
>
> Decisions involving medical considerations "should only be made in consultation with and upon recommendation of a competent physician or medical

expert. It is not the task of the priest or religious counselor to recommend or approve any specific method of contraception."

There was no direct discussion in the report on abortion.

Viewing the Problem with Eyes Closed

In their rush to capitalize on the sensational and distasteful aspects of abortion, the various anti-abortion groups give no consideration whatsoever to the other side of the coin. While they claim massive support from non-Catholic individuals and groups —and wherever possible, put such individuals in executive positions so as to bolster this claim—the truth is that about 60 to 75 percent of the support and membership of all anti-abortion groups come from Roman Catholic individuals and the Catholic hierarchy.

I have met some of the leaders of the Tennessee Volunteers for Life and at their invitation attended one of their chapter meetings as an observer. I don't know whether this group is typical or not, but I found no evidence of the extreme fanaticism that animates so many anti-abortionists, a disturbing aspect of this movement which is discussed above.

They appear to be a normal group of men and women, dedicated to a goal which they pursued, but not in a fanatical manner. The meeting was held in a committee room of St. Joseph Catholic Hospital in Memphis and a Catholic priest was in attendance. The chairman was a Catholic doctor on the staff of the hospital. Like all such groups, they have a ready answer for every question a person could ask, except one: *If they are so strongly opposed to abortion, why don't they attack the problem at its source? Why don't they devote their time, efforts and powerful influence to promoting sex education and birth control for the young and uninitiated instead of doing everything possible to thwart such a logical approach?*

With all due respect for the good intentions of such groups, I must tell why they don't respond to such queries: *They don't know the answer. They haven't thought the problem through to a logical conclusion.*

Instead of being guided by the pragmatic thinking of liberated young Catholics, male and female, who realize that abortion, soul-searing as it may be, is far more desirable than the multifaceted tragedies spawned by an unexpected and unwanted pregnancy, they are guided by the cardinals and bishops,

45

well-meaning old men who have never been forced to face up to the problems haunting the pregnant girls and women on whom they sit in judgment; old men who still adhere to the medieval position of the institutional church as expressed by Dr. Austin O'Malley in his *Ethics of Feticide*: "The first fact in the world is that justice, law, order, should be observed no matter what the cost; *better that ten thousand mothers should die than one fetus should be unjustly killed.*"[12]

While, as I have said before, the anti-abortion movement is dominated by the Catholic institutional church, let no one get the idea that this movement is backed by a majority of the Catholic laity, male and female.

Civil War in the Church

No one with the slightest understanding of the situation can deny there is turmoil and dissension in the Roman church today. This is shown by a loss in the numbers of priests, nuns and lay members, as well as in the sharp decline in regular mass-attending by the laity of all ages.[13]

In 1971 the Catholic bishops of the United States appropriated $500,000 for a study on the relation between the American hierarchy and the clergy, with special emphasis on church discipline, liturgy, and moral teaching. The report of the Chicago Priest-Sociologist Andrew M. Greeley, director of the study, was gall and wormwood to the bishops. "Honesty compels me," noted Father Greeley in a sad prologue, "to say that I believe the present leadership of the church to be morally, intellectually and religiously bankrupt."[14]

In another survey by Father Greeley and Father William C. McCready, with emphasis on the changes in attitude by various groups of Catholics toward legal abortion in specific circumstances, they found: (1) young Catholics were not attending mass with anything like the traditional regularity of their parents; (2) in the area of sex and behavior, young Catholics have departed substantially from that of their parents' generation; (3) the majority of Catholics approve of legal abortion where the woman became pregnant through rape, where there was evidence of a defective child, or where the woman's life would be endangered by bringing the pregnancy to term. Though there were changes in attitude toward abortion by Catholics of all ages except those over sixty, Catholics under thirty reported the greatest change and are practically indistinguishable from Protestants of the same age group.[15]

Still another study made by Father Greeley and three colleagues in the fall of 1974 showed an even further "backsliding" on the part of American Catholics. These interviews tested the attitude of the laity on certain aspects of their faith compared with attitudes revealed in a similar study in 1963, a bit over a decade before.

In the 1963 survey, 71 percent of those interviewed attended weekly mass, compared with 50 percent in the 1974 study. A decade ago 45 percent of Catholics approved of "artificial" contraception; in the new study 84 percent approved. Only 12 percent approved of sexual relations between engaged couples a decade ago; now 43 percent approved. Approval of remarriage after divorce rose from 52 to 73 percent. While 73 percent of those interviewed in the new study said they would not have an abortion themselves, 70 percent said that abortion should be available to married women who didn't want any more children[16]

Juvenile Time Bombs—Male and Female

If one were asked to point out the most glaring mistake made by the various anti-abortion groups, he would be right on target if he mentioned their failure to face up to the revolution in sexual mores on the part of teenagers and sub-teens. Whether we like it or not, we must admit that in the past decade the sexual activities of our children, boys and girls, have reached epidemic proportions. I quote from the findings of 160 delegates from 39 countries at the First Interhemispheric Conference on Adolescent Fertility, Arlie House, Virginia, 1976:

> Close to 13 million of the 60 million women who became mothers in 1975 became parents before they became adults . . . Early childbearing is increasing everywhere, is emerging as a serious problem in many countries, and has reached alarming levels in others (where it is associated) with serious health, socio-economic and demographic implications for young women, young men, their off-spring and, indeed, for the whole society . . . Adolescent pregnancy is a serious threat to the life and health of a young woman . . . whether the birth occurs in or out of marriage.

In a recent article carried by the *New York Times* Special News Service, Dr. Melvin J. Konner, Professor of Biological Anthropology at Harvard University, said that the United States faces a problem that has reached the dimensions of a national disaster comparable to a flood, epidemic or famine, one that results, similarly, from a gigantic flaw of nature. That flaw is the precipitous, unprecedented drop in the age of puberty; the problem is the startling spread of teenage pregnancy.

A bit over a century ago, in 1840, the average young woman in Europe and the United States menstruated for the first time at the age of 17; her modern counterpart reaches the age of menstruation at about 12.

"Human beings are not designed by evolution either physically or spiritually for the experience of adolescent pregnancy," writes Dr. Konner. In the United States, from 1940 to 1960, births in the 15-19 maternal age group about doubled. After 1960, out-of-wedlock births in the 14-17-year age range rose steadily until 1973, when legal abortion halted the rise. But teenage pregnancy has continued to rise to the present rate of one million a year. The fastest rise is in the youngest group, 11-13 years. Dr. Konner continues:

> As maternal age drops from age 20, mortality risk for mother and child rises sharply as does the probability of birth defects. Offspring of adolescent mothers, if they survive, are more likely to have impaired intellectual functioning. Poverty, divorce, inept parenting, child neglect and child abuse are all more frequent in teenage parents . . .
>
> The baby, of course, is not the only sufferer. For women of all ages, the incidence of onset of mental illness increases fivefold to fifteenfold during the first month after delivery. What sort of effect may we expect it to have on a junior high school girl? Little stretch of the imagination is required to conclude that denying her an abortion is in itself a form of child abuse, even leaving aside the kitchen-abortion horror tales.
>
> In every other arena of life, including the criminal court, we absolve her of responsibility for her actions; in the maternity clinic we avert our eyes and condemn her.

Continuing along these lines, Dr. Konner goes on to say:

Consider the plight of these children. Assaulted by culturally sanctioned sexual innuendo and borne along by physical and physiological events that have never before befallen such young children, they are at the mercy of their own and one another's impulses, having five years less experience and mental growth than their pubescent counterparts of a century ago.

To guide them through these biological storms, we offer religions thick with the dust of a past era, parental counsel that is vague, timid, false, irrelevant or negligible, and teachers who, on the subject of contraception, are silenced by the rule of law.

The people who keep children in the dark about contraception have now deprived them of a major source of rescue from the accident caused by this legislative ignorance . . . We may sympathize with the impulse of those whose private views make them oppose abortion on ethical grounds. But their personal reading of the human moral law need not constrain the rest of us from exercising a more complex judgment . . . Modern teenagers are the victims of a physiological blight, the capacity for immature pregnancy—a tragic, anomalous, biological novelty. It is our clear duty to help save them from this blight, not condemn them to it.[17]

Adolescents in the United States have rates of childbearing that are among the world's highest. About 10 percent of United States teenagers get pregnant and 6 percent give birth each year. Among the world's industrialized countries, only Romania, New Zealand, Bulgaria, and East Germany have higher teenage fertility rates. Indeed, adolescent fertility is higher in the Unites States than in many less developed nations, such as the Philippines, Tunisia, and East Malaysia.

The statistics and sexual activities of our juvenile time bombs, taken from authentic studies by responsible organizations in this field, are astounding. There are about 21 million young people in the United States between the ages of 15 and 19 years. Of these, more than half—something like 11 million—are estimated to have had sexual intercourse, almost 7 million young men and 4 million young women. In addition, one-fifth of the eight million 13 and 14-year-old boys and girls are believed to have had intercourse.

As adolescents grow older, the probability that they will have premarital sexual experiences increases sharply. Fewer than one-fourth of unmarried girls aged 15 have had intercourse, compared to more than half of the 19-year-olds. Sexual activity also appears to be commencing at younger ages. Among the predominantly white, middle class teenagers in one midwestern city, the proportion of 14-year-olds who had experienced intercourse grew from 10 percent in 1971 to 17 percent in 1973.

Each year more than one million 15 to 19-year-olds become pregnant, one-tenth of all the women in this age group. (Two-thirds of these pregnancies are out of wedlock.) In addition, something like 30,000 girls younger than 15 get pregnant annually.

Of the million teenagers who get pregnant each year, something like 600,000 give birth. Here is how the million pregnancies were resolved in 1974:

Marital births conceived after marriage: 28 percent
Marital births conceived before marriage: 10 percent
Out-of-wedlock births: 21 percent
Terminated by induced abortion: 27 percent
Miscarriages: 14 percent

Of the additional 30,000 pregnancies experienced by girls younger than 15, 42 percent were terminated by abortion, and 36 percent resulted in out-of-wedlock births. Only 6 percent ended in marital births, and virtually all of these resulted from premarital conceptions. The remaining 13 percent were miscarriages.

Because of the high rate of teenage pregnancies and childbearing, 608,000, or one-fifth of all U.S. births, are to girls in their teens. Of these, 247,000 are to girls 17 or younger, 13,000 to girls younger than 15.

A substantial and growing percentage of adolescent childbearing occurs out-of-wedlock. Between 1961 and 1974 the rate of illegitimacy declined by about one-fourth among women 20 to 24. By contrast, it increased by about a third among those 18 and 19, and three-fourths among 14 to 17-year-olds. More than half of all illegitimate births are to teenagers; one in four to youngsters 17 or less. Since the early 1960's the proportion of all illegitimate births to younger adolescents has risen by 18 percent and to older adolescents by 40 percent.

A government-reported study of sexually active teenage girls in 1976 shows a decline in out-of-wedlock births, a trend "largely influenced by the availability of abortion," Johns Hopkins University researchers reported. They estimated that about one-third of all the nation's girls in the 15-to-19-year-age group are sexually active. Of the girls interviewed in 1976, the proportion who ever experienced a premarital pregnancy was one-third higher than for a comparable group interviewed in 1971.

At the University of Arkansas Medical Center at Little Rock in 1976, there were 15 girls no older than 11 years who gave birth. A UPI dispatch of June 1, 1979 reported the birth of *twins* to a 10-year-old girl at the Indiana University medical Center, Indianapolis. According to medical experts, this was the youngest mother of twins in U.S. history.

Despite the increased number of abortions since 1973, there has been an increase in out-of-wedlock births both among teenagers and adults. An Associated Press dispatch of May 5, 1978, says that "one American child in seven was born out of wedlock in 1976, with the rate exceeding 50 percent among blacks for the first time, the government reports."

Some 468,100 of the 3,168,000 babies born during the year were to unmarried mothers, or 14.8 percent, according to the National Center for Health's statistics. Some 258,800, or 50.3 percent of all births among black mothers were out of wedlock. There were 197,100 births among unmarried white mothers, or 7.7 percent. The percentage of births out of wedlock has been climbing steadily for both races. In 1969, it was 34.9 percent among blacks and 5.5 percent among whites.

Virtually without exception pregnancies among unmarried teenagers and sub-teens are unwanted and unintended. The problems such pregnancies cause these unfortunate girls and their families are too numerous and too well known for further comment. Pregnancy is the cause of most drop-outs among school girls and the younger the girl the more likely she dropped out because of pregnancy. From a health standpoint the problem is even worse. Not only is the infant of a teenage or sub-teen mother at greater risk of death, defect, or illness than one born to a woman in her twenties, but the younger mother herself is more likely to die or suffer illness or injury.

When one considers the countless and overwhelming problems faced by a young girl in this position, one wonders how the so-called "right-to-lifers" can believe they are doing her, the unborn child, or society a favor by insisting that she bring her pregnancy to term.

A Pediatric Bill of Rights

Cognizant of all these complications—serious health, social, and economic problems—the National Association of Children's Hospitals and Related Institutions announced, in 1974, the following Pediatric Bill of Rights:

> Every child. . . shall have the right to receive appropriate medical care and treatment. . . (including) the right to receive medically prescribed contraceptive devices . . . adequate and objective counseling relating to pregnancy and abortion . . . (and) medically accepted treatment which will result in abortion.

Despite the fact that the lives and careers of millions of our children are at stake, six out of ten sex education programs exclude birth control. In what we like to consider an enlightened age, it is a shameful thing to admit that, with the boundless facilities at our command, we are doing so little to protect these hapless youngsters against themselves.

It is doubtful if anyone in America has given as much time, effort, and thought to the abortion controversy as the eminent Catholic writer and editor, Daniel Callahan, author of *Abortion: Law, Choice and Morality*, perhaps the most definitive book on the subject ever written. Dr. Callahan might be described as a "pro-lifer" in its broadest connotation, which means that in arriving at a conclusion, he takes into consideration all the factors involved: the welfare of the fetus, the welfare of the involved woman and her family, along with the welfare of society as a whole. His appraisal of the teenage problem is illuminating:

> What we are facing now . . . is an epidemic. Worse still, it is an epidemic about which something can be done but isn't being done. Teenage pregnancy can, through better education and preventive services, be, if not altogether avoided, at least reduced, and through better maternity, abortion and social services, be reduced in its personal impact on the teenager who does get pregnant. Some may find one or more of the possible means morally repugnant. Life rarely presents us with perfect choices. If we do not provide teenagers with education and services, we surely now know that many will do great harm to themselves—that is both a present reality and a future prospect which cannot also fail to be morally repugnant . . .

52

Our greater obligation is toward their welfare; our other, and competing, convictions should give way at that point. At the very least, teenagers should have as much knowledge of sex, as many and as good services available, and as many choices open to them, as do adults. Adults hardly have all the knowledge they should have, or all the services they need. But whatever they have at least should be shared equally with teenagers. Like adults, teenage girls can get pregnant, and like adults, teenage boys can impregnate girls. Why then should they remain ignorant, unserved and uncared for? [18]

Planned Births, the Future and Quality of American Life

Improvements in family planning methods and practices, along with substantial progress in making such services available to all, wrought a reasonably successful federal program in the past decade. Gratifying as this limited success has been, it is nothing compared with what might be achieved if the government is sincere in its search for "alternatives to abortion" and is willing to invest substantially increased sums to initiate a program that will pay back in added benefits and savings in welfare outlays nearly two dollars for every dollar so invested.

Unfortunately for the nation at large, and especially our teenagers, President Carter's personal aversion to abortion caused him to adopt a "do nothing" policy when it came to pursuing effective alternatives to abortion, but the distaff side of the administration was more receptive. Interviewed by the *Philadelphia Bulletin* (November 10, 1976), Rosalynn Carter said: "I personally don't like abortion, but I am not for an amendment to the Constitution to make it illegal, because I've seen what happens when abortion was made illegal in some states. Abortion mills spring up in neighboring states where it is legal. *We should try to prevent the need for abortion, by pushing for organized family planning, better sex education and less red tape in the adoption procedures."* (Emphasis added).

Taking the Carter Administration up on its frequently expressed preference for "alternatives to abortion," five national health and family planning organizations proposed a comprehensive national program of preventive services in human reproduction which they said, "In as few as five years, could halve the incidence of unwanted and unintended births and pregnancies in this country and have significant ramifications for the quality of American life and the strengthening of the family." The sponsoring organizations include the Alan Guttmacher Institute, the Planned Parenthood Federation of America, the Population Section of the American Public Health Association, the National Family Planning Forum, and Zero Population Growth, Incorporated.

The plan of these organizations called on the federal government to launch a wide range of new health and education initiatives, including expanded family planning services to reach *an additional 3 million sexually-active adolescent* and older low-income persons in need of services over the next three years; federal support of sex education programs in the family, the school, community agencies and the media; preventive programs to reduce the incidence of infant retardation and disability; services to minimize the need for abortion (especially *late* abortions); along with programs to help infertile couples to have the children they want.

The health agencies' plan, which is entitled "Planned Births, The Future of The Family, and The Quality of American Life," called on the administration to commit itself, at minimum, to maintenance of the federally-assisted national family planning program, which provided contraceptive information and services to an estimated 4 million persons in 1977, and to a substantial expansion of the federal effort in medical and behavioral reproductive research for improved contraceptives.

Savings Effected by This Program Would Exceed Costs

While the costs of this proposed plan would be great, the benefits and savings would be much greater. The program could be implemented through "incremental changes in existing federal legislation," at a gross cost of approximately $410 million for the first year, rising to $783 million by the early 1980's. These estimates compare with the (fiscal year 1978) federal spending on family planning of $225 million, say the sponsors of this plan.

Core legislation for the proposed program would be Title X of the Public Health Service Act, the primary source of most current family planning and contraceptive research monies. In addition, changes would be needed in other federal statutes which provide assistance to the states for medical and social services for the poor (principally, Titles XIX and XX of the Social Security Act); in legislation providing health aid to special population groups (e.g. mothers and children); and in the Elementary and Secondary

Education Act.

Against the projected financial costs of the program, say the sponsors, we must place not only the "health, social, economic and emotional benefits to individuals" which it may be expected to yield, but also "anticipated savings to the government which accrue when women are enabled to avert unintended pregnancies and births that would require health and social services at the taxpayer's expense." *They pointed out that cumulative savings under the national family planning program, which cost some $584 million between 1970 and 1975,were $1.1 billion—twice the cost of the program.*

At first glance estimated savings of $1.1 billion may seem overly optimistic, but if one will only consider the tremendous outlays made by the government under the Aid to Families of Dependent Children program, he will see that this estimate is really conservative. The average cost of raising a child to age eighteen under the AFDC program is $35,216—that is, if the child is in average health. If the child is severely retarded, mentally or physically, the cost may be twice that much, or more. In fiscal year 1978, 3,532,398 families and 7,480,666 children were cared for by AFDC, at a total cost of $10,726,866,000. [19] In round numbers the cost of the AFDC program for fiscal year 1979 was $12 billion, the estimated cost for fiscal year 1980 was $13 billion, and the estimated cost for fiscal year 1981 was $14 billion. [20]

Vital Need for Further Research

Because of the problems associated with currently available contraceptives, it is clear that family planning programs, even if fully implemented as projected above, can only do so much to reduce the incidence of unwanted and mistimed pregnancies, or to minimize the need for abortion services. Even our most sophisticated contraceptive methods have disappointing failure rates, and all have persistent and occasionally serious side affects which make them unacceptable to many women.

Clearly federal efforts must be expanded to acquire new knowledge and develop new, more convenient, more effective technologies. Biomedical research efforts designed to produce safer and more acceptable contraceptive methods—including those for men—are vital, and they should be accompanied by behavioral research efforts to aquire a better understanding of the social, economic, demographic, and psychological aspects of reproduction. [21]

Federal expenditures for biomedical and behavioral research in human reproduction, including expenditures for the development of new contraceptive methods, are currently about $60 million—*less than two percent of the total research efforts of the National Institutes of Health [NIH]*. This is unconscionable, especially in view of the increasing concern among millions of American women over the safety of current contraceptive methods. Therefore, the authorization under Title X for the nation's population science research program, at a minimum, should be increased to at least $175 million in fiscal year 1981.

A Giant Step for Mankind

A unique opportunity for the nation's well-being has been created by four developments of the past decade:

Widespread distribution and use of contraceptive methods, which further research could make even more effective.

An overwhelming consensus in favor of family planning among Americans in all socio-economic and ethnic groups.

Legalization of termination of unwanted pregnancies.

A successful federal program to equalize access to family planning services.

As a result of these developments, our society now has the opportunity to move forward decisively to assist women and men in all walks of life to have their children at times and under conditions that are optimal for the social, physical, economic, and emotional well-being of both parents and children. Such an opportunity is rare in our history: Never before have Americans regulated fertility to the extent that they do today. Moreover, few other nations now have within their grasp the opportunity we have to solve the remaining critical problems of unregulated child-bearing and to ensure that future generations are born wanted by their parents, free of handicapping social and health conditions, and launched in life with the best skills and knowledge that modern medicine and humane social policy can offer.

Realization of this family planning objective could have significant ramifications for the quality of American life and the strengthening of the family. By resolving the quantitative problems of childbearing, it could free families and communities to concentrate resources on enriching the quality of life for children. Helping young people postpone childbearing until they are ready to become parents could reduce the number of teenagers who form single-parent households and who often are forced into unstable marriages. Enabling couples to avoid more children than they want and can rear could ease a major stress leading to broken families. In these and many other ways, family planning could multiply the impact of other efforts to improve individual and social well-being.

In addition to these important benefits for our own people and nation, the implementation of such a policy here could also have significant influence worldwide, both in industrialized nations faced with similar problems of unregulated fertility and in developing nations struggling to curb rapid rates of population growth.

If we are to achieve these gratifying objectives we must reverse the trends of the past few years when the national family planning program, initiated under President Johnson, became a casualty of the "New Federalism." By withdrawing the commitment to a national priority effort, federal policy since 1973 cut by two-thirds the program's annual rate of growth in patients served and threatened to leave implementation of the constitutional right to regulate fertility to each state's varying interpretation. It also became impossible to achieve the goals of the 1971 Department of Health, Education and Welfare five-year plan for family planning services or to design new initiatives to deal effectively with the remaining problems of fertility regulation in the United States. Whether intended or not, the New Federalist policy precluded a comprehensive effort to reduce the need for abortion by coping with unintended pregnancy. The incoming administration (1981-1985) has an unprecedented opportunity to provide leadership and support for a national effort which, in as few as five years, as the sponsors have pointed out, could halve the incidence of unwanted and unintended pregnancies and births. Such an effort would be relatively inexpensive compared with other major programs and would return benefits both to individuals and to society far in excess of the costs.

5

Weep for the Unwanted Child—At Birth!

In concluding his penetrating book, *Mandatory Motherhood,* Garrett Hardin, Professor of Biology at the University of California at Santa Barbara, asked: "What would be the consequence if the number of psychologically warped adults could be reduced to a tenth of the present population by seeing to it that no mothers ever were compelled to bear an unwanted child, and every child born was a *wanted* child?"

While such a boon would not change our crime-ridden society into a Utopia, it would certainly bring about a tremendous improvement. It is common knowledge that the *unwanted* child is too often the *abused* child. Applied to the unwanted child, Montesquieu's epigram "Weep not for men at death: weep for them at birth!" is all the more pertinent. Even for the most fortunate families life in this vale of tears is no bargain; but when you consider the plight of the unwanted child—the out-of-wedlock child, the child born to a subteen or early teenage mother, the child born into a large, poverty-stricken family—one can't help questioning the sagacity of those who fight incessantly for the "right" of such a child to be born. Granted that even in the early stages of pregnancy an aborted fetus can feel pain, what is the momentary twinge suffered by the aborted fetus compared with a lifetime of mental and physical degradation, extreme poverty, hunger, ill-health, sexual or physical abuse, in one degree or another, that is almost always the fate of the unwanted child?

58

Better Unborn Than Unwanted

In *The Diary of an Unwanted Child*, little Melisha Gibson gives us some idea of the kind of life thousands of children suffer each year at the hands of brutal, neurotic parents or step-parents, the kind of life the anti-abortionists are fighting so hard to "save":

> When I was eleven months old my mom and stepdaddy were sent to jail for burning and beating me and an older sister. We were sent to a foster home, along with mom's three other children.
>
> After mom and my stepdaddy had served their term, 11 months and 29 days, my four sisters and brothers were returned to their home, but I was left with my foster parents. Nearly three years later my parents asked for my return and the authorities granted their request.
>
> My parents were drunk a big part of the time. My sisters and brothers were big enough to get out of their way when they were on one of their jags, but I was too little, so I took many a beating when they were drunk.
>
> Whenever I wet the bed, or did something they didn't like, my step-daddy would beat me with a stick and force me to walk the floor for hours at a time, never stopping to give me a moment's rest. When I'd fall to the floor he'd just beat me all the harder, make me get up and walk some more. He kept hitting me again and again, until my body was nothing but one mass of bruises. I begged my mom for help, but she just gave me an icy stare. When I asked for water my tormentor forced tabasco sauce down my throat. He was almost too drunk to stand up, but he wasn't too drunk to beat me unmercifully.
>
> This went on for months. Every time I'd wet the bed he'd get out that stick—said he'd learn me a lesson if it killed me. Then one night, when I was nearly four years old . . .

Of course, this "diary" wasn't actually written by the unfortunate little girl, but it is the true story of her short and tragic life. Four-year-old Melisha Gibson, of Cleveland, Tennessee, died October 30, 1976, after her step-father had marched her back and forth in the house during waking hours for two days and nights, beating her all the time with a metal-tipped club, while her mother looked on. An autopsy showed that her liver had been split and a kidney ruptured. Ronald Maddux, the step-father, and Wanda Gibson Maddux, the mother, were convicted of murder shortly afterwards and are now serving a ninety-nine year sentence in the Tennessee penitentiary.

In March of 1969 a similar case was the scandal of the year in New York City and the nation at large. Three days after she disappeared, the body of three-year-old Roxanne Felumero was found in the East River at 10th Street, weighted down with concrete slabs. Her stepfather, George Poplis, was charged with beating the little girl to death, and her mother was held as a material witness.

Poplis confessed that for several days he had been beating the child with his fists "for wetting the bed." A witness who saw the child a day or two before she died testified that her head was swollen "to twice the normal size." After the final beating, Roxanne threw up her dinner and fell lifeless to the floor. When the child's mother cried, "What are we going to do?" Poplis replied, "I think I'll have to throw her in the river." He walked down to the river with the child in his arms, while the mother pushed their 18-month-old in a stroller. After weighting the body down with cement slabs from the crumbling sidewalk, Poplis tossed the dead child in the river. He received a sentence of twenty years to life.

Are these exceptional cases? Not at all. Two similar cases were reported in the February 16 and 18, 1978, issues of the *Memphis Commercial Appeal*, one from east Tennessee, the other from north Mississippi. Each year in the United States, according to dependable authorities, 4,000 children are beaten to death. Each year, estimates the U.S. Children's Bureau, there are 50,000 to 75,000 cases of serious child abuse. Dr. Vincent DeFrancis of the American Humane Association estimates that 10,000 children are severely beaten each year, at least 50,000 to 75,000 sexually abused, 100,000 emotionally neglected, and another 100,000 physically, morally, and educationally neglected. David Gil, Brandeis professor of sociology, basing his figures on a study he did some years ago for the National Opinion Research Center, estimates the number of severely abused children at between 2.5 and 4 million each year.

Dr. Gil's figures cover physical abuse only. There is no survey data for the incidence of child neglect and sexual abuse, although studies in both New York State and New York City show that neglect and sexual abuse occur more than twice as cften as physical abuse.

The National Center on Child Abuse and Neglect estimates that there are at least 100,000 cases of sexual abuse each year and says it is the least reported of all criminal activities, largely because the father or some relative is so often to blame. Hank Giarretto, director of the Santa Clara Child Abuse Treatment Program in San Jose, considers a quarter of a million cases a conservative estimate. [1]

"Who are reported abusers and neglecters?" asks Naomi Feigelson Chase in her alarming book, *A Child Is Being Beaten.* "Overwhelmingly they are poor people, black people, Hispanic people, very young mothers. Mothers with illegitimate children. Alcoholics. Junkies. People on public assistance. People with no friends. People with no resources. People with emotional problems, with medical problems, with poor physical health, with poor mental health." [2]

Social, financial, and physical pressures often become so overwhelming that even intelligent, relatively stable men and women cruelly abuse their children. Some authorities say that 10 percent of our population is sufficiently disturbed to need psychiatric treatment at one time or another in their lives. The incidence of alcoholism is high, and many young people who have turned to large-scale use of drugs have now become parents. That's why today we find so many parents who are psychotic, neurotic, drunk, or under the influence of drugs attempting to cope with their stress-filled roles; why their reaction to their child's annoying behavior is often so brutal.

In a study reported in the *Journal of the American Medical Association*, Dr. Henry Kempe, a pioneer in the field of child abuse, said: "Those who practice child abuse are immature, impulsive, self-centered, hypersensitive and quick to react with poorly controlled aggression. *Not infrequently the beaten infant is a product of an unwanted pregnancy, a pregnancy which began before marriage, too soon after marriage, or at some other time felt to be extremely inconvenient.*" (Emphasis added).

One of the worst things about child abuse is that it is more or less self-perpetuating. More often than not the abusing parents have been badly raised by their own parents. Abused children not only tend to develop characteristics that make them less attractive, such as fear of being alone, excessive whimpering, shyness, abnormal hostility and the like, but if these abused children become parents themselves, the likelihood of a repetition of the abusive practice is very great. Abuse and neglect are passed on from generation to generation.

A Life Of Pain and Fear

Perhaps those children who die as a result of parental violence are more fortunate than those who live, those who are destined to spend their entire childhoold in pain and fear. According to a national survey on child abuse, conducted in 1975 by Dr. Richard Gelles, Dr. Murray Straus and Dr. Suzanne Steinmetz, more than three million children in a year's time had been kicked, hit or punched at some time in their short lives by their parents. In the year of the study, 460,000 to 750,000 children had been beaten to the point of serious injury by their parents. More dramatically, 46,000 were threatened or injured by their parents with a gun or knife.

The number of children abused in the United States is increasing every year. Dr. Trude Lash and Dr. Heide Sigal found in their study of child abuse in New York City that the incidence of child abuse increased 1026 percent in the decade 1964 to 1974. No doubt a big percentage of this increase can be attributed to a growing willingness to report child abuse, but obviously most of this increase indicates a substantially higher incidence of abuse. The Office of Child Development of the Department of Health, Education and Welfare said, "An epidemic of child abuse is occurring in this counry."

In this situation one problem often begets another. Statistics show that unwanted births are a major factor contributing to the murder of infants and children and to child abuse in general. In a study of 37 infants killed within the first 24 hours after birth, Dr. Phillip J. Resnick found that 83 percent of the victims were unwanted by the mother.[3] Despite the legalization of abortion the incidence of unwanted births in this country is still very high. A fertility study by Dr. Larry Bumpass and Dr. Charles Westoff reported that for the years 1960 to 1965, 22 percent of all births were unwanted by at least one spouse. Among low-income and poorly educated families, the rate of unwanted births was even higher.

By careless and indifferent breeding we are literally setting the stage for more crime and disorder. The recent U. S. Supreme Court decision against the use of federal Medicaid funds for abortion will result in a loss of federal and state funds for poor women who wish to terminate an unwanted pregnancy. This insures an increase in unwanted and abandoned babies, in infant and child mortality, and in the human reservoir of crime, violence, child abuse, and drug and alcohol addiction fifteen to twenty years from now. But who will be held responsible for the consequences of an unwise decision made a generation before? The people in the White House, current members of Congress and the Supreme Court majority responsible for that decision will all be gone. Tragically, no one will be held responsible but the unwanted, neglected child, tomorrow's social offender.

It is estimated that more than a million of our children run away from home each year because they find their home lives intolerable. As a result, Congress passed the Runaway Youth Act to provide halfway houses and other support programs for children. The studies of Dr. Rocco D'Angelo, of Ohio State University's School of Social Work, found that runaway children are physically punished two-and-a-half times as often as non-runaway children. Naturally children who live in happy, affectionate homes are not so apt to run away. On the other hand, children who are deprived of physical affection by their parents are more likely to receive a great deal of physical punishment from them. Such children become extremely vulnerable to exploitation, especially sexual exploitation. So it is not surprising to find so many of these runaways involved in child prostitution and pornography.

Child Abuse—The Sleeping Sickness

Unless a person is actively involved with the problem—such as a social worker, juvenile court judge or officer, a delinquent parent or the like—he is pretty apt to regard child abuse and neglect as he would a dormant volcano. He knows it's there, he knows it's dangerous, but so long as it doesn't erupt, he should worry!

John Donne could have had such a problem in mind centuries ago when he wrote, "No man is an island . . . never send to find for whom the bell tolls; it tolls for Thee."

The joint problem of child abuse and child neglect is perhaps the most malignant cancer afflicting our nation today. It is the fountain source of juvenile delinquency, which itself is the breeding ground for most of this nation's crime of every description.

Not only is the problem getting worse year by year, but it is virtually insoluble. A mere listing of the countless ramifications would carry us too far afield, but I feel it essential to comment, at least briefly, on two avenues of approach that have turned out in too many cases to be dead-end streets: the foster parent plan and youth detention centers.

Foster care is a custodial arrangement for children whose natural parents are dead, missing, ill, or delinquent. No doubt many foster parents have the most charitable intentions, are thinking only of the foster child's well-being. On the other hand there are a great many who look on such an arrangement mainly as a chance to make a little extra money. Too often they agree to take care of a problem child with little understanding of what the problem is all about, and before long the situation becomes intolerable.

Even where there is a warm rapport between foster child and foster parent, problems are bound to arise. Frequently even brutal parents have a certain affection for their children and bitterly resent a court order that takes the children out of their hands. If the natural parents request it, the judge invariably grants at least limited visitation rights and that usually leads to endless complications. Most foster parents don't like it and neither do the social workers, because it inevitably upsets the child. As a rule the child is angry with the parents, and the parents feel guilty about the child. Often the foster parents don't know too much about the child they have agreed to shelter and soon find many incompatibilities. Many a problem child is tossed from haven to haven as the spheroid in a hard-fought game of basketball. In time, if the delinquent parents ask for their child's return and show even the slightest evidence of mending their ways, the court is pretty apt to grant their request. And this often happens just when the temporary parents have begun to establish an affectionate relationship with the child.

If the foster parent plan seldom works to advantage among whites, what must be its chances when black children and parents are involved? Infinitesimal, if not impossible.

Now a few words about the care that children get in custodial institutions. No doubt there are exceptions, but in most cases it is not a pretty picture. In 1969 Howard James of the *Christian Science Monitor* toured the country, visiting children's jails and detention facilities. His report, later published in book form, is sickening. Children beaten with truncheons, fists, belt buckles. Children left hungry, humiliated, caged like animals, put in dungeons, anything but cared for, anything but "rehabilitated." Two years later Larry Cole visited such institutions in New York, Louisiana, Colorado and California, described by him in *Our Children's Keepers*, and found similar conditions, but even worse: children "hog-tied," hands to feet, kept face down in solitary dungeons for days at a time; children raped and sodomized by guards; three-year-old babies penned up in cages.

Describing a school for girls in Denver, Cole tells about "troublesome children" being locked in solitary, sometimes for as long as eighty days. Often unruly girls were handcuffed, with their feet bound to their hands and made to lie face down on a bed in solitary for days. As a result of such inhumane treatment, several girls became psychotic, as one might expect.

Corporal punishment is fairly common in children's jails and detention centers. The emphasis in most of these institutions is not on helping children but on making them adjust to the rules and regulations, while giving as little trouble as possible. If they conform they are rated "improved." If they don't, they are punished, often transferred to an even worse environment.

These are not rare cases or "horrible examples," but are quite typical of most of the children's detention centers in the United States.

By Their Fruits Ye Shall Know Them

While it is true that *wanted* children are often neglected and abused, common sense tells us that the incidence of neglect and abuse among *unwanted* children is many times as great.

Criminal history gives us some good examples of children spawned by unwanted pregnancies carried to term through the myoptic mentality of self-styled "pro-lifers"—some illegitimate, some born in wedlock, all mistreated as they grew up. Among them are Charles Manson and many of his "family," most of whom after many years imprisonment don't seem the least bit repentant. Then there is Lee Harvey Oswald who assassinated President Kennedy and Jack Ruby who assassinated the assassin for reasons best known to himself. Another shining example is Charles Whitman, the Texas marksman who proved his skill by picking off fourteen innocent victims from his perch high atop an Austin tower; to say nothing of David Berkowitz, Greater New York great killer who, with something like thirteen victims, was front page news in 1977 from coast to coast: *"Born Richard David Falco, but given up for adoption at birth."*

Judging from the history of these criminals, most of whom were unwanted but adopted, "Birthright" and similar organizations that would solve the abortion problem by forcing pregnancies to term and "adopting" the unwanted child, don't seem to have a leg to stand on.'

For those who aren't convinced that it's better to be unborn than

65

unwanted here are several more glaring examples:

Arthur Bremer. With the passage of time most of us have forgotten this man, but he is the youth who tried to assassinate Governor George Wallace of Alabama, May 15, 1972. He failed to kill the hardy Wallace but crippled him for life. "My future was small, my past an insult to any human being," he wrote in his diary. The second youngest of five children, Bremer was raised in a run-down working-class section of Milwaukee's south side. Court records and service agency files show that the Bremers were a problem family in which child abuse and neglect were every day occurrences. Abused and neglected, Arthur grew up a social misfit bolstered by his own weird dreams which he eventually acted out. Before his attempt on Wallace's life he had planned to assassinate President Nixon.

Sirhan B. Sirhan. His claim to fame is the assassination of Robert Kennedy on June 6, 1968. Investigating his background in Palestine, reporters learned from neighbors that the senior Sirhan was said to have been in the habit of beating his children severely when they disobeyed. After the Arab-Israeli war the family came to the United States, but the father soon abandoned the family and returned to Palestine.

James Earl Ray. The Ray family were "ne'er-do-wells" who were unable to handle the everyday problems of living. James, the oldest of nine children, was about forty years old when he shot and killed Dr. Martin Luther King on April 4, 1968. The shiftless, indigent family drifted from one shabby home to another. The children drifted too, wandered off, and wound up in various foster homes. Those who stayed home suffered unspeakable poverty and neglect. From an early age James was regarded by his teachers as a thief and a vicious bully, destined to be a killer.

Guiseppe Zangara. One must go back nearly half a century to remember the man who tried to assassinate President-elect Franklin D. Roosevelt February 15, 1933, but fatally wounded Mayor Cermak of Chicago instead. Zangara was born in Italy in 1900. His mother died when he was two years old and his father remarried shortly afterwards. Two months after he started school at the age of six, his father took him out of school and put him to work. Is it any wonder that he turned out to be an unbalanced, social misfit?

William D. Carroll. This man has never been in the national headlines as have the others mentioned above; he is just an obscure, middle-aged convict who has spent much of his life in prison. I mention him because he is so typical of the desperately poor, unwanted child. The fifth of eleven children, he started shining shoes and selling magazines before he was seven. By the time he was twelve he had a record of petty thefts. He was sent to a reform school three times and eventually graduated as a long-term criminal who will be eligible for parole in 1986. In telling a reporter about his bleak, love-starved childhood, Carroll said, "Kids need love. Ninety percent of the guys in these prisons, sometime back in their childhoods there was a lack of love or concern. So they go out to get it. They want attention. They want to belong, and they've got to do something."[4]

Leontine Young, in her classic book, *Wednesday's Children*, cites the case of an emotionally and physically abused girl who is typical of thousands of children in the same situation. A social worker asked the little girl what she wanted to be "when she grew up." The child replied that she had thought of jumping into a bottomless lake. Then she added: *"I don't want to be!"*

In this chapter I have touched upon a small fraction of the countless problems faced by unwanted children and unwilling or unworthy parents. It would take many pages to treat in depth each case, many volumes to explore the endless complications in a fair measure of detail. In view of the tragic, miserable lives faced by nine out of ten unwanted children, again I say, "Weep for the unwanted child—*at birth!*"

Again I ask, "Why are the anti-abortionists so intransigent in fighting for the 'right-to-life' of the disaster-prone, unwanted child, when that child—if he could speak for himself—would most likely say with the little girl mentioned above, *"I don't want to be!"*

Must we go on forever condemning the unwanted child to life?

6

Abortion as the Last Resort

The Roman Catholic Canon Law and the restrictive abortion laws nullified by the United States Supreme Court in 1973 were generally considered to be as permanent a part of the social fabric as the Ten Commandments, yet both were comparatively recent innovations. Abortion was scarcely an issue in Britain until 1803, and not until shortly after the Civil War in the United States.

The practice of abortion has existed from time immemorial, but for our purpose we need go back no further than Aristotle (383-322 B.C.), who held that all forms of population control, including infanticide, were valid. "When couples have children in excess and there is an aversion to exposure (infanticide)," he urged, "let abortion be procurred before life and sense have begun."

Neither Roman law nor morality opposed abortion, since the basic legal principle was that the fetus was not a human being but merely a part of the mother's body. Tertullian, St. Basil, and most of the Church Fathers, however, were bitterly opposed to the Roman custom and condemned all abortion as "murder."

The exact moment at which a fetus was "infused with a soul" has never been determined, but earlier theologians followed Aristotle's view that the "soul developed in three stages," and the church generally punished abortion as murder only if performed after the soul became rational, or "animated." This stage, no doubt also taken from Aristotle, was set at forty days after conception for a male child, and eighty or ninety days for a female—though no one ever explained how the fetal sex was determined. This distinction was adopted in the Decretals of Pope Gregory IX (1227-1241), with the forty and eighty day theory generally accepted as the dividing line. In time, practical English jurists were replacing the theological theory of animation with another line of demarcation for the beginning of fetal life, which they called "quickening." This concept was most likely adopted from St. Thomas Aquinas, who added *motion* as a principle of life in Aristotle's "three stage souls." From then on, common law would punish abortion only if performed after the mother could feel the child jumping in her womb—a tolerant approach, since only the mother or father could testify in court as to the exact moment of "quickening."

After England's break with the Roman Catholic church both the ecclesiastical courts and those responsible for enforcing the civil law seem to have lost interest in abortion and it was not until 1803 that modern legislation on abortion was enacted in England.

In the Catholic church the Decretals of Gregory IX remained in effect until 1588, when Pope Sixtus V, an even more pronounced extremist than Paul VI, issued a bull that wiped out the old forty- and eighty-day rule and declared that all abortion was murder regardless of the stage of fetal development, a "crime" punishable by excommunication which could be removed only by the pope—a serious punishment in those days.

Interestingly enough, the leading theologians of that day and most of the laity took the same position toward Sixtus's bull as their counterparts today have taken toward Paul VI's encyclical banning contraception. They ignored it!

When Gregory XIV succeeded Sixtus, less than three years later (1591), he didn't worry about compromising "papal infallibility" (which did not become an official doctrine of the Church until the Vatican Council of 1869-1870), nor the theoretical "infrangibility of Roman Catholic doctrine"; he just did what Paul's first intelligent successor will most likely do: he announced that Sixtus's bull had not produced the hoped-for results, set it aside, and revoked all the penalties applied by Sixtus except those for an abortion performed after forty days!

The centuries-old system, now back in effect, was to last nearly three more centuries. It was not until 1869—after almost eighteen centuries of debate within the church—that another extremist, Pope Pius IX, returned to the sanctions of Sixtus V, eliminated the distinction between a non-animated and an animated fetus, and decreed that all abortion would be regarded as murder.

Although some theologians still hold that the old forty and eighty day rule is applicable for canonical penalties, the majority view among the hierarchy is that punishment should be based on abortion from the moment of conception.

The history of abortion in the United States during the past hundred years is much the same as that of contraception, treated at length in chapter four. At the time of the First Vatican Council (1869-1870) few American Protestants would have given Pope Pius IX a pleasant smile; but when he decreed abortion *under any circumstances* to be a crime, a big part of the "separated brethren," led by the jubilant Anthony Comstock (1844-1915), were about ready to hit the sawdust trail to Rome. The autocratic pope played right into the hands of the autocratic Comstock who, just at that time, was mobilizing his forces for an attack on American morals that was to put this nation under his menacing thumb for more than forty years.

In 1873, about three years after the pope's attack on abortion, Congress—egged on by the neurotic crusader—passed the so-called Comstock Law, which not only barred "obscene" matter from the mails, but also the sale or interstate transportation of contraceptives of any type.

In today's relaxed, liberal atmosphere it is hard for anyone who didn't live in the Comstock era or who is not a student of that period to comprehend the incredible fanaticism of that incredible despot during the four decades he reigned as arbiter of morals in these more or less united states. In those days politicians were politicians no less than they are today: never mind their personal morals, votes were to be found in confronting evil, so they lined up in force to help the lily white St. George slay the dragon.

Early in his sin-chasing career, Comstock was designated a Special Federal Agent with powers that would make a current FBI wire-tapper green with envy. Over a period of forty years, as secretary of the New York Society for the Suppression of Vice, he was paid a substantial salary to supplement his modest income as a salesman for a dry goods house. No child was too young, no malefactor too powerful to stay the intrepid avenger's malice. Among his first victims were two boys, ages eleven and thirteen, clerks in a variety store, arrested because Comstock said the owners were selling "obscene" books, the kind you might find today in the library of a genteel woman. (The three owners were sentenced for three months to a year.) In their intriguing biography, *Anthony Comstock: Roundsman of the Lord,* (1927), Heywood Broun and

Margaret Leech said, "He stood like a rock in the path of American art and literature." Commenting on his immaturity they quipped, "His religion is that of Paul, but on occasion he robs Paul to play Peter Pan."

In a pamphlet proudly published by his colleagues in the Society for the Suppression of Vice, Comstock was credited with destroying 134,000 pounds of "impure" books; 194,000 "obscene" pictures and photographs; 14,000 pounds of stereotype plates; 60,300 "rubber articles intended for immoral use"; 5,500 packs of "indecent" playing cards, along with 3,150 boxes of "pills and powders." It was Comstock's proud boast that he convicted "enough persons (men, women, and children) to fill 61 passenger coaches holding 60 persons each."

After hounding Madame Restell, famous Fifth Avenue abortionist, for years and finally causing her to cut her throat, he boasted that she was the fifteenth person he had driven to suicide. In a letter to that keeper of the nation's conscience, the Reverend Dr. Rainsford said, "You have hounded an honest, not a bad woman, to her death. I would not like to answer to God for what you have done."

Comstock, a big, powerfully built man, had the courage of the convictions he so avidly sought. He never flinched from physically attacking and arresting the victim he stalked, but he finally met his Waterloo at the feet of a small town doctor he was trying to arrest. Fleeing up the stairs of his Connecticut home with Comstock nipping at his heels, the quarry suddenly turned and kicked his pursuer down the steps. That fall took the wind out of the avenging angel's sails and twelve months later he died, in the year of our Lord 1915, and the year of our Lord's roundsman the seventy-first. May he rest in turmoil!

Anthony Comstock has been dead these many years, but the Comstock Law—though no longer enforced so strictly—is still on the books, and Comstockery lingers on. *Vide,* the "Tennessee Obscenity Act of 1978," recently bull-dozed through that state's legislature by the Honorable Larry Parrish, former Assistant U.S. District Attorney and a modern day Comstock, and approved April 12, 1978 by Governor Ray Blanton.

The penalties provided by this complex, forty-seven page statute for the first and second convictions were very severe, but the *third* conviction called for a fine of "no less than fifty thousand ($50,000) dollars, nor more than one hundred and fifty thousand ($150,000) dollars," *plus* imprisonment in the state penitentiary, "without possibility of probation, parole, or any other program whereby such person is released, permanently or temporarily, prior to his expiration date, for a period of not less than three (3), nor more than twenty (20) years."

This absurd statute was unconstitutional on its face and was so declared by the Tennessee Supreme Court about a year after enactment.

Contraception Comes Out of the Closet

Despite millions of unwanted pregnancies and countless deaths from illegal abortions, despite the valiant efforts of Margaret Sanger and other humanitarians for several decades, it was not until the Lambeth Conference of 1930 that contraception began to take on an aura of respectability, and "this nation under God," along with the civilized world, began to see the birth control problem in its true light.

In his revolutionary book *Abortion*, written several years before the Supreme Court legalized the practice, crusader Lawrence Lader says:

> The importance of this seemingly endless debate (on abortion) is its impact on our civil laws. The Catholic hierarchy, in violent opposition to any change in the present system, has constantly resorted to the argument that all abortion is against "the precept of God" or "the law of nature . . ."
>
> Far from being natural law going back to the dawn of history, or even to early Christianity, the present Church law on abortion (discounting the three year interlude under Sixtus V) is less than a hundred years old. Through the centuries popes have clashed with popes, theologians with theologians. When the church itself could not reach a reasonably permanent decision until 1869, it is obviously absurd for the non-Catholic to accept such claims of "natural law." [1]

Polls taken in the United States show that attitudes toward abortion have changed so radically in the past decade that it really amounts to a revolution. Of course, in the past few years there has been a counter-revolution led by the Catholic hierarchy. Taking advantage of a certain apathy on the part of the pro-choice advocates, who were inclined to rest on their oars after their 1973 victory, the anti's have done a phenomenal job of intimidating Congress and winning the battle over government funding of abortions for indigent women, as we pointed out in the opening chapter.

Just what the final outcome will be is hard to say, but with 65 to 88 percent of the general public, including the majority of Catholics, in favor of legalized abortion, it is hardly possible that the anti's current victory will prove to be anything more than temporary.

Abortion to save the mother's life has long had the approval of 85 percent of the general public and more than 60 percent of Roman Catholics. A poll taken early in 1969 asked a slightly different question: "Should an abortion be available to any woman who requests it?" In apparent contradiction of earlier opinions, more than half of those interviewed said: Yes. Though many did not approve of abortion except for such reasons as danger to the mother, rape, incest, or the possibility of a deformed or retarded child, the majority felt that prospective mothers should be free to make their own decisions.[2] (When some Catholic nuns were raped in the Congo in the 1960's the Church reversed its position and permitted them to be aborted.)

According to a survey made for the Planned Parenthood-World Population Organization, reported in the *Memphis Commercial Appeal* of September 30, 1974, almost one-fourth of the Roman Catholic priests in the state of New York did not agree with or had serious doubts about the Church's traditional teaching on abortion. More than one-fourth of the priests either favored no abortion laws at all or supported the liberal New York state law.

This survey also showed that the younger and better educated the priest, the less likely was he to agree with his Church's teaching on abortion. More than half of those ages twenty-five to thirty-four disagreed or had doubts about the traditional teaching, compared with fewer than one in eight of those over sixty-five. It should be noted, however, that this study was made a year before the American hierarchy formally declared war on abortion. Under pressure from the institutional Church, it is most likely that many priests have retreated from this liberal stand regarding abortion.

Of the 40,089 United States physicians who answered a poll by *Modern Medicine* a few years ago, 87 percent favored liberalizing the abortion laws, including 49 percent of the Roman Catholic doctors who answered.[3] A UPI dispatch dated at Detroit, November 14, 1968, said: "The nation's organization of Public Health Workers Thursday demanded laws be changed to allow 'safe, legal abortions' for all women." The 23,000-member

American Public Health Association (APHA), in a resolution adopted with little debate by its governing council, went on record in favor of the woman's "right" to abortion. [4]

What is responsible for this revolutionary change in the nation's attitude toward abortion during the past decade? First of all it is *enlightenment*, due largely to improvements in surgical procedures. Stringent laws against abortion were passed before the medical profession knew much about antisepsis, when any kind of surgery usually produced complications and often ended fatally. The purpose of such laws was chiefly to protect the prospective mother, not the fetus. With our modern techniques an abortion, except in the final stages of pregnancy, is much safer than childbirth. [5] For generations we have been so imbued with the "horrors" and the "criminality" of abortion that it has taken a revolution to replace the deep-seated feeling of guilt with a common sense viewpoint. [6]

A Humane Revolution

A listing of the many courageous, dedicated men and women, lay and professional, responsible for this revolutionary change in attitude would take many pages, but no one has done more than Lawrence Lader, freelance writer and college professor, who did for abortion what Margaret Sanger did for birth control: made it *respectable*. Lader's crusade is graphically depicted in his book *Abortion II: Making the Revolution*, a book every student of sociology should by all means read. Commenting on the change in attitude toward abortion, Lader says:

> What distinguishes abortion from most other social campaigns is that it became a people's revolt, developed at the precinct level of politics. Striking deep into the national conscience, enveloping our most fundamental instincts on sex and procreation, it galvanized the democratic political process as no other issue but the Vietnam war. But in contrast to Vietnam, where the individual's will, and often that of his representatives in Congress, were thwarted by the power of the White House and Pentagon, abortion provided a rare chance for decision-making by the people.
>
> By the very nature of its base in the individual's right of free choice in childbearing and the individual's opposition to dictation by church or state, the abortion movement soon took in a broad range of support from

every economic, social, and political stratum. . .

By guaranteeing that no child comes into this world unwanted, unloved, and uncared for, legalized abortion produced immeasurable gains in psychiatric and social health. . . Above all, the abortion movement destroyed to a large extent the system of exploitation in which generations of women had been trapped. The savage ordeal of underworld abortions, its generally substandard medical care at exaggerated prices, its debasing secrecy and harassment by the police, even the hypocrisy of so-called "therapeutic" abortion where women crawled and begged before hospital committees—these had been largely replaced by the dignity and safety of legalized abortion. [7]

In "A Scientist's Case for Abortion," (*Redbook*, May 1967) Dr. Garrett Hardin, eminent biologist, said:

Contrary to widespread belief, a properly performed abortion is *not dangerous*. Amateur abortion is dangerous, of course . . . But in Hungary, where the best medical procedures are employed, E. Szabady reports a death rate of only three per 100,000 cases, less than 20 percent of the death rate for normal childbirth in the United States. The pain of an early abortion seems to be that of a difficult menstruation. Sterility no more frequently follows abortion than it does childbirth—which is the alternative if abortion is rejected.

A few years ago a widely publicized tragedy focused the eyes of the thinking world on this problem. In 1963 a German measles epidemic affected 82,000 women in the first three months of pregnancy. Thirty thousand babies were born dead or died in early infancy. More than 20,000 came into this valley of tears with major abnormalities such as blindness, deafness, heart disease and severe mental retardation.[8]

One fallacy that is swallowed whole by a great many people is the claim by the Roman hierarchy that the destruction of a zygote—the union of the cells that produce the fetus, or the fetus itself—is murder. If this be true then Mother Nature herself is the greatest mass-murderer of all time since she destroys more than a third of the zygotes or fetuses capable of producing life, a process known as "miscarriage." [9] Be that as it may, to say that destroying a zygote or fetus in the early stages is "murder" is saying that in crushing an acorn you are felling an oak tree; that in setting fire to the blueprints of a projected house you are guilty of "arson."

Commenting on the hierarchy's never-ending attempt to force on the general public legislation that conforms to Roman Catholic tenets, the Reverend Lester Kinsolving, an Episcopal minister, says, "This is no more valid than if the legislature were asked to outlaw pork because of Jewish beliefs; or imposing the Christian Scientist's view on medicine, or the Jehovah's Witnesses' objection to blood transfusions for everyone." [10]

In the *Redbook* article referred to above, Dr. Hardin explains that the most effective types of contraception now available fail in about one case in a hundred, which means that every year there are more than 200,000 unwanted, often tragic pregnancies, among the women who used the best available birth control, to say nothing of about a million, mostly respectable married women, who used less reliable methods, or none at all. After going into some technical details, Hardin says:

> (Just as) a set of blueprints is not a house (so) . . . a zygote (or the zygote after it has reached the fetus stage) is not a human being. . . A favorite argument of abortion prohibitionists is: "What if Beethoven's mother had had an abortion?" The question moves us; but when we think it over we realize we can just as relevantly ask: "What if Hitler's mother had had an abortion?" Each conceptus is unique, but the *expected* potential value of an aborted fetus is exactly that of the average child born. It is meaningless to say that humanity loses when a *particular* child is born or is not conceived. A human female at birth has about 30,000 eggs in her ovaries. If she bears only three children in her lifetime, can we meaningfully say that mankind has suffered a loss in those other 29,997 fruitless eggs? (Yet one of them might have been a super-Beethoven!) (Original emphasis).

For a long time one of the most common arguments against abortion has been the supposed emotional trauma suffered by a normal woman following a deliberate termination of pregnancy. A recent study reported in an Associated Press dispatch published in the *Memphis Commercial Appeal of* January 14, 1974 lays that misconception to rest: "Women who have had abortions show no greater depression or emotional stress than women who carry their babies to birth, according to a Johns Hopkins study . . . Patients who obtained. . . abortions or decided to continue their pregnancies to term were no more alientated or lower in self-esteem either before or after hospitalization."

Another myth that has won acceptance in certain quarters is that abortions cause serious physiological problems if a woman later decides to have a child. It causes no such problems an exhaustive study at the University of Washington medical school shows.

Reviewing the case records of 4,900 pregnancies handled at University Hospital in Seattle, researchers found that women who previously had abortions were no more likely to have miscarriages or malformed babies than women who never had an abortion. Nor were the rates of premature delivery, low birth rates, or the incidence of general complications any different. If anything, the researchers said, women who had had abortions tended to have *healthier* babies. [11]

A Great Success in New York

In the fall of 1972 a UPI dispatch reported that the death rate for mothers and infants in New York City dropped sharply since July 1, 1970, when a state law made abortions legal. A summary of more than 400,000 abortions in that city indicated a reduced incidence of complications in abortion operations performed in early pregnancy. Out-of-wedlock births in the city declined in 1971 for the first time since such records were begun in 1954, and city officials said they believed the number of criminal abortions was declining.

Referring to the 1970 New York abortion law, Gordon Chase, New York's Health Services administrator, said:

> Overall, the law has been an enormous success in New York City . . . The gross death rate for mothers in the two-year period was 37.7 per 100,000 live births, a substantially significant decline from the preceding two-year period, when it was at the rate of 52.2 . . . Infant mortality . . . has now dropped to an all time low. [12]

The overall death rate from legal abortion was 4.7 deaths per 100,000 abortions in the first year of legislative reform and this figure dropped to 3.7 during the last half of 1971. This rate is well under that for deaths associated with live delivery (less than half) and compares very favorably with death rates for other industrialized countries with longer experience under legal abortion.

Medical complications associated with abortion procedures in New York City dropped from a rate of 12.7 per 1,000 abortions in the first six months of reform to 6.4 in the second half of the first year, and were reduced even further to 5.7 in the last half of 1971.

In Kings County Hospital, New York, incomplete (botched) abortions dropped from 2694 in 1965 to 1182 in 1971. In that city's Harlem Hospital during the same period, such incomplete abortions dropped from 1054 to 292.

Contrary to the belief of some people, the impact of legalizing abortion is largely a shift from dangerous and costly illegal procedures, rather than the generating of abortions which would not otherwise have occurred. An analysis of New York's experience with legalized abortion by the associate director of the biomedical division of the Population Council revealed that 7 out of 10 abortions replaced illegal procedures. [13]

In Great Britain, as well as in the United States, an intelligent approach to abortion has proved a boon to a great segment of the population. A recent article in *Family Planning Perspectives* says:

> After studying the operation of Great Britain's 1967 Abortion Act for nearly three years, a special government-appointed committee of doctors, lawyers and social scientists has concluded that the law " . . . has relieved a vast amount of individual suffering . . . has helped . . . to focus attention on the paramount need for preventive action, for more education in sexual life and its responsibilities, and for the widespread provision of contraceptive advice and facilities . . . and (has stimulated) research into all aspects of abortion and the development of safer operative techniques . . . "
> The committee concluded that "the gains facilitated by the Act have much outweighed any disadvantages for which it has been criticised." [14]

Breakthrough in the Courts

While the crusaders for legalized abortion were gradually gaining through the legislative process—losing in one state, winning in another—the real breakthrough, as everyone knows, came through the courts. A monumental victory came September 5, 1969 when the California Supreme Court, in a four to three decision, declared the old state law unconstitutional. Just two months later (November 10, 1969), Judge Gesell of the Federal District Court declared the District of Columbia law unconstitutional. For its immediate impact alone, this decision exceeded in importance even that of California. It made Washington the first area in the country where abortion was completely legalized.

Both decisions were most gratifying to the proponents of legalized abortion, but the greatest triumph of all came with the decision of the United States Supreme Court, January 22, 1973, striking down all state laws that prohibit or restrict a woman's right to obtain an abortion during the first three months of pregnancy. Of course no one can say to what extent the Supreme Court Justices were influenced by the gratifying results that followed New York's repeal of legal restrictions, but no doubt they carried a great deal of weight. Six Justices—Chief Justice Burger, Justices Douglas, Brennan, Stewart, Marshall, and Powell—concurred with Justice Blackmun, who wrote the majority opinion. It is to be noted that here again Justice Brennan, a Roman Catholic, voted in accordance with his convictions and not with the tenets of his church. It is also to be noted that R. M. Pennover, one of the lawyers in the abortion issue, said that the New York Archdiocese does not speak for the majority of Christians or even for all Catholics in its opinion on abortion.[15]

The Supreme Court's ruling has been so widely publicized that no detailed exposition is necessary here, but it should be noted that while it drafted a new set of guidelines that resulted in broadly liberalized anti-abortion laws in the forty-six states that retained the old restrictions, it did not abolish restrictions entirely. The decision established detailed timetables for related legal rights of pregnant women and states that will control their acts. The ruling specified that for the first three months of pregnancy the decision to have an abortion lies with the woman and her doctor; for the next three months of pregnancy the state may regulate abortion procedures in ways that are reasonably related to maternal health, and for the last ten weeks of pregnancy, the period during which the fetus is judged capable of surviving if born, any state may prohibit abortions, except where they may be necessary to preserve the life or health of the woman.

A Gallup poll made sixty days before the 1972 presidential election found that 64 percent of all Americans were in favor of legalized abortion. Even Catholics approved by 56 percent. Three years before this study only 40 percent of those polled favored legalized abortion. [16]

In its November 21, 1969 issue, *Time* magazine said: "The case for more permissive abortion laws is strengthened by a new study revealing that 22 percent of all legitimate births in the United States are unwanted by either the husband or wife. This conclusion is based on a survey of 5,600 married women throughout the country by Dr. Charles F. Westoff of Princeton's Office of Population Research. As expected, he found there are more unwanted births among the poor (42 percent) than among the near-poor (26 percent), or the more affluent (17 percent).

In a survey made in the fall of 1973 by the National Opinion Research Center, with some 1500 face-to-face interviews on a national scale, it was found that the number of Catholics favoring abortion in cases where the woman's health was in danger increased from 80 to 88 percent during the preceding year. Similarly, 75 percent approved of abortion in cases of rape, compared with 70 percent the previous year, and 77 percent of the Catholics surveyed condoned abortion when "there is a chance of a defective child." The figure was 67 percent the previous year. [17]

A Breakthrough in Science

A revolutionary method that causes uterine spasms shows great promise as the easiest and simplest abortion technique ever developed, according to Dr. K. Sune D. Bergstrom, head of Stockholm's Karolinska Institute and chairman of the World Health Organization (WHO) Council on Medical Research. It is a synthetic prostaglandin in the form of a suppository, about an inch long with the thickness of two felt-tipped pens, which melts from body heat after insertion, and starts up a new menstrual cycle within one to five hours after a "missed period."

Dr. Bergstrom says the WHO-sponsored trials with the new suppository are now being conducted in a dozen countries, including Britain, Russia, Yugoslavia, and India.

The early abortion suppository has been classed as an "investigative new drug" by the U.S. Food and Drug Administration, and as such is now undergoing tests directed by scientists at medical centers at Harvard, Cornell, and the University of North Carolina.

Dr. Bergstrom recently received the Albert Lasker Medical Research Award for identifying prostaglandins—minute, hormone-like substances that regulate many vital processes—including pregnancy, blood pressure, and circulation. He said the new synthetic prostaglandin was developed for early abortion (first three months) to avoid side affects caused by natural prostaglandin, which upset the digestive system.

The president of the pharmaceutical house that produces this new suppository said it would probably be developed sufficiently for FDA approval "in a little over a year, but not more than two."

According to Dr. Mark Abramowicz, editor of *The Medical Letter*, this new simple way to start a missed period may soon make debate about abortion "purely academic."

When the birth control pill first came on the market, it was such a great improvement over contraceptives then in use that many researchers in that field began to rest on their oars. In time, however, the medical profession discovered serious after effects from its long continued use and their warning brought a new era of research. An injectable, time-release contraceptive that could be effective for six months is being developed at the University of Alabama at Birmingham. Under way at the University of Tennessee at Knoxville is a contraceptive vaccine that "someday" may enable women to discard daily birth control pills for "a shot in the arm once every two years."

Both these developments are in the initial stages and it will probably be years before they come into general use. I mention them, however, because there is every reason to believe that sooner or later scientific developments such as these will end the abortion controversy.

A Boon to Mankind

Another revolutionary development that could eliminate many private tragedies and go a long way toward improving the general quality of the human race is described in *Psychology Today* by Amitai Etzioni, Professor of Sociology at Columbia University and Director of the Center for Policy Research in New York City. A relatively simple test called amniocentesis can tell with an extremely high degree of accuracy whether or not a *specific* fetus a woman is carrying is deformed or mentally defective.[18]

The test consists of inserting a hollow needle into the sac in which the fetus floats, withdrawing some of the fluid and sending it to a laboratory for intensive study. The fetal cells found in the fluid are grown in a culture and microscopically examined to determine whether they carry any one of sixty or more genetic abnormalities. If the test is negative, the parents can be quite sure their child will be born free from any such diseases. If positive, the situation is explained to the prospective parents who may or may not decide to have an abortion. If they opt for abortion, experience has shown that in most cases where the couple really want a child another pregnancy eventually follows. The new embryo can also be tested. By this procedure even a woman with a high predisposition to mongolism can have healthy children. In virtually every case amniocentesis can assure a pregnant woman of a child free not only from mongolism but from other tragic diseases like Turner's syndrome, galactosemia, Tay Sachs disease, and scores of other metabolic and genetic related abnormalities, such as blindness, deafness, or other serious disabilities.

The general application of this test was delayed for several years due to doubt of its safety by some doctors, but a four-year clinical study by the National Institute of Child Health and Human Development, reported in a UPI dispatch of October 22, 1975, proved that neither the woman nor her child was harmed by amniocentesis. Furthermore, the study proved the test better than 99 percent accurate. Dr. Duane Alexander, one of two government doctors in charge of the study, said 3,000 such examinations were made in the United States last year. He predicted that many more such tests will be carried out in future now that the safety of amniocentesis has been clinically proven.[19]

Though amniocentesis can disclose scores of genetic abnormalities, mongolism is the most common disease it detects. It occurs once in every 680 births in the United States, but the chance of a woman bearing a child with mongolism or a similar genetic defect increases rapidly after the age of 35. According to Dr. Virginia Apgar, Clinical Professor of Pediatrics at Cornell Medical College, the risk of mongolism is one in 280 childbirths for women 35 to 39, one in 80 for ages 40 to 44, and *one in 40 for ages 44 or over.* There are 300,000 pregnant women over age 35 in the United States each year, and they produce half the children afflicted with mongolism. It may be true that "life begins at forty," but if *fetal* life begins at this age the red flag of caution should always be flying high! Studies by the National Institute of Health show that about 70 percent of childhood deafness and 80 percent of blindness in nontropical countries is caused by genetic related diseases. A total of about 15 million American children are thought to be affected by various genetic-related diseases, one of the most common being diabetes, an important factor in blindness.

While insulin proved to be a godsend for diabetics, at the same

82

time it is largely responsible for the alarming increase in diabetes since it was discovered in 1922. It has kept alive through their child-bearing years hundreds of thousands of diabetics who would otherwise have died young. The genes that cause, or help to cause or increase the proneness to diabetes are increasing in our population at an unprecedented rate. The number of diabetics will multiply accordingly if drastic steps aren't soon taken to limit through the process of amniocentesis the procreation of children by parents who are afflicted with diabetes.

"Probably amniocentesis should be done on all pregnant women over the age of 35," says Dr. Alexander. He said this test should also be carried out on women who already have a child afflicted with a genetic abnormality or who have a family history of such disorders. In virtually all cases where a genetic defect is found no cure is possible, so the only alternative is abortion.

Anti-abortionists Oppose Amniocentesis

Nothing shows the anti-abortionists' one-sided approach and their callous disregard for the individual's distress or the well-being of the general public more than their fanatical opposition to amniocentesis. On the NBC "Evening News" of February 14, 1978, John Chancellor announced that, as a result of pressure from anti-abortion groups, the National Foundation of the March of Dimes would no longer devote any part of the funds collected from the American public to the support or development of any phase of the amniocentesis program. Shortly afterwards a high official of the foundation appeared on the screen; he confirmed Chancellor's statement, but denied that pressure from the anti-abortion groups had anything to do with the change in their position. Next on the screen came Dr. Mildred Jefferson of Boston, a black surgeon who is one of the leaders of the anti-abortionists, president of the National Right To Life Educational Foundations, with headquarters in Tulsa, Oklahoma. She was jubilant over the decision of the March of Dimes, saying in effect that if this country could spend billions "to put a man on the moon" it could afford to spend billions taking care of the physically and mentally defective children that would come into this world if the amniocentesis program were phased out.

Any doubt about the position of the March of Dimes National Foundation was dissipated by publication of an Associated Press dispatch in the Memphis *Commercial Appeal* of March 9, 1978. This dispatch confirmed statements made on television newscasts.

While still denying that their decision was prompted by pressure from anti-abortion groups, spokesmen for the National Foundation of the March of Dimes said they would no longer devote any part of their income to further experiments or development of the amniocentesis technique. [20]

Despite the opposition of the anti-abortionists, any reasonable, fairminded person is bound to admit that amniocentesis is one of the greatest gifts that science has ever made to the human race, a turning point that could eliminate for the individual parents the heartbreak of a mentally or physically retarded child, a boon that in time could cut deeply into the billions the public pays each year for the care of the mentally ill who now occupy more than half the hospital beds in this country. Incidentally the cost of maintaining each inmate in the mental institutions of this country is estimated at \$25,000 to \$35,000 per year. Even more important than economic considerations, however, is the intelligence factor. Amniocentesis could go a long way towards bolstering the sagging IQ of our nation.

A Call to Concern

Following is an excerpt from a statement entitled "A Call To Concern" which was issued by a group of more than 200 national leaders in the field of religious ethics and printed in *The Christian Century,* October 12, 1977:

The increasing urgency of the issue of abortion rights requires us as leaders of religious groups in America to speak out.

Abortion is a serious and sometimes tragic procedure for dealing with fetal life. It raises important ethical issues and cannot be blandly legitimized by the mere whim of an individual. Nevertheless, it belongs in that large realm of often tragic actions where circumstances can render it a less destructive procedure than the rigid prolongation of pregnancy.

We support the Supreme Court decisions of 1973 which had the affect of removing abortion from the criminal law codes. The Court did not appeal to religion or ethics in arriving at its judgment, but we believe the decision to have been in accord with sound ethical judgment. Taking note of the fact that theologians, as welll as other experts, disagree on the fundamental moral question of when life begins, the Court decided that the law ought not to compel the conscience of those who believe abortion to be in harmony with their moral convictions.

In the last four years, however, those decisions have been subjected to a relentless attack from those who take the absolutist position that it is always wrong to terminate a pregnancy at any time after the moment of conception. Those who take this absolutist position have not hesitated to equate abortion at any stage of pregnancy with murder or manslaughter. From such an extreme viewpoint, all legal means are considered justified if they limit abortions, no matter what the human consequences for poor women and others—as in the recent efforts to deny Medicaid funds and to prohibit use of public hospitals for abortion services.

We feel compelled to affirm an alternative position as a matter of conscience and professional responsibility.

1. The most compelling argument against the inflexibility of the absolutist position is its cost in human misery. The absolutist position does not concern itself about the quality of the entire life cycle, the health and well-being of the mother and family, the question of emotional and economic resources, the cases of extreme deformity. Its total preoccupation with the status of the unborn renders it blind to the well-being and freedom of choice of persons in community.

2. *"Pro-life" must not be limited to concern for the unborn; it must also include a concern for the quality of life as a whole.* The affirmation of life in Judeo-Christian ethics requires a commitment to make life healthy and whole from beginning to end. Considering the best medical advice, the best moral insight, and a concern for the total quality of the whole life cycle for the born and the unborn, we believe that abortion may in some instances be the most loving act possible.

3. We believe it is wrong to deny medical assistance to poor women seeking abortions. This denial makes it difficult for those who need it most to exercise a legal right, and it implies public censure of a form of medical service which in fact has the moral support of major religious groups. [21]

Obviously no sensitive person can approach the problem of abortion without fear and trepidation. At best it is an unpleasant topic, a traumatic experience. It is a practice that no one with high ethical standards would advocate—except as a means of avoiding much greater evils. But when one takes a realistic view of the situation, when he considers all the tragic complications that haunt the lives and futures of those involved, it behooves every thinking person to adopt a pragmatic approach to the problem.

Every couple, every woman who does not want to bear a child, should feel morally bound to take the most effective, medically approved method of contraception at her disposal; but that failing, it should be her inalienable right to choose abortion as a last resort.

7

Anything But the Truth

A vivid account of the national campaign being waged by the anti-abortionists is given by Marion K. Sanders in *Harper's* magazine. After telling about "scare tactics" and feelings so intense that the life of one liberal physician was threatened and a priest "in full clerical dress" called another opponent a "foul murderer" and tried to push him down the Capitol steps, she tells about Dr. J. C. Willke, "a dapper and articulate Cincinnati general practitioner" who leads the fight and furnishes inflammatory literature (available also in French, German, Spanish, and Italian) "the stable ammunition of the movement throughout the world." [1]

Among their best-selling items is a paperback *Handbook on Abortion*, written by Dr. Willke and his wife Barbara, a registered nurse. [2] It is illustrated with shocking color photographs of disintegrating fetuses and is replete with questionable "information." I have read the revised, 1975 edition carefully and while I can't vouch for the authors' veracity, I must report that, as propagandists, they are in a class by themselves. Here is an example: "Legalizing abortion does not, has not, and apparently will not reduce the number of self-induced, back-street abortions" (p. 104).

In the *Harper's* article, Mrs. Sanders thus quotes the Willkes: "Isn't abortion safer than childbirth?" . . . (Answer) "No, in the late stages it is far more dangerous. Even in the first stages at least twice as many mothers die from legal abortions as from childbirth."

Since that article was written in 1974, obviously this quotation was from an earlier edition of the Willkes book. Apparently the authors finally realized they couldn't "get away" with such a blatant misstatement, for I was unable to find it in the 1975 edition. As a matter of fact the U.S. Center for Disease Control (CDC) Abortion Surveillance statistics for 1976 show 1.0 death per 100,000 abortions (regardless of gestation period), compared with 11.8 deaths per 100,000 childbirth deliveries. When official statistics don't jibe with their statements, the Willkes get around that little difficulty by claiming that the statistics are "manipulated."

On page 178 of the aforementioned *Handbook on Abortion* we find this gem: "Instead of destroying life (with abortion), we should destroy the conditions which make life intolerable." Following this line of thought, one might well ask the Willkes, "Instead of destroying life (with abortion) why not destroy opposition to birth control and thus virtually destroy the *need* for abortion?"

Some of the "authorities" Dr. Willke uses to bolster his arguments are outdated. In a plea for permitting unlimited births of mental and physically defective babies, he quoted Nobel Laureate James Watson, "the man who cracked the genetic code": "Because of the present limits of such (pre-natal) detection methods, most birth defects are not discovered until birth." (pp. 113-114). Obviously this statement by the eminent Dr. Watson was made before the development of amniocentesis.

Much the same thing may be said of the authors' account of the detrimental after-affects of abortion (pp. 90-97), e.g., increased sterility, problems during pregnancy and delivery, low birth weight of infants, severe psychological repercussions and the like. As I have pointed out before, such misinformation has been refuted by several reputable studies, most recently by a World Health Organization (WHO) study summarized in the July 1978 *International Family Planning Perspectives and Digest.*

Throughout their book the Willkes use the question-and-answer method. In dealing with a controversial subject like abortion there is hardly a question for which you can't dig up some "authority" who will give you the answer you want. Most of the answers in the Willkes' book come from foreign sources, which is understandable since many foreign countries legalized abortion long before the United States did. Regardless of one's position on abortion, he can't help but admire Dr. Willke's diligence in searching the medical literature of the world for the answers he needs to shore up his argument. One must also commend Dr. Wilke for following his own advice: "never use the word 'fetus'; always say 'baby'". This series includes a ghastly color-photo of a dismembered ten-week-old fetus, actually only two inches long but enlarged to make it appear the same size as a nine-week-old infant shown on the same page.

It is doubtful if Dr. Willke finds much time to devote to his private practice. "In an average year," says the blurb on the back cover of his book, "they (the husband-wife team) will speak in 50 cities, face 50,000 people, and appear on over 100 radio and TV programs."

Anyone who saw Dr. Willke on NBC's "Weekend," January 21, 1979 commemorating the sixth anniversary of the Supreme Court's decision, has to admit that he puts on a marvelous show. Viewers will also admit that NBC was grossly partial to the anti-abortionists, giving them three times as much exposure as they gave their pro-choice opponents.

On TV and radio programs and local meetings, Dr. Willke explains how to get maximum results from his propaganda. Here are some highlights: Never use the word "fetus" or "embryo"; always say "baby." Always start with the slide of a live baby and move backward at two-week intervals, asking at each change, "Is it still human?" If you start at the other end, the ovum, observers will see it only as a "glob," not a baby from the beginning.

The next set shows the actual abortion—bloody and bloodcurdling—ending up with a garbage pail filled with "dead babies." For the finale the good doctor offers the scene of a concentration camp showing a truckload of Jews headed for the incinerator—the inference being that abortion is only the first step toward compulsory "abortion" for undesirables, raising the specter of genocide for black people and compulsory "euthanasia" for the aged.

In countering such questionable tactics one is tempted to resort to similar tactics himself, but I feel the most effective rebuttal is to be found in the statements of more responsible Roman Catholics who are objective enough to see both sides of the picture.

Liberal Catholic spokesmen have already pointed out that the laws of a nation should treat men who favor legal abortion as a mature segment of a pluralistic society. Father Robert F. Drinan, until recently a member of Congress from Massachusetts and former dean of the Boston College of Law, speaks for the liberal element in the Roman church:

> It is submitted that episcopal statements going beyond
> the morality of abortion and entering the question of
> jurisprudence of the best legal arrangement are
> inappropriate intrusions in a pluralistic society by an
> ecclesiastical official who wrongly assumes that he can
> pronounce a moral and uniform position for his church
> on a legal-political question. [3]

A Daniel Come to Judgment

For all his early life, Dr. Daniel Callahan, Roman Catholic
director of the Institute of Society, Ethics and Life Sciences, upheld
the traditional viewpoint of his church on abortion. After studying
abortion laws and their consequences in all regions of the United
States and many foreign countries, however, he began to favor
more permissive laws and the inalienable right of women to govern
their own lives. After years of monumental research he produced
what is probably the most comprehensive and objective book ever
written on the subject: *Abortion: Law, Choice and Morality*.
Although he is still a conservative at heart, an advocate of giving
moral consideration to every decision on abortion, he is an
outstanding example of traditional Catholic intolerance giving way
to a viewpoint that tolerates a multiplicity of considerations.

Writing about Catholic opposition to California's attempt to
repeal its restrictive abortion law several years ago, he cites a
prominent Catholic theologian as saying, "If we are going to
murder we should call it by that name . . . for abortion is exactly
murder." Then he adds, "Francis Cardinal McIntyre asked that
the state 'not consent to contract a responsibility in conscience for
a carnage of untold numbers of innocent and unborn in the years
to come. Surely a wail from eternity will arise from those souls
forbidden and denied life.' "

In his reply, Callahan says: "Language like this throws sand in
your eyes. It excites each side to escalate its own rhetoric; and it
misleads just about everyone. By reducing the problem to a level of
crude polemics, people are invited to emote rather than to think.
Where subtlety and discrimination are called for, a bludgeon is
used." [4]

Callahan then discusses his church's traditional doctrine that a
zygote, an embryo or a fetus is a "human being from the moment
of conception." He says that while a fetus, *statistically speaking*,

may have "a better than even chance of developing," it is not certain that it will so develop.[5] He criticizes the intransigent position Pius XI took in *Casti connubii*, pointing out that the pope made no allowance for such problems as desperate poverty, mental illness, crippling physical disease, grave family responsibilities, incapacity for motherhood, nor violent impregnation. "Any position that leads to so many exclusions, to so narrow a focus, merits rejection. The good it would accomplish is at the expense of other goods; the price exacted for the protection of fetal life is too high a price . . . (such) a rigid exclusion of experience and social data is an untenable position."[6]

Regarding the harm done by restrictive abortion laws, Callahan says, "The worst possible laws on abortion are those which are highly restrictive. They lead to a large number of illegal abortions, hazardous enough in affluent countries, but all the more so in underdeveloped countries . . . Society ought to have a high regard for nascent life . . . but restrictive abortion laws have not proved an effective way of exhibiting this regard."[7]

After setting forth his conception of an "ideal abortion law," (pp. 488-490) Dr. Callahan thus concludes his objective and informative book:

> It may be counted a social and technological advance that abortion is becoming legally possible and medically safe as a method of procreation control where other methods have failed. But it is at best an advance to be looked upon with ambivalence. A single and faint cheer only is in order. Any method which requires the taking of human life, even though that life be far more potential than actual, falls short of the human aspiration, in mankind's better moments, of dignifying and protecting life. The time for loud cheering will come when, through a still more refined technological development, a method of birth control is discovered which does not require that we make a choice between the life of a conceptus and those other human values and goods we count important. It is possible to settle for and become comfortable with bad choices. It is better to seek good ones.[8]

Roman Catholic Dissent

While it is true that the "Right To Life" movement reflects the *official* stand of the institutional Roman Catholic church, a look at any of the recent polls proves conclusively that this vociferous group represents a minority of American Roman Catholics as I have pointed out before. Despite the great difference between organizations supporting or opposing voluntary abortion, a Gallup poll showed no appreciable differnce between *individual members* of the two main Christian groupings. In June 1972 pollsters asked this question: "Do you agree that the decision to have an abortion should be made solely by a woman and her physician?" Of the Protestants, 65 percent answered Yes; of the Catholics, 56 percent. [9]

As Professor Garrett Hardin points out in his book *Mandatory Motherhood*, since the right-to-lifers try to give the impression that theirs is *the* religious position, it is important to note the large number of religious and ethical organizations that oppose them. He lists sixty-three such religious and ethical groups. [10] The fact that there is not a single Roman Catholic organization in this list only proves what we have said before: that the opposition comes chiefly from the American hierarchy, representing the *official* position of the church, not from the rank and file who, since Vatican II, are inclined to think for themselves. The anti-abortionists are chiefly *men*, and their women followers are mainly those beyond the child-bearing age. Furthermore, in their protest demonstrations they march their children into the fray. In one such demonstration in Memphis, marking the fifth anniversary of the 1973 Supreme Court decision, there were six or eight children to every adult.

The rapidly increasing approval of legalized abortion on the part of the American public is shown by a "plebiscite" sponsored by the mass-circulation weekly, *National Observer,* reported in a March 7, 1976 UPI dispatch. Long before all replies were in, of 13,572 ballots received from its million-plus readers across the United States, 9,683 or 71.4 percent voted to let stand the Supreme Court's decision legalizing abortion in the first trimester.

In a more recent poll, a nationwide survey made by the Knight newspapers, 82% of Protestants and 98% of Jews agreed with the right to abortion; while 76% of Catholics agreed, 21% disagreed, and 3% said they didn't know. Overall 81% agreed.

Regarding the intransigence of the right-to-lifers, two veteran sociologists, Arlene Carmen and Howard Moody, say:

> The action of the hierarchy of the Roman Catholic church in the excessiveness of its language on the issue of abortion and its all-out warfare to win *the abortion*

issue is forsaking some basic tenets of our living together in an open society. Now the issue that suddenly needs open dialogue and serious debate is *not* "when does life begin in the womb?" but "when does freedom of choice and conscience end in society?" The question is not whether "feticide is homicide," but whether in this society any group can impose moral and religious beliefs by legal sanction upon *all* of society. Analogous to the abortion issue would be the passing of a law that forces a woman, against her religious convictions, to terminate a pregnancy or to be sterilized. That law would also be a violation of the belief in the freedom *of* religious practices even when those practices go against the seeming best interest of the state or, in another's view, seem erroneous. The principle of religious liberty to follow the dictates of one's own conscience on matters of faith and morals can never be forsaken regardless of the zeal or conviction with which one holds another's conscience to be wrong. [11] (Original emphasis).

Amid all the confusion and name-calling by the anti-abortionists, a statement by the eminent biologist Garrett Hardin is as logical as two plus two make four: what the world needs now is not therapeutic abortion but *humane* abortion: "Today, the qualitatively important reasons for abortion are to preserve the mental health of the mother, to reduce marital stress and to make it possible for children to be born into families in which they are wanted. Abortion is needed to help minimize divorce, child-abandonment, child-neglect and child-beating." [12]

Christianity's Debt to Judaism

In my opinion one of the greatest mistakes made by orthodox Christianity, and there have been many, was turning its back on the roots from which it sprang—Judaism. While many of the ancient rituals of orthodox Judaism seem meaningless and obsolete to the modern mind, no serious student of world religions can fail to respect the rationality of modern Judaism, nor to honor that faith as the progenitor of Christianity, the source of the believing world's basic tenet—monotheism. If the devotees of Judaism, like those of all other denominations, have their shortcomings, they are also rich in redeeming qualities. They don't proselytize; they don't try to force their beliefs on others; and for the most part they have a down-to-earth, rationalistic attitude toward sex and countless other problems of life. In no area is this viewpoint more evident than in their approach to abortion. In *A General Guide to Abortion*, Dr. R. Bruce Sloane and Diana Frank Horvitz say:

> In the United States the position of the Jewish religion and the collective Protestant churches has never posed a real threat to the free practice of therapeutic abortion for the benefit of the mother and child, and certainly not in modern times. Jewish liberalism, or a laissez faire attitude, derives in part from a Biblical and historic tradition in which abortion was rarely legislated against and a theology which considers the unborn fetus a part of the mother's body until it breathes independently . . . The question of actual moment of ensoulment of the fetus has never been of great significance in the Jewish faith and certainly not in regard to the permissibility of abortion. Judaism has always espoused the fundamental legal and ethical principle of the sanctity of all human life as the highest good and the creation of God, and, as recorded in the Old Testament, has praised the "begetting of children" as a blessing and reward from God; however, Jewish law has usually favored the well-being of the mother over that of the unborn fetus. [13]

Certain Jewish organizations that have adopted a rational attitude toward abortion include the American Jewish Congress, the National Council of Jewish Women, the Union of American Hebrew Congregations, the New York Association of Reform Rabbis, and the New York Federation of Reform Synagogues. In my opinion the following statement of the reform rabbi, Israel Margolies, is one of the most admirable expositions I have ever encountered:

> As long as men and women find it in their hearts to fulfill their love for and joy in each other through sexual intercourse, there is no law of nature or of God, no ethical imperative or moral compulsion, that requires that such love and joy must perforce lead to conception and birth . . . Until a child is actually born into the world, it is literally part of its mother's body, and

belongs to her and her mate. It does not belong to society at all, nor has it been accepted into any faith. Its existence is entirely and exclusively the business and concern of its parents, whether they are married or not. It is men and women who alone must decide whether or not they wish their union to lead to the birth of a child, not the synagogue or church, and certainly not the state. [14]

Contrasting the rational viewpoint of Judaism with the stoicism of Christianity, which "to this very day is characterized by elements of monasticism, reclusion, and austerity," David M. Feldman tells us that "such other-worldliness, again quite aside from sexual continence, is alien to Judaism. Temperance and self-control are always recommended, and the medieval Jewish philosophers made a virtue of discipline and of the curbing of appetites, but all within the framework articulated by Maimonides, (who) gave hearty endorsement to the Talmudic observation: 'Are not the prohibitions of the Torah sufficient for you, that you seek additional ones?' "

In his informative book *Birth Control in Jewish Law*, David M. Feldman gives us further insights to the charming earthiness of that faith's philosophers:

Renunciation of the pleasures of this world is characteristically regarded as sinful ingratitude to its Creator. No lesser a Sage than Rav, founder of leading academies of Talmudic learning, is the authority for the declaration: "Man will have to render an account (to God) for all the good things which his eyes beheld but which he refused to enjoy."

Of the "good things," however, sex seems to have a status of its own. Early Christianity had departed from Judaism not only in its attitude to all pleasures of this world but in giving special preeminence to sexual abstinence. To achieve spiritual perfection through renunciation of the world and the bodily appetites, every means was to be employed—fasting, solitude, prayer, mortification; "but always," our Anglican authority, D.S.Bailey writes, "the decisive test, the critical discipline, was that of sexual continence. This cult of virginity followed inevitably from the dualism implicit in St. Paul's comparison of the married with the single state to the advantage of the latter." The Church Fathers, he continues, treat continence as "the first fruit of faith" and, significantly, regard it as "a new and distinctly Christian virtue." The coital act was singled out for special contempt by Tertullian, Arnobius, and Jerome, but it remained for Augustine to designate it as the vehicle of original sin. All of this is the more remarkable in view of the fact that in those instances when asceticism did invade the Jewish community, such as in moments of national calamity and spiritual stress, sexual abstemiousness was still not prescribed. [15]

After commenting that from the Jewish point of view, "original sin" is an unfortunate and untenable concept, "the result of an orientation foreign to biblical and certainly post-biblical Judaism," Feldman quotes the Anglican Dr. Bailey: "It is futile to speculate how Christian thought might have developed, in this and other realms of theology, had the early church clung more closely to its Hebraic roots." [16]

A Protestant-Jewish Protest

In less than a year after the passage of New York's liberal abortion law of 1970, New York Protestant and Jewish clergymen joined to endorse the free practice of abortion and challenged the policy of the Catholic leadership in that state:

We must begin by an affirmation of the sanctity of and concern for human life, which is no less precious for Protestants and Jews than it is for our Roman Catholic brethren. On the contrary, we see in last year's law the opposite of an "erosion of respect" for human life. The countless unwanted children who are abused by their parents and society; the sickly and poor who are shunned by all and closed up in orphanages without love; the malformed by disease also deserve to live, but in the fetal form they are only the possibility of life rather than life itself. To decide when ensoulment takes place is a theological problem which must be decided by the individual church and cannot be a dictated dogma to all other religious faiths. To ask mothers to return to illegal and dangerous methods to avoid unwanted children is foolhardy. We are life affirmers who cherish

96

the very concept of life. Our traditions glorify and emphasize it. Therefore, we resent the implication of being murderers. In an age of ever-increasing inter-religious understanding and cooperation, we feel that mutual respect will better mark the time than name-calling.

We firmly believe that the decision to bear a child lies within the realm of one's own conscience and religious faith. It should be further predicated on the woman's civil right to determine her own reproductive life.

If our Roman Catholic brethren believe differently, it is their responsibility to be heard. There is no question about their right to speak to their followers. But we do question their right to make the choice for everyone else. In a free and democratic America, one religious discipline should not force its theological views on another. Since our belief is different and, we believe, equally humanitarian, we too want the right to speak to our constituency. [17]

In commenting on this war on abortion, which is backed to the hilt by the Catholic League for Religious and Civil Rights, organized and led by the reactionary Father Virgil Blum, one can't resist trotting out that old aphorism, "In every war, Truth is the first casualty." One example is the attempt by the Catholic League to intimidate *Harper's* magazine for publishing Marion K. Sanders' article "Enemies of Abortion," referred to above. It was a simple, factual article exposing many patent misrepresentations by the fanatical anti-abortionists, but the Catholic League characterized it as a "bitterly anti-Catholic article" and castigated *Harper's* editors for refusing to repudiate it.

In this particular war the second casualty is Christian Ecumenity. In the past decade, due chiefly to the spirit of Pope John and the Second Vatican Council, there has been a gratifying dissipation of the anti-Catholicism that tore the Christian world apart since the Reformation. Now, greatly to the embarrassment of millions of Catholics, the American bishops and the Catholic League are out to stir up a hornet's nest and destroy all the inter-faith good will built up during the past decade. Terming itself "a Catholic anti-defamation organization, a Catholic civil rights union," the League opts for many special privileges in defiance of the First Amendment, such as tax aid for Catholic schools, but its chief objective is to substitute the Roman church's traditional laws against abortion for this country's civil law as defined by the Supreme Court of the United States.

By castigating as "murderers" all those who don't agree with their position on abortion, and trying to overrule with a constitutional amendment our Supreme Court, naturally these fanatics have stirred up a lot of resentment, but one questions their right to call this resentment "anti-Catholicism," especially since more than half of the American Catholic laity disagree with them. The correct term for the general public's resentment of such high-handed measures is not "anti-Catholicism" but "anti-fanaticism." Whatever you may call it, by alienating millions of progressive Catholics and antagonizing all who take a rational view of this problem, these reactionaries are not reducing "anti-Catholicism"—they are *asking* for it!

While the American Catholic bishops and the Catholic League are organizing political strategies to make abortion illegal, policy trends in European nations, including several predominantly Catholic ones, appear to be headed in the opposite direction. In Italy some years ago, more than 557,000 signatures were validated on petitions calling for a referendum on abolishing all abortion laws. After a parliamentary committee approved a bill that would give a woman the right to make a decision on abortion, political observers predicted full approval for the proposed law, but they underestimated the power of the Vatican. Pope Paul and the Italian hierarchy pulled out all the stops and forced Premier Aldo Moro and the ruling Christian Democratic Party to substitute a watered-down version that would permit abortion only in cases of rape or when the woman's life was in danger.

The reaction was cataclysmic. The next day thousands of Italian women marched through Rome, protesting Parliament's action. It was the biggest feminine rally ever staged in Rome. Women flocked to the city in cars, buses and trains from all over the country, marching for three hours through the churches and palaces of old Rome, disrupting traffic everywhere. Estimates of the marchers ranged from 50,000 to 100,000. [18]

In less than a month, as predicted by political observers, Premier Moro was forced to resign. As a result of Moro's fall, President Leone Giovanni called for new elections and set a tentative date of June 20, 1978, a full year ahead of the original schedule.

Under date of April 15, 1978 a UPI dispatch said:

> The Chamber of Deputies voted Friday to legalize abortion for the first time in this homeland of Roman

Catholicism. The Chamber voted 308-275 to pass a Vatican-opposed bill introducing free state subsidies for abortion on demand in the first 90 days of pregnancy for any woman over 18 who says childbirth would endanger her physical or mental health. The measure must now be approved by the Senate before becoming law. (Note: This bill was approved by the Senate a month later.) [19]

Earlier in 1975 other European nations either adopted or implemented abortion laws. In France abortion during the first ten weeks following conception has been legal since January of 1975. In Cyprus abortion was legalized on grounds of rape or adverse socio-economic and psychological conditions. In Austria abortion is now legal on request during the first three months and later in pregnancy if the woman's life is in danger, if there is serious risk of fetal abnormalities, or if the woman was under age fourteen at the time of conception. In Sweden abortion is legal during the first nineteen weeks from the last menstrual period. Swiss law was liberalized in early October 1975, permitting abortion when there would be a "serious and long-lasting danger to the physical, psychic or mental health," of the woman or if she would face a state of "social distress." Although the West German Constitutional Court prevented implementation of a liberalized abortion law, the governing Coalition of Social Democrats and Free Democrats has proposed new legislation that would permit abortion after a three-day waiting period. Thus we see that a commonsensical attitude toward abortion, not only in America but in most of the Western World, is "an idea whose time has come," and these American reactionaries are not doing their church a good turn by fighting this rational trend. [20]

With the full weight and vast financial resources of the Catholic church behind it, the hierarchy's "Pastoral Plan" is the most serious attack on the Supreme Court's decision since it was announced in January of 1973. Even before the plan was officially adopted the Religious Coalition for Abortion Rights, an organization of twenty-three Protestant, Jewish, and other religious groups called it "an abrogation of our First Amendment rights to practice our own religions," and expressed the hope that "our Catholic brethren will consider the ramifications of the ecumenical community of enacting into law one religious viewpoint." As I pointed out in the opening chapter, the three leading Catholic magazines, *America, Commonweal,* and *National Catholic*

Reporter are strongly opposed to the hierarchy's attack.

With the passage of time, more and more people see for themselves the real needs and real problems of unwanted pregnancies in a very personal way. Since as many as six or seven lives may be directly touched by each unwanted pregnancy—husbands, lovers, parents, friends, physicians, ministers, and other professional counselors—*as many as six or seven million people* may be involved each year in the decision to have an abortion.

Countless men and women feel that abortion clinics should be outlawed—*until the need comes home to them!* In his down-to-earth book, *A Woman's Choice*, referred to above, Dr. Barr tells of such an incident.

"I've picketed your clinic for years and I thought anyone who came here had no standards of their own," one grandmother said to him. She hesitated, the tears welled up in her eyes and she couldn't finish what she started out to say. "Until . . . my grand-daughter . . . well . . . thank you!" [21]

"The pressures to make abortion a political issue represent the voices of a well-financed, *small minority*," says Dr. Barr. "The majority of these people are Republicans—yet a Republican family rushes their pregnant teenage daughter to my clinic for an abortion just as fast as a Democrat's family." [22]

Among the questions most often asked of him, Dr. Barr mentions, "When and what is life?" and "When does the fetus have a soul?" To the first question, he replies:

> Life is medically accepted as beginning at the point of the ability for survival. In obstetrics that point occurs at approximately thirty-three weeks of gestation. From the standpoint of abortion, no responsible physician to my knowledge has the least interest in terminating a pregnancy beyond twenty-two to twenty-four weeks, the upper limit of the second trimester. [23]

To the second question, Dr. Barr answered:

> Discussion of a soul is difficult because a definition of a soul is almost impossible to agree upon. The most realistic medical answer to this philosophical question is the equation of a soul with twenty-eight weeks, at which time it is estimated that the brain is capable of functioning. [24]

Long ago one of the Roman church's keenest observers said that Pope Paul's flight from reality—his refusal to take a rational position on the problem of contraception and abortion—would not bring about a "schism" in the Church, but would cause a gradual falling away of millions who have lost confidence in their leaders; a prediction that Father Greeley's surveys, quoted above, have proved to be only too true. In the light of that exodus—along with the socio-economic-emotional tragedies resulting from the forced births of millions of unwanted children—one is justified in recommending to the right-to-lifers that they change the name of their organization to "The Right to *Wreck a Woman's* Life."

(Author's Note: In a two-day referendum held May 17-18, 1981, in which 80 percent of Italy's 43 million voters took part, the citizens of that country overwhelmingly defeated motions that would have overturned that nation's abortion law, soundly rejecting Pope John Paul's vigorous campaign against the practice. A church-backed proposal to ban abortion, except in extreme cases of danger to a woman's life, was defeated with 69 percent against and 31 percent in favor, late returns showed. This referendum left intact Italy's 1978 abortion law, which allows women to get abortions at state-run clinics if two doctors agree.

This referendum, in the heart of Roman Catholicism, would seem to indicate that a sane approach to abortion is here to stay).

PART TWO

Pope Paul's *Humanae Vitae* poses a serious question and it does not give a serious answer. . . . It falls very far short of justifying the teaching it attempts to convey. (Such) teaching affects the lives of millions of married Catholics everywhere . . . in countries which desperately need to curb their population growth to prevent economic stagnation, malnutrition and starvation.

Editorial
National Catholic Reporter
August 7, 1968

8

Liberated Women vs. Male Chauvinist Prigs

"A woman preaching," said the sagacious Doctor Johnson in a quip long cherished by male chauvinist prigs, "is like a dog's walking on his hind legs. It is not done well; but you are surprised to find it done at all."

It's a good thing the legendary wit uttered this gem two centuries ago. In this day of the "liberated woman" he would not only be afraid to make such a remark, but he would be too smart. Whether it be through the pulpit, the forum, or the written word, "preaching women" have turned this staid old world around, made it a better place to live in, and brought a measure of enlightenment that even the most optimistic could hardly have imagined only a few decades ago.

In the late 1930's Amiee Semple McPherson, a "female Billy Graham," beat the devil around Southern California and built up an enormous congregation, to say nothing of a hefty bank account. On the serious side, Mary Baker G. Eddy, more of an organizer and writer than preacher, is revered by Christian Scientists the world over as the founder of their religion. A hundred years ago Susan B. Anthony and Elizabeth Cady Stanton "preached" woman suffrage from Maine to California and eventually won the vote for women. Today we have Ann Landers solving problems for millions, while Betty Friedan, Gloria Steinem, and scores of associates are constantly preaching rights for women. These and countless other "women preachers" have left their imprint on every facet of our lives today, but it is doubtful that any woman in this century has ever had as potent and direct effect on the intimate lives and well-being of women and families the world over as the high priestess of contraception—Margaret Sanger.

Margaret Sanger Against the World

The fight the courageous Margaret Sanger waged to make birth control respectable in America and throughout the world deserves a chapter to itself, but her story is too recent, too well known to need retelling here. At the start, shortly after the turn of the century, contraception was a dirty word, contraceptive devices anathema, and she had everybody and everything lined up against her—incredibly stupid laws foisted on the public by the neurotic Anthony Comstock, the medical profession, the judiciary, Congress, all the state legislatures, all Christian denominations, Protestant as well as Catholic. Her long drawn out struggle is told dramatically by Lawrence Lader and Milton Meltzer in *Margaret Sanger: Pioneer of Birth Control* and Alvah W. Sulloway in *Birth Control and Catholic Doctrine.* After trying unsuccessfully for year after year to have the restrictive state and federal laws repealed, or at least modified to permit dissemination of contraceptive information by the medical profession in hardship cases, the tide began to turn in 1936 when, in the case of *United States* vs. *One Package,* Federal District Judge Grover Moskovitz decided that the Tariff Act of 1930, containing a provision that grew out of the earlier Comstock law—barring the importation of contraceptives—should be construed to permit such importation by physicians. In affirming his decision, the Circuit Court of Appeals held that contraceptive articles should not be confiscated unless they were intended for an immoral purpose. In delivering the opinion of the Court, Judge Augustus Hand said:

> We are satisfied that this statute, as well as all of the acts we have referred to, embraced only such articles as Congress would have denounced as immoral if it had understood all the conditions under which they were to be used. Its design, in our opinion, was not to prevent the importation, sale or carriage by mail of things which might intelligently be employed by conscientious and competent physicians for the purpose of saving life or promoting the well being of their patients. [1]

While this decision did not invalidate the Comstock Law, as author Sulloway implied, it did initiate a much more liberal and intelligent approach to the problem on the part of the courts. It should also be noted here that penalties under the 1930 Tariff Act were much less severe than those imposed by the Comstock Law. The former called only for instigation of a civil action in which the penalty was confiscation of the "immoral" object, while action under the latter was in the criminal courts, with stiff fines and or imprisonment upon conviction.

While until recent years most Protestant denominations were against birth control as a matter of principle, they never put up such determined, active opposition as did the Catholic hierarchy, and gradually as the clouds began to clear, they could see the problem of contraception in its true light. It would be interesting to recount the running battles staged by Catholic authorities who were determined to break up every meeting Mrs. Sanger scheduled, going all out to "have the law on her" whenever and wherever she set up a birth control clinic, if only to show the drastic change in the Catholic position since those early days; but that would take us too far afield. Margaret Sanger was not only chiefly responsible for a rational solution of the problem here in the United States, but she was also largely responsible for breaking the fetters in Japan, India, Great Britain, Germany, the Netherlands, and other foreign countries.

Contraception Regarded as Homicide

In this day and age it is hard for an intelligent person to realize how fanatical the Church Fathers were on sex. Apart from child-bearing, said St. Augustine, "the marriage chamber is a brothel. . . husbands are shameful lovers, wives are harlots." [2]

In his *Si aliquis,* that reformed sensualist went so far as to characterize contraception as homicide and thus a mortal sin. Fortunately there were others who found such teaching objectionable, notably St. Albert the Great, but Augustine's ukase was defended by many prominent theologians of the Middle Ages and "the branding of contraception as a mortal sin," writes Noonan, "must have been the most powerful sanction against the practice." [3]

In the Middle Ages when theologians wrote about "the sin against nature" they didn't mean beastiality or unnatural modes of intercourse as we use the expression today; they meant any form of contraception, including the most commonly used, *coitus inter-*

ruptus. It was sheer insanity, as shown by these quotations from Professor Noonan's book *Contraception:*

> The theologians and canonists proclaimed that non-procreative marital intercourse, including coitus inter-ruptus, was a form of sin against nature. Peter Cantor, John Gerson, Bernadine, and Antoninus assimilated such intercourse to the even uglier category of sodomy. *Aliquando* proclaimed that the users of contraceptives were adulterers. *Si aliquis* condemned them as homicides. Bernardine labeled spouses frustrating insemination "the killers of their own children."
>
> In the ranking of sins of lechery, the sin against nature was said by *Adulterii malum* to be worse than incest. Gratian's ordering was maintained by the standard works of theology. In Thomas' *Summa theologica,* the sin against nature, including the sin in marriage, is the greatest of sexual vices, being worse than fornication, seduction, rape, incest, or sacrilege. (2-2. 154.12). This abstract ordering of vices is put concretely in preaching by Bernardine: "It is better for a wife to permit herself to copulate with her own father in a natural way than with her husband against nature." (The Christian Religion, 17.1.1) [4]

In the thirteenth century, Alexander of Hales was teaching, "The woman ought not at all consent to the man in the sin against nature, and if she consents, she sins mortally." In France, nearly a hundred years later, John Gerson said if one spouse seeks something "indecent" in intercourse, the other is to resist "to death." In Italy, as we have just seen, St. Bernadine was equally as fanatical: if the sin against nature is involved, "you women ought to die rather than consent"; even if the husband threatens to seek other women or other men for intercourse, the wife must stand firm. [5]

In this modern age intelligent men and women are inclined to laugh at such fanaticism, but to the faithful in the Middle Ages it was no laughing matter. Priests in hearing confessions were urged by their superiors to question their penitents on the most intimate details of their married life. One shudders to think of the thousands, tens of thousands of marriages wrecked, countless homes broken up, innumerable lives ruined by these fanatics who, obeying the orders of their superiors, were determined to ferret out the hapless "sinners against nature," setting husband against wife and wife against husband—*all for the greater glory of God!*

Fortunately for the hapless victims there were some theologians who realized that too detailed inquiry could bring a backlash. In his *Manual for Confessors,* John Nider advised caution in asking about sins of the flesh, especially sins against nature, "lest something be disclosed to the simple of which they were ignorant." But "with caution," the interrogation was to be made. [6]

A New Look at Marriage

It would be tedious to trace the gradual development of the doctrine of contraception all through the Middle Ages. Suffice it to say with Professor Noonan:

> Between 1450 and 1750 the doctrine on the purpose of marital intercourse evolved—not in a straight linear motion, not to a point of final perfection—but, with difficulties and setbacks, to a new synthesis distinguishable from the medieval balance. The Augustinian theory of intercourse was seriously impaired. The idea of limiting intercourse in order to avoid excessive births was introduced and given theological approval. *Amplexus reservatus* was increasingly discussed as a lawful alternative to contraception. The innovations accepted amount to a partial triumph of the theories and values labeled, in terms of the medieval synthesis, "counter approaches." [7]

Though neither St. Albert nor any of his colleagues went all out for unbridled pleasure in marital intercourse, they were quite instrumental in projecting a more rational viewpoint. A much greater influence, however, was Martin LeMaistre (1432-1481), an intellectual leader at the University of Paris whose thesis might have been written yesterday: "It sometimes happens that the desire of lust is so vehement, and so disturbs the mind, that a man is scarcely master of himself." Then no law prohibits intercourse with the wife, "given to him for the sake of solace and remedy." [8]

LeMaistre then goes on to his most radical position: "I say that someone can wish to take pleasure, first for the love of that pleasure, secondly, to avoid tedium and the ache of melancholy caused by the lack of pleasure. Conjugal intercourse to avoid the sadness coming from the absence of veneral pleasure is not culpable." [9] With admirable courage and logic he pointed out that the old doctrine—copulation for the sake of pleasure may be a mortal sin—was much more dangerous for human morals. Given that doctrine, LeMaistre said, a simple man will as readily have intercourse with any woman as with his wife when he feels the impulse to pleasure. [10]

LeMaistre's appeal to the dilemma of married Christians, joined with the open, penetrating, and comprehensive application of Aristotelian reasoning in marriage, led to a sweeping legitimation of the nonprocreative purposes of intercourse. On a strictly common sense approach LeMaistre ended the tie between procreative purpose and lawful intercourse. Almost single-handed by he brought about a new stage in the Catholic approach to marriage. [11]

By the mid-eighteenth century the shift in the Church's position whereby contraception was regarded not as homicide but as a violation of the purpose of marriage had relaxed the stringent teaching of the canon law and the Roman catechism. Despite the strong pro-Augustinian leanings among some French and Belgian die-hards, the trend was away from the rigors of the medieval position on sexual intercourse. Contraception was still unmistakably condemned, but by the end of the period 1450-1750, the reasons for opposing the contraceptive act, and the application of sanctions against it, lacked the vitality which the denunciation of contraception by St. Augustine and his school had once communicated. [12]

Toward the end of the eighteenth century we find further evolution in this history of the doctrine of contraception. Two phenomena marked this change: the steady decline of the birth rate in France, "eldest daughter of the Church" and most populous country in Europe; along with the open advocacy of birth control as a socially desirable practice, especially in England and the United States. In France the birth rate began to fall about 1750. By 1771 it was 38.6 per thousand persons, only 32 in 1800, from which it dropped to 26.3 in the mid-1850's. Since infectious fatal diseases were still uncontrolled, by 1850 the French nation was failing to reproduce itself. [13]

In England, where Thomas Malthus with his *Essay on the Principles of Population* (1798) had alerted the world to the problem of overpopulation, there was considerable opposition to contraception, but year by year the more rational viewpoint was adopted, not only in England but in most of the enlightened countries. Birth control leagues under various names were organized in England, the Netherlands, France, and other countries. In the twentieth century the birth control movement reached worldwide proportions. International congresses were held in Paris (1900), Liege (1905), The Hague (1910), Dresden (1911), London (1922), and New York (1925). In 1927 the advocates of birth control promoted and held at Geneva a World Conference on Population, which brought great impetus to the organization of world population studies. In 1930 the first international clinic on contraceptive methods was staged at Zurich. These international congresses did much to publicize the advantages of birth control, in stimulating public opinion for birth control, and in making birth control a social objective in the Western World.

As new and more dependable contraceptive methods were developed, the birth control movement gradually won over a substantial number of doctors. In time the humanist arguments of birth control advocates began to convert the learned worlds of science, sociology, and economics, as well as the Protestant denominations. In 1921 Edward M. East, a professor at Harvard wrote, "The world confronts the fulfillment of the Malthusian prediction here and now." In *Mankind at the Crossroads,* Professor East predicted that, if not checked, world population would reach an insupportable three billion by the year 2000. If Professor East is alive today, he will be amazed to learn that the United Nations estimated the 1975 world population at *four* billion; that it projects the year 2000 population at *seven* billion, *more than twice Professor East's estimate of half a century ago!*

Along with the shift in medical, scientific and academic opinion noted above, there was a drastic change in the position of the Anglican Church. In both 1908 and 1920 that church's Lambeth's Conference of Bishops had condemned contraception, as had also the American House of Bishops of the Protestant Episcopal Church in 1925. At the Lambeth Conference of 1930, in spite of determined opposition, the following resolution was adopted on August 14, by a vote of 193 to 67, with 46 abstaining:

> Where there is a clearly felt moral obligation to limit or avoid parenthood, the method must be decided on Christian principles. The primary and obvious method is complete abstinence from intercourse (as far as may be necessary) in a life of discipline and self-control lived in the power of the Holy Spirit. Nevertheless in those cases where there is such a clearly felt moral obligation to limit or avoid parenthood and where there is a

morally sound reason for avoiding complete abstinence, the Conference agrees that other methods may be used, provided that this is done in the light of the same Christian principles. The Conference records its strong condemnation of the use of any methods of conception control from motives of selfishness, luxury, or mere convenience. (Resolution 15, Lambeth Conference of 1930).[14]

Thus the bishops of the denomination whose theology was closest to that of the Roman Catholic church no longer adhered to an absolute prohibition of contraception. It wasn't long before most of the other non-Catholic denominations followed the Anglican lead, among them the Federal Council of Churches of Christ (1931), the Church of Sweden, Presbyterian Church of Ireland, the Calvinist Church of Holland, the United Lutheran Church of America, Methodist Church, U.S.A., Reformed Church of France, Lutheran Church of Finland, Baptist Church of Denmark, United Presbyterian Church, U.S.A. In time virtually all the Christian churches, with the exception of the Greek Orthodox, approved of birth control.

Pius XI's Casti Connubii

Facts and figures on the birth rate in the United States and other countries will be discussed in a later chapter. Here we are concerned primarily with the evolution of Roman Catholic doctrines pertaining to marriage, procreation, and contraception.

A little over four months after the Anglican bishops announced their stand at the Lambeth Conference Pope Pius XI retaliated with the famous encyclical, *Casti Connubii* (On Christian Marriage). Referring to the Anglican bishops the pope said, "Certain persons have openly withdrawn from the Christian doctrine as it has been transmitted from the beginning and always faithfully kept." Therefore:

The Catholic church, to whom God himself has committed the integrity and decency of morals, now standing in this ruin of morals, raises her voice aloud through Our mouth, in sign of her divine mission, in order to keep the chastity of the nuptial bond from this foul slip, and again promulgates:

110

Any use whatever of marriage, in the exercise of which the act by human effort is deprived of its natural power of procreating life, violates the law of God and nature, and those who do such a thing are stained by a grave and mortal flaw.

Summing up Pius XI's restrictive encyclical, Noonan says: "Here, in the small compass of a single document, was a synthesis of themes which this book has explored at length.... The encyclical. . . was not history. Yet if not history, it had immense doctrinal authority as a solemn declaration by the pope." [15]

Like Paul VI's *Humanae Vitae,* Pius XI's *Casti connubii* had its opponents, but it served as the Church's guide for the next thirty-four years and still remains the most solemn, complete, and authoritative presentation of the Catholic doctrine on contraceptive practice. [16]

So far as the evolution of the doctrine of contraception is concerned, the most important thing about *Casti connubii* is that it did give a limited, somewhat cryptic approval of the rhythm method and thus at least admitted procreation was not the sole purpose of marriage; that in certain situations a married couple was justified in limiting the size of their family. Any doubt about the right of dedicated Catholics to use the rhythm method was dispelled by Pope Pius XII in October 1951 when, addressing the Italian Catholic Society of Midwives, he made the fullest statement on contraception since *Casti connubii.* A new spirit appeared. For the first time rhythm was greeted by papal authority not as an alternative to be cautiously proffered to Onanists, but as a method open to all Catholic couples. Pius XII said that rhythm, for a good reason, could be used. It would be a sin to have intercourse and avoid the duty of procreation without serious reasons, but he admitted there could be compelling motives for avoiding contraception. In the presence of such reasons—medical, eugenic, economic, and social—"observance of the sterile period can be licit." [17]

While in one sense this slight concession to a most unreliable method was a step forward, most observers say that rhythm produces more problems than it solves. Among practicing Catholics it would be hard to find a husband or wife as enthusiastic about this gamble as the hierarchy and the clergy. "We practiced rhythm for the last four children," a mother of six told her pediatrician. "It was a nightmare. It bred distrust and hate of the very one you love. You live by the calendar, under the constant threat that the whole world will collapse if there's another pregnancy." [18]

One of the most brilliant crusaders against the rhythm method is a young Catholic writer, Sidney Cornelia Callahan, wife of the well-known author and editor, Daniel Callahan, mother of six children and incidentally a head-turning beauty. In her book *Beyond Birth Control*, this young "writer-preacher" doesn't waste any time getting down to the nitty-gritty of her sermon and no doubt has St. Augustine and the other Church Fathers spinning in their graves.

"Tinkering with the rules and patching up doctrines does not work," she says in her opening paragraph. "A radical reappraisal and a new synthesis is needed." In the next paragraph: "This generation needs a whole new 'philosophy' or 'theology' or 'structured approach' to human sexuality."

In prose that is both emphatic and eloquent she tells the Church Fathers, past, present, and future that the better half of Catholicism is sick and tired of playing the underbitch, sick and tired of being forced to have children when they are sick and tired; that the institutional church's sack-cloth-and-ashes approach to the marital bed is strictly for the birds—not meaning the storks. "A lover can welcome eroticism and passion," says this spokeswoman for her modern sisters, "just as a mother in childbirth can consciously and exultingly welcome the waves coming from within." [19]

As lover, wife, and mother, the author touches on so many phases of the procreation-family-planning problem that one is tempted to quote almost every paragraph. Skeptics of both sexes who are puzzled over some phases of the woman's liberation movement should read every line of this book, for if there is any group of women who need liberating it is the distaff side of the Roman Catholic church.

Scientists Warn Against Rhythm

Aside from its uncertainty, scientists have recently found a far greater objection to the rhythm method. Two eminent gynecologists, one Irish and the other Italian, say that when the rhythm method fails it carries an added risk that the baby may be fatally malformed, suffering from anencephaly—literally, absence of a brain. Says *Time:*

> Dublin's Dr. Raymond G. Cross noted that the
> incidence of anencephaly and a comparable abnormal-

ity, spina bifida (failure of the spinal column to close), varied with religion. Records of 700 cases of these abnormalities showed that the rate was 2.8 per 1000 births among Catholics, 2 per 1000 among Protestants, and only .7 per 1000 among Jews. (Few Protestants and fewer Jews practice rhythm).

Cross's original concern was to help subfertile couples to have normal babies. Now he has come to believe as have other embryologists and physiologists that an unusually high incidence of abnormal births may result from couples' using the rhythm method for birth control and miscalculating the date of ovulation. An ovum may remain fertile for at least two days, and the sperm for about 36 hours. Cross says that in the first half of the ovulation cycle, a stale sperm may fertilize a normal egg, and in the second half, a normal sperm may fertilize a stale egg. Either way, he believes, the stale component may contain a deteriorated chromosome and cause a fetal abnormality. . .

Milan's Professor Carlo Sirtori agrees with Cross and adds mongolism to the list of congenital defects associated with outdated ova. The conventional Ogino-Knaus schedule for contraceptive rhythm bars intercourse from the twelfth to the fifteenth day of the cycle; Sirtori would prolong the ban through the seventeenth day. This way, says Sirtori, both the risk of an unwanted pregnancy and the possibility of a malformed baby are reduced. [20]

In the eyes of many a hard-pressed family of today the discovery of fire, the wheel, America, gold in California, or atomic energy is nothing compared with the discovery and development of the birth control pill. So revolutionary is it that many couples would be in favor of indicating time by "B.P." (Before Pill) and "A.P." (After Pill).

In commenting on the advantages of the "pill," however, it should be noted that today the medical profession is not as enthusistic about this method of birth control as it was a few years ago. Recent research has found some disturbing after-affects resulting from its long-continued use. In many cases specialists are now recommending the condom, since recent revolutionary improvements have overcome most objections and greatly increased the safety factor. New developments are coming so fast that instead of relying on measures commonly accepted in recent years, every concerned woman should consult a recognized specialist to insure the safest and most suitable method for her particular use.

(Author's Note: While some medical authorities have expressed reservations about the safety of the "pill," as we have just noted, new studies now show a more optimistic trend. "The overwhelming majority of studies so far have found no evidence that 'pill' use causes cancer of the ovaries, uterus or breast, as was earlier thought," says the report by Dr. Howard W. Ory and associates. To the contrary, studies they examined presented evidence that the pill may protect against ovarian and uterine cancer. Dr. Ory, who headed the review team, is chief of the Epidemiologic Studies Branch, Family Planning Evaluation division, at the U. S. Center for Disease Control in Atlanta).

9

Pope Paul's Flight from Reality

Commenting on Pope Paul's ban on priesthood for women, Sister Margaret Ellen Traxler of the National Coalition of American Nuns said: "These men in the Vatican, operating out of a wholly male environment, are totally out of communication with the world of reality." [1]

The monumental example of Paul's flight from reality came on July 29, 1968, the day he published *Humanae Vitae,* his encyclical banning birth control. Time may well prove that day to have been more fateful for the Roman church than the historical October 31, 1517, when Martin Luther nailed his Ninety-five Theses to the door of Wittenberg's Castle Church. The latter produced a reformation; the former a *revolution.*

My crystal ball doesn't give me the complete prognosis, but I'm inclined to agree with Father Andrew M. Greeley, internationally known sociologist and acidulous critic of the institutional church, who predicts that scholars of the future will judge Paul's encyclical as "one of the greatest mistakes in the history of Catholic Christianity."

Since Pope Paul's controversial encyclical was issued more than a decade ago, many look on it as "ancient history" and hardly worth further comment, but we must bear in mind that a decade, even a century, is but a moment in the long history of the Roman church; that its official position on contraception is so closely related to its position on abortion and world population control that a brief review is timely here.

In a recent book *Catholic Schools in a Declining Church,* Father Greeley and his two Catholic co-authors declared that the birth control decree was "a shattering blow" to the loyalty of U. S. Catholics, may have cost the church more than one billion dollars a year in contributions, and may be largely responsible for drastic declines at mass, monthly confessions, and parochial school enrollment in the past few years. [2]

If the vascillating pope had deliberately set out to destroy Catholic unity, he could hardly have picked a more propitious time, a more potent weapon. In the years since his colossal blunder the institutional church has lost more members than in the fifty years following Luther's attack. While Paul was nobody's fool, at the same time, as the eminent Catholic theologian Hans Küng pointed out in a magazine article some years ago, "He lives largely in the past, always gets nervous if you want to change something that had been decided by the Council of Trent in 1545." [3]

For the first time in American history, as the late Catholic editor and publisher John Cogley said in his book *Catholic America,* priests refused to accept what the pope clearly defined as binding on the Catholic conscience. Millions of laymen dismissed the encyclical as merely wrong-headed and unrealistic. For thousands of them it meant the breaking point. Apparently the new generation of Catholics would forgive almost anything but irrelevance and obscurantism, and they felt that Paul's encyclical was promoting both. [4]

In the years since Paul published his encyclical—the shot that was heard around the world—leading Catholic theologians and writers have produced a veritable flood of protests, books, and magazine articles, chiefly on the theme that a papal encyclical, while entitled to thoughtful consideration, is not infallible and therefore the individual's appeal to his own conscience takes precedence over the words of the pope. These authorities hold that in following his own conscience, the Catholic who feels that using artifical means of contraception is morally superior to bringing into the world children who will endanger the life or health of the mother, children whose father is incapable of educating and caring for properly, or more children than is necessary to "stablize" the world population, is not beyond the pale; that such a Catholic can and should remain in the good graces of the church, entitled to all the rights, privileges, and spiritual emoluments that the most favored Catholic enjoys.

Paul's unrealistic approach to the problem, his flagrant intrusion into the most intimate areas of a married couple's private life, were galling both to the laity and to those practical theologians who understood better than Paul the consequences of his intransigence. [5]

The naive pope and his closest advisors seemed to think that time had stood still since the middle of the 1500's when the art of printing, though a century old, was still in swaddling clothes, when few of the rank and file could read or write, when the papacy rode herd on most of the civilized world, when in order to end the most violent controversy—Rome had only to speak. They failed to consider the incredible advances in communications since the Council of Trent; that today, by means of the printed word and flashing airwaves a position announced in Rome before noon is known to a more or less literate world before dark. The pontiff failed to realize that he, Paul VI, was not Boniface VIII, not even Pius IX, no longer the omnipotent Shepherd of a worldwide flock of docile sheep; that Vatican II had opened the eyes and stiffened the backbones of millions of Catholics throughout the world, especially the better educated, more intelligent Catholics who were no longer afraid to think and speak for themselves. He failed to realize that millions of Catholic couples, plagued by poor health or financial pressure, took heart at Vatican II's discussion of birth control, along with rumors of the Papal Commission's favorable report, and thus felt justified in taking a common sense approach to the problem—only to be stunned by the bomb that Paul dropped two years after they thought they had been given the green light to manage their own marital affairs.

Among the laity a segment of traditionalists took Paul's encyclical as inviolable law, but for millions of Catholics now living in the latter half of the twentieth century there was no turning back to the Middle Ages—another case of "How you gonna keep 'em down on the farm after they've seen Paree."

It goes without saying that Paul found no comfort in the charge made by Magdalen Goffin, prominent Catholic writer, in *Objections to Roman Catholicism:* "If contraceptives had been dropped on Japan instead of bombs which merely killed, maimed and shrivelled up thousands alive, there would have been a squeal of outrage from the Vatican to the remotest mass center of Alaska." [6] Nor in the prediction of *Christian Century,* America's leading ecumenical weekly: "Pope Paul's birth control encyclical has contributed to the decline, perhaps to the demise, of the papacy." [7]

In his book *A Question of Conscience,* Charles Davis, one of the most eminent theologians ever to leave the Roman church, sharply criticizes the autocratic pope:

> The unyielding stand of the Church against contraception has caused great hardship and personal suffering... Had there been open discussion within the Church over birth control, the moral teaching on the subject would have gradually evolved. Instead, an acute crisis has been provoked, because Church authority has resisted change to the breaking point. Meanwhile, the cost in human suffering has steadily mounted. . . Because Pope Paul is acting upon the archaic absolutist conception that he personally for the whole Church must decide so intricate an issue and come up with a solution, because he thinks that the faithful must be directed even in the intimacies of their married life by authoritative laws promulgated by the Church. . . he failed to show justice and love to the people suffering under the existing norms.[8]

In the Sweet Bye and Bye

Before going into a more detailed discussion of the Roman hierarchy's official position on contraception, it might be well to comment briefly on two major theses on which this position, now rejected by progressive Catholics, is based. The first is the centuries-old ambition of the institutional church to conquer the world, that is, to convert the whole world to Catholicism. The simplest way is to outbreed the rest of the world. The more Catholics the more votes, the greater the political clout, the easier it is to achieve this ambition.

The second pertains to the future world. The trials and tribulations of individual Catholics—wretched lives, broken marriages, juvenile delinquency, nervous breakdowns resulting from breeding like rabbits—is of no concern to the institutional church. "The more offspring, the bigger the population, the bigger the population of heaven."[9]

The importance of this future-world approach is shown most graphically by comments on birth control in the Jesuit magazine *America,* from its first issue in 1909 to the 1960's. Up until 1930, when Pius XI made a slight concession to the rhythm method in his encyclical *Casti connubii,* the overwhelming emphasis was on the simple value of procreation, the moral worth of large families irrespective of any personal considerations.

118

Suppose a child is born deaf, dumb, blind, idiotic, in utter poverty, and that its parents knew beforehand that such would be its condition. Suppose, in another example, that there is a "tubercular father with no prospects of supporting the family." Suppose, in a third example, that a wife is told by "a very modern physician" that "she could not give birth to her child without imperiling her own life." In all these cases, *America's* answer was the biblical injunction to "increase and multiply." "To be born, even with a strong probability of future infirmity, is better than not to be born." Similarly: "We must make every effort to accommodate the increased numbers which God, in His wisdom, sees fit to place upon the earth through men". . . ."The family which courageously and even heroically rears a large number of children in an over-populated area merits special praise for its virtues." [10]

It is only fair to say that in recent years the editors of this magazine have admitted there are situations in which "some use of contraception" by a genuinely Catholic family may be necessary. [11]

Ever since Pius XI gave a somewhat equivocal approval of the rhythm method in *Casti connubii* (1930), the Church has been gradually revising its doctrine on the purpose of marriage and easing a trifle its adamant stand against birth control. Before giving its blessing to the rhythm method, the Church looked on marriage chiefly as a license to procreate. Of course there were certain "fringe benefits" offered by the married state: mutual love and consideration, a sharing of fortunes and misfortunes, a means of avoiding or minimizing extramarital adventures for both partners, and the like, but in the fifteen centuries since the neurotic St. Augustine laid down his Spartan ukase—not only that the primary purpose of marriage was procreation, but that it was sinful to take pleasure in the marital act—the Church had hardly budged an inch. In the early 1930's when the Japanese scientist Ogino and the Austrian scientist Knaus, working independently, discovered the rhythm method, the faithful were getting restless and, realizing that something "had to give," the Church was reluctantly forced to admit a limited approval of the new "invention." What if it wasn't fool-proof? What if wags did call it "Vatican roulette"? What if it did bring a generous measure of surprises, especially for "good" women who weren't good at mathematics? It was just this element of chance that endeared rhythm to Catholic theologians and canonists of the old school. Had it not presented at least some element of chance, its approval would have bordered on an about-face, much too precipitous a step for the Church to take. These uncertainties made it possible for the Church, pressured on one side by the modern approach to sex, and hampered on the other by its traditional resistance to doctrinal change, to chart its course in the middle.

After Paul the Deluge

A mere listing of the flood of books that followed Paul's *Humanae Vitae,* mostly by Catholic writers, would take pages. The enlightened approach by the majority of these authors and editors is most gratifying. Amid so much excellence one hesitates to mention only a few, but without disparagement of the others, I have been most impressed by the following: *Contraception: The History of Its Treatment by Theologians and Canonists,* by John T. Noonan, Jr., a veritable "bible" on the subject; *Beyond Birth Control,* by Sidney Cornelia Callahan, a brilliant exposition of the modern Catholic woman's viewpoint on conjugal love, marriage, and contraception; *Dissent In and For the Church,* an account of the storm that centered around the Catholic University of America, edited by Charles E. Curran, Robert E. Hunt, and others; *The Catholic Case for Contraception*, edited by Daniel Callahan, a paperback that is worth its weight in radium; and *Contraception: Authority and Dissent,* a symposium by leading Catholic theologians and professors, plus one Protestant, Robert McAfee Brown. I have based this and the following chapter largely on these five books.

In *Contraception,* a masterpiece of erudition and research, John T. Noonan, Jr., late of Notre Dame but at this writing, professor of law at Berkeley's University of California, and one of the original consultants to the Papal Birth Control Commission, starts with the early Church Fathers who regarded women as a necessary evil, little more than breeding machines, and looked on sexual intercourse, even between man and wife, as a sin. From there he carries the Catholic doctrine on marriage, procreation, and contraception step by step through the Middle Ages, tells how it was modified and toned down by Vatican II and brings us to the eve of Pope Paul's heaven-and-earth-shattering encyclical. It is a most comprehensive and lucid treatment of the subject and is required reading for anyone who wants extensive and authentic information on this difficult and little understood problem.

120

As Professor Noonan points out, the Bible shows explicit post-Exilic legislation against marital intercourse during menstruation, homosexuality, beastiality and temple prostitution, but other than the precept to "increase and multiply," nothing is said about contraception. [12] The most famous passage on marital intercourse, "It is better to marry than to burn," (1 Cor. 7) says nothing about procreation, nor does the Bible lay any stress on the subject, yet the early Church Fathers were obsessed with both contraception and procreation. As Noonan tells us, the Church Fathers got their ideas about marriage, intercourse, and contraception from the Stoics and from Judaism's Philo, the foremost philosopher of the first-century diaspora, who condemned "the passion of love" as the origin of lustful wickedness. The Stoic Musonious taught that marital intercourse was morally right only if the purpose was procreative. Seneca rated as "shameful" too much love of one's own wife.

The epigram "an adulterer is also everyone who is shameless with his own wife" is symbolic of Stoic influence says Noonan and was destined to echo through a thousand years of Christian writing on marriage.[13]

The Tragedy of *Humanae Vitae*

It is doubtful that any book on the struggle over Paul's *Humanae Vitae* gives a fairer, sharper picture of the battle among the various elements of the Church than *Dissent In and For the Church.* In the preface it shows how this upheaval differed from the great disputes of the past. "Never before in history has an authoritative papal teaching met such widespread, immediate and public dissent. . . Theologians and clerics, laymen and laywomen from all over the globe voiced their disagreement. Surprisingly, the most concerted opposition came from theologians in the United States. [14]

The statement of the theologians in the United States, a masterpiece of logic, is a bit too long to quote here. It was published in full in the August 7, 1968 issue of the *National Catholic Reporter* and reprinted in *The Catholic Case for Contraception.*

To straight-thinking Catholics as well as to non-Catholics, one of the most offensive things in Paul's encyclical was classifying artificial contraception as a violation of "the natural law." It reminded them of Humpty Dumpty's reply to Alice in *Through the Looking Glass,* when she questioned his use of a certain word.

"When *I* use a word it means just what I choose it to mean—neither more or less."

A recent survey among American priests conducted by Father Andrew M. Greeley of the University of Chicago, director of the National Opinion Research Center, corroborated these Catholic opponents of Pope Paul's position. He found that only forty percent of the priests of this country supported the Catholic official teaching on birth control. Eighty-three percent of the bishops did, as opposed to thirteen percent of priests under thirty-five and thirty percent of those between 36 and 45. In commenting on this survey, Father Greeley says:

> There isn't much doubt on the basis of (these) find-ings. . . that the traditional sexual teachings of the Catholic Church are in serious, probably fatal, trouble. Despite the steady stream of warnings issued by Rome and the national hierarchy, the majority of American clergy no longer are willing to concede credibility to the Church's official position on birth control, divorce and masturbation. . . While we do not know what priests would have said on the subjects of birth control and divorce in 1960, we do know, at least in so far as a retrospective question can tell us, that about one-quarter of the priests in the country have moved to the left on both birth control theory and birth control procedure in the confessional since the issuance of *Humanae Vitae*. . . In less than half a decade the majority has swung away from support of this central moral position to refusal to try to enforce it. It may be one of the most dramatic shifts in the entire history of human ethics. . .
>
> *Humanae Vitae* was a tragedy. . . because it destroyed for many Catholics and for many priests their confidence in ecclesiastical leadership and the optimism and euphoria which Vatican II had engendered.[15]

The tragedy of *Humanae Vitae* is shown most dramatically by the sharp decline in attendance at mass in the past few years. A report commissioned by the Federation of Diocesan Liturgical Commissions attributes almost half this decline to the laity's dissatisfaction with Pope Paul's opposition to contraception. The report, entitled "Changing Attitudes of American Catholics toward the Liturgy, A National Survey, 1974," was prepared by the

National Opinion Research Center on the basis of a national survey of Catholics. Presented at a mid-October (1975) meeting of the federation in Boston, the research notes that when reasons for nonattendance are probed, 48 percent of the decline in weekly attendance at Mass is accounted for by attitudes toward contraception, 26 percent by changing attitudes toward divorce and 26 percent by changing attitudes toward the pope as head of the Church. "In other words," the report states, "the entire decline in Mass attendance can be explained using only those variables which are linked to the kinds of issues discussed in the encyclical *Humanae Vitae* or to the authority of the pope." [16]

10

Revolt of the Angels

Of the many books I have read on the subject, I believe a short paperback of 236 pages, *The Catholic Case for Contraception,* gives the clearest and most pertinent information on the birth control controversy. In his introduction, editor Daniel Callahan pictures the consternation, frustration, and bitterness felt by so many of his fellow Catholics over Pope Paul's autocratic action in banning effective measures of birth control. After giving many rational objections, Dr. Callahan says: "I think the encyclical is wrong on all these points. Put positively, I think there are many occasions when Christian couples may use contraceptives and do so with sufficient Catholic support to set their conscience at rest." [1]

All the essays in *The Catholic Case for Contraception* are so enlightening that it is required reading for any who are seriously interested in this problem. If only Pope Paul and those of his advisers who put authority above humanity could have talked with some of the victims of his heartless action, it might have been a different story. Unlike Paul, Dr. Thomas F. Draper, a distinguished Catholic pediatrician who contributed to this symposium, didn't learn about marriage and contraception by reading the papers. He quotes a young mother, a victim of the rhythm method. Obviously she was speaking for millions of fellow Catholics who shared her experience:

I had five children in six years. We had wanted the first baby right away and I do love all my children. But when the last one was born, our fifth, I had "that terrible feeling" that I couldn't take care of any of the children. I couldn't take care of the house; I couldn't cook the meals; I couldn't even change the baby. . . For almost a year my husband, neighbors, and friends took care of everything. Life seemed hopeless, babies would keep coming and I would be unable to take care of them. I think I wanted to die. Then a doctor prescribed some birth control pills, but two priests told me I wasn't allowed to take them. Someone told me of a priest who would give permission. I went to him and he told me it was like taking aspirin. I didn't believe him, but I took the pills.[2]

Dr. Draper asked how the pills had affected her life. No theologian could have condemned Paul's position in sharper terms:

The first six years of my married life were torment. I wasn't a wife. I was afraid to give myself to my husband. I was afraid of intercourse because it meant pregnancy. I resented my husband coming home at night. I was afraid to smile at him, to show affection, even to hold his hand lest it lead to something more. Now I can smile again. I think all I ever want to do is make my husband happy. When he's happy, I'm happy and the children are happy.[3]

In its issue of August 7, 1968, scarcely a fortnight after Paul dropped his bomb, the *National Catholic Reporter* condemned his encyclical in no uncertain terms. Commenting on the faithful's explosive reaction, the editorial said, "the birth control issue poses a serious question and the encyclical does not give a serious answer. . . it falls very far short of justifying the teaching it attempts to convey."

Catholic teaching on contraception affects the lives of millions of married Catholics everywhere. It influences the population policies of governments and the United Nations, as well as the personal decision of hundreds of thousands of couples in countries which desperately need to curb their population growth to prevent

125

economic stagnation, malnutrition and starvation. Finally, this encyclical purports to express the mind of Catholicism on sex in marriage; by failing to present a respectable rationale for the stand it takes, it imposes an impossible burden on Catholic teachers and confessors and creates a formidable new obstacle to theological exchange with other churches.[4]

The majority report of the Papal Commission is a priceless compendium of common sense which I should like to quote in full, though I can give only a few highlights. These excerpts are from *The Catholic Case For Contraception,* which reprinted the Commission's report in full:

> The *regulation of conception* appears necessary for many couples who wish to achieve a responsible, open and reasonable parenthood in today's circumstances. If they are to observe and cultivate all the essential values of marriage, married people need decent and human means for the regulation of conception. They should be able to expect the collaboration of all, especially from men of learning and science, in order that they can have at their disposal means agreeable and worthy of man in the fulfilling of his responsible parenthood. (Original emphasis) (pp. 157-158)

After commenting at some length on the advantage of a rational approach to the problem, the report goes on to say:

> The reasons in favor of this affirmation are of several kinds: social changes in matrimony and the family, especially in the role of the woman; lowering of the infant mortality rate; new bodies of knowledge in biology, psychology, sexuality and demography; a changed estimation of the value and meaning of human sexuality and of conjugal relations; most of all, a better grasp of the duty of man to humanize and bring to greater perfection for the life of man what is given in nature. Then must be considered the sense of the faithful: according to it, condemnation of a couple to long and often heroic abstinence as a means to regulate conception, cannot be founded on the truth. (p. 187)

126

The minority report of the Commission is a masterpiece of negation, its chief argument: *Contraception is wrong because the Church says it's wrong.* After quoting *Casti connubii* at great length, the report goes on to say:

> The Church cannot change her answer *because this answer is true.* Whatever may pertain to a more perfect formulation of the teaching or its possible genuine development, the teaching itself cannot not be substantially true. It is true because the Catholic Church, instituted by Christ to show men a secure way to eternal life, could not have so wrongly erred during all those centuries of its history. The Church cannot substantially err in teaching doctrine which is most serious in its import for faith and morals, throughout all centuries or even for one century, if it has been constantly and forcefully proposed as necessarily to be followed in order to obtain eternal salvation. The Church could not have erred through so many centuries, even through one century, by imposing under serious obligation very grave burdens in the name of Jesus Christ, if Jesus Christ did not actually impose these burdens. The Catholic Church could not have furnished in the name of Jesus Christ to so many of the faithful everywhere in the world, through so many centuries, the occasion of formal sin and spiritual ruin, because of a false doctrine promulgated in the name of Jesus Christ. (Original emphasis).

The Fateful Encyclical

The last item in *The Catholic Case for Contraception* is a translation of *Humanae Vitae* by the National Catholic News Service. A careful reading doesn't add anything to the late Pope Paul's stature. As the brilliant Catholic theologian, Hans Küng, said in a magazine article while Paul was still trying to make up his mind: "I think the Pope ought to say simply that *Casti connubii* was a mistake. He ought to try to explain how it was an understanding mistake for Pope Pius XI to make. The world will not make a big furor over this. Everybody makes mistakes." [5]

Instead of taking a progressive view in line with the needs and conditions of the times Paul retreated to the Tridentine era, rehashed the worn-out dogmas of a forgotten age, stationed a prying priest at the head of every Catholic marital bed and forged the chains once again on all the faithful who hadn't the gumption to think and act for themselves. Along with a plethora of priceless advice on marriage offered by the celibate pope, we find this gem: "This discipline (periodic continence) which is proper to the purity of married couples, far from harming conjugal love, rather confers on it a higher human value. . . Let (married couples) not be discouraged, but rather have recourse with humble preserverance to the mercy of God, which is poured forth in the sacrament of penance. In this way they will be enabled to achieve the fullness of conjugal life described by the Apostle: 'husbands love your wives, as Christ loved the Church.' " [6]

There are few married men or women, Catholic or other, who won't agree that the "joys of periodic continence" and similar "advantages" proffered by Paul are vastly exaggerated.

Pope Paul even had the nerve to call on public authorities outside the Catholic fold to help forge the chains on all mankind:

> To rulers, who are those principally responsible for the common good, and who can do so much to safeguard moral customs, we say: Do not allow the morality of your peoples to be degraded; do not permit that by legal means practices contrary to the natural and divine law be introduced into that fundamental cell, the family. Quite other is the way in which public authorities can and must contribute to the solution of the demographic problem: namely, the way of a provident policy for the family, of a wise education of peoples in respect of moral law and the liberty of citizens. [7]

Science Versus Fanaticism

A stinging rebuke to Pope Paul came during the 135th meeting of the American Association for the Advancement of Science, held at Dallas at the end of the year 1968. About 2000 scientists, including four Nobel Prize winners, signed the protest which read in part:

> More than half the world is hungry and the environment of the world is deteriorating rapidly because of over-population. Any action which impedes efforts to halt the world population growth perpetuates the misery in which millions now live and promotes

death by starvation of millions this year and many more millions in the next few decades.

It has been stated by Roman Catholics that the Pope is not evil, but simply unenlightened, and we must agree. But, whatever the motives, the evil consequences of his encyclical are manifest. [8]

The scientists, in signing the protest, pledged they "will no longer be impressed by appeals for world peace or compassion for the poor from a man whose deeds help to promote war and make poverty inevitable."

The scientists' statement concludes:

> *The world must quickly come to realize that Pope Paul VI has sanctioned the deaths of countless numbers of human beings with his misguided and immoral encyclical. The fact that this incredible document was put forth in the name of a religious figure whose teachings embodies the highest respect for the value of human dignity and life should serve to make the situation even more repugnant to mankind.* [9]

As noted above, recent surveys prove that in the United States the great majority of Roman Catholics are paying little attention to Paul's archaic and arbitrary appeal; but in Latin America, parts of Asia, Africa and other underdeveloped countries, in which the Roman hierarchy holds the upper hand, the results are disastrous. Commenting on this situation, The *New York Times* said editorially:

> *When the Church presumes to speak for one-sixth of mankind, on an issue that could affect the very survival of the human race, others cannot remain indifferent. The papal encyclical is bound to retard recently promising efforts to check a population explosion that threatens in the next few decades to plunge the world into hopeless poverty and chaos.* [10] (Emphasis added).

Universal Rejection of the Papal Ban

While, as we have seen, the strongest dissent from Paul's ban on contraception came from America's Catholic theologians, clergy, and laity, the opposition was worldwide and far more vocal among Catholics than non-Catholics. The hierarchies in most countries of Western Europe, while not directly repudiating the encyclical, came out with statements that it is not infallible and that Catholic couples may use contraceptives "if their conscience permits it." This is the position of hierarchies in The Netherlands, Belgium, Federal Republic of West Germany, Austria. Canada, Switzerland, the Scandinavian countries and France.[11]

Reflecting the feelings of innumerable Catholic mothers was the statement by Ann Gerrard of Fairfax, Virginia, who said she would pay no attention to the pope. "I have seven kids and can barely feed them already, and without the pill I'd have seven more. The Pope isn't going to feed them. So why should he say I should keep on having babies?"[12]

Catholic physicians were even more articulate in their dissent. Dr. Robert B. McCready, a fifty-four-year-old Chicago obstetrician, reported that 38 out of 40 Catholic patients, for whom he had been prescribing contraceptives before the encyclical was issued, declared their intention to continue their use.

One of the sharpest rebukes came with the resignation of James P. Shannon, Auxiliary Bishop of the Archdiocese of St. Paul-Minneapolis. Out of loyalty to the pope he tried for several months to uphold the Church's teaching, but he finally had to give up. In a letter to the pope, Bishop Shannon said he had found the birth control teaching "simply impossible of observance by many faithful and generous spouses. I cannot believe that God binds man to impossible standards. I must now reluctantly admit that I am ashamed of the kind of advice I gave some of these good people, ashamed because it has been bad theology, bad psychology, and because it has not been an honest reflection of my inner convictions."[13]

While Paul was greatly surprised and concerned over the strong opposition from Catholic theologians, teachers, and priests in America, he probably had even more cause to be concerned over the big percentage of Catholic women—especially those between the ages of 18 and 39—who were not saying much but were quietly going about their business of family planning.

In a magazine article entitled, "The Revolution in Birth Control Practices of U.S. Roman Catholics," pollsters Charles F. Westhoff and Larry Bumpass point out that the proportion of Catholic women between the ages of eighteen and thirty-nine who use methods of conraception other than rhythm increased from 30 percent in 1955 to 68 percent in 1970.

The greatest changes occurred between 1965 and 1970; the

percentage of women deviating from official teaching rising from 51 percent to 68 percent. In the lower age groups (ages twenty to twenty-four), the percentage of non-conforming women in 1970 was 78 percent. The authors note that their most significant finding is that the defection has been most pronounced among women who receive Communion at least once a month. Noting that in 1970 two-thirds of all Catholic women used methods disapproved by the Church, that the figure becomes three-fourths for women under thirty, Westhoff-Bumpass conclude that "it seems abundantly clear that U.S. Catholics have rejected the 1968 papal encyclical's statement on birth control and that there exists a wide gulf between the behavior of most Catholic women on the one hand, and the position of the more conservative clergy and the official stand of the Church itself on the other." [14]

11
An Orchid for President Kennedy

In the early 1960's the National Institute of Health made a study of birth control and came up with a voluminous report favoring the practice. But "religious pressures" were exerted on Dr. Luther L. Terry, surgeon general of the United States Public Health Service and the report was suppressed. "Its publication might result in religious controversy!"

When word of the decision leaked to the press, a real storm blew up. Greatly to his credit, when the matter came to the attention of Anthony J. Celebrezze, Roman Catholic secretary of HEW, he ordered the report to be published.

Ironically, it was a Catholic president who took the first step toward establishing a national policy on population and family planning programs. In December, 1962, President Kennedy authorized our United Nations delegation to support a United Nations' proposal to permit the World Health Organization to provide birth control help to countries requesting it. Since that day progress on both the domestic and international scale has been arduous and snail-like. President Johnson gave the idea his moral support, but it was scores of billions for the war in Vietnam, wars on poverty and getting to the moon, but pennies for solving the world's population problem. Beginning with Senators Ernest Gruening and Joseph Clark in the mid-1960's, there has been a small group of dedicated men in Congress who have been trying to get some government action on these matters. In the late 1960's Senator Joseph Tydings was interested enough to visit many of the hungry nations, a trip that resulted in *Born to Starve*, one of the finest books on the subject yet to appear.[1] Senators Packwood, Eagleton and Gruening and Congressmen McClosky, Bush and Scheuer, along with a few other Congressional leaders have shown real concern for population problems. Their fight against the American hierarchy and the entrenched bureaucracy has been uphill all the way. Too many of our leading legislators are too much concerned with "vote control" to bother about the real problem—population control. Most of them are deathly afraid of opposition from the Roman Catholic hierarchy, with which, on the question of population control, the great majority of the Catholic laity and at least half the clergy are at odds.

The story of the snail-like progress of the federal government's efforts to slow down world population growth is too complex and too fluid for recounting here. As might be expected, Richard Nixon, when in the White House, gave some lip service to family planning but no leadership.

Some years ago President Nixon appointed a Commission, headed by John D. Rockefeller III, to make a study of the situation and report its finding. The distinguished Commission, after an exhaustive two-year survey, came up with some realistic and logical recommendations, including abortion on request, free contraceptive information and supplies for all, including minors, and a national policy of zero population growth. Married couples would be encouraged to have an average of only two children. (The average was 2.3 when the report was published in May of 1972.) Nixon responded to his Commission's report by attacking both the legalization of abortion and the distribution of contraceptive information and supplies to minors, the ones who needed such help the most. In a rare intrusion into state affairs, he also sent a letter to Cardinal Terrence Cooke, endorsing an effort to repeal New York's liberal abortion law of 1970.

Chairman Rockefeller and members of the Commission wanted to present their recommendations on a national TV network but Nixon, catering as always to the Roman hierarchy, used his influence to prevent it. Some months later a documentary film, in which the opposition was given equal time, was aired on the Public Broadcasting Service, but the Commission's recommendations never did get the broad exposure they deserved. It was another case of "love's labor lost."[2]

The current crises in energy and food production may be gall and wormwood to the nation, but sooner or later the reckoning had to come; sooner or later these forewarnings of national and worldwide catastrophes had to show up the false prophets who won wide publicity by telling people what they wanted to hear, by discounting as "myths" the solemn warnings of public spirited students of the problem like John D. Rockefeller III, genuine scientists like George Borgstrom, Paul Ehrlich, the Paddock brothers, and other experts whose writings have been confined strictly to their own specialized fields—men whose dire predictions of a few years ago have already come home to roost.

By contrast to the foot-dragging of the Nixon and Ford administrations, such organizations as Planned Parenthood Federation, the Population Council, Planned Parenthood—World Population, and the Population Reference Bureau have been doing yeoman service for the population control cause. A big part of the work of these organizations was to press Congress and the administration for research and development appropriations, an uphill battle in which they were fairly successful; but their greatest success was in alerting the public, especially women of child-bearing age, to the need for containing the population explosion. To them goes the chief credit for the drastic decline in the American birth rate announced in the mass media some years ago.

In its December 18, 1972 issue, under the heading "ZPG Achieved," *Time* magazine said:

> According to newly released federal statistics the birth rate in the U. S. has declined to a level of 2.08 children per family—or just below the 2.1 plateau needed to achieve zero population growth. That marks a precipitous decline from the palmy days of 1957, when the birth rate stood at a staggering 3.8 children per family.
>
> Zero population growth is the ultimate goal of family-planning groups concerned with the implications of spiraling overpopulation. This marks the first time the U. S. has reached the optimum figure; given the dire Malthusian forecasts advanced by many scientists and sociologists, that is an encouraging sign. It does not mean, however, that population growth will level off significantly in the near future. Since there are now so many young child-producing families in U. S. society, the maintenance of the 2.1 figure really means that the population will level off at around 280 million in 2037.

To those who realize what an impossible problem would be posed for the United States by unrestricted population growth during the remainder of this century, this decline is most gratifying; yet one victory does not mean we have won the war. Before we get complacent over this boon we must give some thought to another aspect of our population problem: *immigration.*

Should We Take Another Look?

Throughout our colonial days, through the early years of our republic, and for many generations thereafter, our gates were wide open to all comers. "Give me your tired, your poor, your huddled masses," said the Statue of Liberty—and we got them by the millions. To be sure, America was built by immigrants—47,601,000 of them from 1820 to 1976, according to the latest figures available. But now that our frontiers are closed and America is bursting at the seams, isn't it about time—for the benefit of the Third World as well as our own—to pause and take another look?

In spite of restrictions imposed in recent years, immigraton to the United States between 1960 and 1970 accounted for 16 percent of our annual growth. In 1971 it was responsible for 18 percent, and by 1972 it had jumped to 23 percent. Compared with our total population the effect seems slight, one immigrant for every 500 residents, but in terms of its impact on our *annual growth* it is truly substantial. In fact, *it amounts to nearly one out of every four persons added to our population each year.* This takes into consideration *only legal immigrants,* which have been averaging about 300,000 to 400,000 each year in the past decade. Estimates of illegal aliens now in the United States vary greatly, but some authorities estimate the number of "illegals" at twenty to thirty times the average annual influx of legal immigrants!

In 1973 the U.S. Immigration and Naturalization Service (INS) reported that 655,928 illegal aliens had been located and deported from the United States. By 1974 the figure had grown to 788,145, a 20.1 percent increase. In 1975, after a year of severe recession, the number decreased to 766,600. Officials of the service admit that the number of illegals located is only a fraction of those who enter the country. They estimate that close to 3 million illegal aliens entered the U.S. undetected in 1973. The INS believes the number of illegal immigrants now residing in this country lies somewhere between 7 and 12 million!

As everyone knows, the bulk of illegal immigration to the United States comes from Mexico. During the last two decades this illegal immigration has been growing rapidly. Since 1964 the number of illegal Mexican aliens *apprehended* has grown from 41,500 to 680,392, a 1,600 percent increase! Legal immigration from Mexico has also grown rapidly in recent years. The 62,205 Mexican immigrants admitted in 1975 amounted to 16.2 percent of total legal immigration, by far the largest national contingent.

There is a consensus among experts that inability to cope with the illegal flow of immigrants is due less to technical impossibility than to political restraint. Once the thin line of enforcement has been bypassed, the illegal alien encounters few obstacles in his way to employment. Social Security cards are presently issued to anyone without proof of citizenship, and employers face no penalties in making use of this cheaper source of labor. Some estimates place the costs of illegal alien participation in Medicaid, the food stamp program, and other welfare services as high as $13 billion a year.[3]

Some time ago Senator Charles H. Percy (R-Ill) requested a report from the General Accounting Office (GAO) on the abuses of the nation's welfare system by aliens and it was shocking. Percy told his colleagues:

> I recently received a report which I had requested from the U.S. General Accounting Office showing that abuses of the nation's welfare system by aliens cost taxpayers as much as $73 million a year in five states alone. The report shows that over three-fifths of all aliens who collect payments under one of the major welfare programs, Supplementary Security Income (SSI), do so within one year of entering the United States, even though entry normally requires that aliens not become public charges.

Here are some of the highlights of the GAO report:

Of aliens who collect welfare under the SSI program, an estimated 8 percent enroll within thirty days of arrival in this country, 41 percent enroll within six months of arrival and 63 percent enroll before residing in this country for one year. All told, 96 percent of those who enroll do so within three years of arrival.

In five states alone—California, Florida, Illinois, New York, and New Jersey—over 37,000 aliens collect SSI welfare payments of $73.2 million a year, says the GAO report.

"These dollar figures are probably low, because they do not include Medicaid payments," said Percy. "Enrolling for SSI generally makes an alien automatically eligible for Medicaid.

Current law permits aliens legally admitted for permanent residence to begin collecting SSI within thirty days after arriving in the United States if they otherwise qualify." With these welfare figures in mind, if President Carter had been serious about balancing the budget, he could have considered the situation south of the border.

"If you consider the problem this country already has with illegal immigrants," says Philip Trezise of the Brookings Institution in Washington, "you can imagine how that problem will grow as the Mexican population reaches something like 100 million by the end of the century. Mexico simply won't be able to cope, and the poor will move across the border in increasing numbers in search of work."

President Carter took a giant step towards halting illegal immigration by appointing Leonel Castillo, a Mexican-American as commissioner of immigration! Disregarding the illegal immigrants, the choice at this moment seems to be this: When the year 2000 rolls around, do we want 250 million people without immigration, or 266 million with it?

Because of all the young people now on hand, we won't stop growing until the year 2040, even at the present rate of 2.1 births per family. If stabilization becomes a reality by 2040, would we want 276 million population without immigration, or 300 million with it?

In other words we have to decide whether our natural compassion for uniting families, the desire to offer a haven for refugees, and the nostalgia for our melting-pot background justifies adding eight percent more people despite the cut in our own fertility rate.

Because of our superior educational facilities, the United States has long been a mecca for doctors, educators, scientists, and other professional people. During the twenty years from 1946 to 1965, our universities and research laboratories were enriched by thousands of professionals, largely from Great Britain and West Germany. In 1960 eight percent of our immigrants were professional people; by 1970 it was twelve percent. But the 1965 revision of our immigration laws abolished preference for people originating in northern Europe and permitted a greater number from southern Europe, Asia, and Africa. Now we have a preponderance of professional immigrants from those localities and fewer from northern Europe. More than a fourth of all Asian immigrants and a third of all African immigrants are professional workers.

While our country has been greatly enriched by this influx of professional talent, what has this "brain drain" done to those developing nations, where physicians, scientists, educators, statesmen and trained leaders are so vitally needed? Among our 1971 immigrants there were 5,756 medical doctors. This was a boon for us—we can use all the doctors we can get—but what about the hapless millions who were left in the lurch? Isn't their need for these emigrants incomparably greater than ours?

In the Philippines there is only one doctor for every 1,300 people. In Iran only one for every 4,000 people, in India one for every 5,000. Many of the Third World countries have as few as one doctor for every 20,000 people. By contrast, here in the United States we have one physician for every 600 people.

No one can blame these Third World professionals—doctors, lawyers, educators, scientists—for wanting to live and work in the United States, where life is a breeze compared to what they would have at home; but what a tragic loss for these underdeveloped nations that have such a vital need for leadership in all areas of the medical, educational, scientific, and political worlds! These countries may not be justified in demanding more food, agricultural and financial assistance from us, but they have every right to protest when we rob them of the very bootstraps by which they are trying to pull themselves abreast of the modern world!

While this "brain drain" has tragic consequences for the Third World, there is of course another side to the coin. Most of our immigrants are nonprofessionals (30 percent), or those with no occupation: housewives, children, freeloaders (55 percent). And there has been a drastic change in their countries of origin since the 1965 immigration laws. Just before this change 113,000 immigrants came from northern Europe and only 21,000 from Asia. But in 1972 many more came from Asia (121,000) and only 90,000 from Europe. The United Kingdom, Germany and Canada now send one-half to one-third as many as before 1965, while Italy sends twice as many, Greece five times as many, the Philippines ten times, and India *seventeen times as many!*

Three-quarters of all immigrants of working age enter the labor market, most of them heading for the larger cities, to be close to relatives and employment, where they compete for housing, educational facilities, and—unhappily for our taxpayers—welfare. With hundreds of thousands of immigrants flooding the job markets, adding to the congestion of slum areas, and putting unbearable pressure on school and welfare programs, is it any wonder that every state in the union and all our major cities—New York, Los Angeles, Miami, Chicago, San Francisco, Detroit, and all points north, south, east and west—are scraping the bottom of the barrel?

It may sound a bit selfish, but with millions and millions of Americans out of work and jobs getting harder every year to find; with millions of Americans suffering from malnutrition, if not actual starvation; with millions of our poverty-stricken and elderly citizens unable to obtain the medical care they so badly need, isn't it time for us to become a bit more realistic? Isn't it about time for us to pause and take a good, hard look at our absurd immigration laws?[4]

Catholic vs. Catholic

The sharp decline in the American birth rate, noted above, plus the 1973 decision of the Supreme Court legalizing abortion, are most encouraging so far as population control for our country is concerned, but worldwide—especially in the teeming areas of India, China, Latin American, and Africa—the situation holds little cause for optimism. Much of the problem in these areas can be charged to the intransigence of the Roman hierarchy.

As I have noted before, there is no area in which the two factions of Catholicism are at such loggerheads here in America as in that of procreation. The laity and most of the clergy are on one side and the hierarchy on the other.

In his epoch-making book *The Time Has Come,* Dr. John Rock, a practicing Catholic, carries the banner for an intelligent approach to the problem. He says, "Nine out of ten fertile American couples are thought to use some voluntary means of limiting family size, and more than seven out of ten American adults have been reported to believe that our government should aid other nations which ask for help in curbing population growth."[5]

Another devout Catholic who was most critical of Paul's opposition to effective birth control is Dr. John H. Thomas, professor of biology at Stanford University:

My first duty as a Catholic is to do what I believe is morally correct. There is no doubt in my mind that the position of the Church with respect to birth control is morally wrong. The price of doctrinaire insistence on unworkable methods of birth control is high. It

139

contributes to misery and starvation for billions, and perhaps the end of civilivation as we know it. As a scientist I also know that Catholic doctrine in this area is without biological foundation. It is therefore my duty both to myself and to the Church not just to ignore this doctrine, but to do everything in my power to change it. After all, without drastic worldwide measures for population control in the near future, there will be no Church anyway. [6]

Pope Paul came in for a great deal of criticism on many phases of his pontificate, chiefly from Catholic sources, but no stand he ever took brought such drastic opposition as his ban on contraception.

"It is almost beyond belief," says George N. Lindsay, chairman of Planned Parenthood Federation of America, "that a man of sensitivity, who has walked the streets of Bombay and seen how overpopulation reduces human beings to misery and despair, can now feel compelled to limit the application of family planning." [7]

Against the background of all this ferment, the Catholic liberals' new thinking on birth control is most significant. One after another, liberal priests are emphasizing these thoughts. "Many Catholics have been oversold on procreation and undereducated on the responsibilities it entails," warns Jesuit Father William J. Gobbons. Jesuit Father John L. Thomas believes that no country can long make reasonable provision for its population increase unless a good percentage of its couples take effective steps to regulate family size. [8]

Mass Production of Indigent Children

Of course, the attitudes of progressive and conservative Catholics are diametrically opposed. Perhaps the most reactionary and distrubing attack on population control in the United States was made by the body of Catholic bishops in Washington, D.C., on November 15, 1966. In a statement entitled "The Government and Birth Control," issued "without audible dissent," the bishops castigated all plans, government or private, for putting any curbs on fertility, and upheld the right of all couples to have an unlimited number of children regardless of their ability to feed, clothe, or educate them. In the opinion of the bishops it was clearly the duty of the general public to pick up the tab for all these indigent couples and their progeny. "Free decision is curtailed when spouses feel constrained to choose birth limitation because of poverty, inadequate and inhumane housing, or lack of proper medical services. Here we must insist that it is the positive duty of government to help bring about conditions of family freedom which will relieve spouses from such material and physical pressures to limit family size. . . We reject, most emphatically, the suggestion that any family should be adjudged too poor to have the children it conscientiously desires". [9]

This shocking irresponsibility speaks for itself. The Aid to Families of Dependent Children program is spreading like a forest fire, bleeding our taxpayers white. The proliferation is almost incredible. In fiscal year 1950 a total of 651,000 families with 1,661,000 children—an average of 2.55 per family—were paid by state and federal governments, in round numbers, $556,000,000. In fiscal year 1978, twenty-eight years later, this program was supporting 7,480,666 children in 3,532,398 families at a cost to taxpayers of $10,726,866,000, nearly twenty times as much! [10]

Incredible as it seems, this payment of nearly $11 billion is *less than half the story!* More than *twice that much* was paid out in that year for Aid to Families with Dependent Children (AFDC), Medicaid, food stamps, Supplementary Security Income (SSI), and other relief programs by federal, state, and local governments!

In submitting his resignation as secretary of HEW, Caspar W. Weinberg said current welfare programs threaten to destroy the nation economically and are not doing the job for which they were intended. Weinberg adds:

> If social programs continue to grow for the next two decades at the same pace as they have in the last two, we will spend more than half our Gross National Product for domestic social programs alone by the year 2000. . . Half the American people will be working to support the other half. [11]

An article in the December 21, 1976 issue of the *Memphis Commercial Appeal* quotes Professor Donald J. Bogue, director of the University of Chicago's Community and Family Study Center, as saying that lack of birth control information among black young people is the single biggest reason for the many mothers on public aid. With little more than 11 percent of this country's population, blacks provide 45.8 percent of the AFDC beneficiaries.

An adequate contraception program among blacks would reduce AFDC rolls by 35 to 40 percent, said Bogue, writing in *Social Science Review*. In contending that a discussion of AFDC is largely a discussion of blacks, Bogue wrote, "Except for those receiving AFDCU (for families with unemployed fathers), all but a comparatively small fraction of the women on AFDC are divorced or separated from a husband who lives elsewhere or are never-married mothers who had a child or children out of wedlock. . ."

Bogue based his argument on in-depth interviews in 1972-73 with 315 Chicago AFDC mothers, 82 percent of whom were black. Because the sample was so homogenous, he said, it was as reliable as a much larger sample. Of the 315 welfare mothers he found:

> Nearly two out of three had sexual relations by the time they were seventeen.
>
> Two out of three, or 66.6 percent, became pregnant outside marriage, compared with the national average of 20 percent.
>
> Fifty percent had a child by the time they were eighteen.
>
> Two out of three said that at the time they conceived they didn't know how to practice birth control.

In addition, Bogue said, some 45 percent of all first pregnancies were both extramarital and unwanted by the mother. Forty percent of the extramarital fathers either "wanted an abortion or simply shrugged off any responsibility."

The "Right" To Be Born

A few quotations from an article by Julius Horwitz, consultant on public welfare to the New York State Senate Majority Leader, will give us some light on the future prospects of those innocents for whose "right to be born" the American Catholic hierarchy is contending "most emphatically." Though he uses fictitious names, the author assures us that everything else is factual. This article was written about sixteen years ago. Today conditions are much worse—and New York City is bankrupt, largely because of its generous "welfare" program. Horwitz begins his article with a brief description of the fatherless "families" that inhabit a "pigsty" in the Bronx and then goes on to tell about the difficulty young, unmarried girls and women have in getting enough welfare to live on if they don't have enough babies:

> The (teenage) Colon girls will soon learn that it is barely possible to support one baby on welfare allotments, but easier to support two and much easier to support three.

Considering the delapidated condition of their living quarters the rent is exhorbitant. Horwitz goes on to say:

> Who would pay $30 a week for two rooms chopped out of a railroad flat, with broken walls, vermin, furniture that belongs in an incinerator, a front door through which rats enter as freely as the swarming children?. . . The City of New York would and does. Why? The landlords know the answer. And the answer makes them inviolate. One of them said, "I run a pigsty for the City of New York. We're partners. See? The city pays me to keep these people off the streets and out of everybody's sight, period. They aren't people. They're drunken, filthy, baby-producing pigs, and as soon as they die off, there are more to take their places. *Nobody in City Hall would dare mention 'birth control.'* They might lose votes, but they don't care about losing the whole city to these pigs. (If the public knew) how these people live (the city) would close down tomorrow. . . but they won't, because there's no place else to put the 150 babies I've got urinating in my halls."

Referring to another group the author says:

> (Mrs. Gilbort's daughter) Roberta is 14, and pregnant. Mrs. Gilbort is 41 and pregnant. This is Roberta's first pregnancy. It's Mrs. Gilbort's 16th. Her ten living children (one, Louis, is in prison) had seven different fathers — all with whereabouts unknown, except for George Williams in Pilgrim State Hospital and John Green in Manhattan State Hospital.

"Where are you going to put the new baby?" asked Mr. Horwitz. "In the dresser drawer," Mrs. Gilbort replied. "She'll grow up all right." [12]

Because of the massive overcrowding in New York the problem of dependent children is a bit worse there than in most of our cities, but the same thing is going on in metropolitan areas throughout the country; impossible situations stoutly defended by an intransigent Roman hierarchy, but not by intelligent Catholics.

On the subject of birth control the divergent attitudes are getting sharper as time goes on. A year after the bishops' statement quoted above, a Gallup survey proved that 81 percent of Catholics, compared with 86 percent of non-Catholics, thought that birth control information and practical help should be available to any married person wanting it. [13]

Even though poll after poll proves that most Catholics are strongly in favor of birth control — as we have shown before — the Church has traditionally used its great influence to enact its own sectarian beliefs into laws carrying penalties for non-Catholics as well as Catholics, as well as to obstruct legislation which it disapproves. "The Church," said Pope Pius XI, "never can relinquish her God-given task of imposing her authority. . . in all those matters that have a bearing on moral conduct." [14]

In his book referred to above, Father John A. O'Brien says:

> (Here in the United States) it is unrealistic to try to deal with the problem of children who are without families or whose families cannot afford to rear them properly by a federally supported program of Aid to Dependent Children. The problem and its costs have been mounting year after year. It is obvious that it could be largely cured at the source by a program of assisting in the prevention of the birth of unwanted children, who comprise the largest group in the ranks of dependent children. This is only one of many problems related to population that are raising our taxes and making life less attractive for many of our citizens. [15]

Congress Lends a Hand

In the latter part of 1970 Congress passed an act known as the "Family Planning Services and Population Research Act of 1970," which President Nixon reluctantly signed on December 24 of that year. The authorized appropriations, in millions, for the following three years were:

	1971	1972	1973
Family Planning Services (project grants)	$30	$60	$90
Family Planning Services (formula grants)	10	15	20
Training Grants and Contracts	2	3	4
Population Research Grants and Contracts	30	50	65
Information and Education Grants, Contracts	.75	1	1.25
Totals:	$72.75	$129	$180.25

144

This act expressly provided in Sec. 1008: "None of the funds appropriated under this Title shall be used in programs where abortion is a method of family planning."

While this act brought a great improvement in the situation, the funding was inadequate for such a colossal undertaking and there was considerable discord between Congress and the Nixon administration, as well as among those members of Congress who wanted to increase the appropriation and those who wanted to hold the line. In the spring of 1975 Congress voted to increase the appropriation for family planning and related medical services from $100 million to $115 million for the following two fiscal years (to September 30, 1977), while the admistration requested only $79 million for that year. President Ford promptly vetoed the bill but his veto was just as promptly overridden by a great majority of Congress.

Despite the opposition of Rep. Robert Dornan (R.-Ca.) and other dedicated opponents of family planning, the appropriations for the next three fiscal years were increased (in millions) as follows:

	1979	1980	1981
Family Planning, Project Grants and Contracts	$200.0	230.0	$264.5
Training	3.1	3.6	4.1
Information and Education	.7	.8	.9
Population Research	105.0	120.8	138.9
Totals:	308.8	$355.2	$408.4

In view of the fact that every dollar spent for providing such services produces a saving of two dollars in costs of public welfare, education, health and housing programs, the advocates of fiscal economy and family planning were not elated over this increase. At the same time, taking into consideration President Carter's reactionary stand on procreation and world population problems, they were willing to settle for what they could get.

Caution—Danger Ahead

The mass production of indigent children by indigent mothers is a frightful burden on our taxpayers today, but without a radical change in our approach the burden is going to get heavier generation by generation as time goes on, not just in money but in the level of our nation's intelligence. A detailed discussion of this problem is beyond the province of this book, but in *Human Fertility*, published in 1951, the eminent biologist Robert C. Cook pointed out that if the next three generations continue to reproduce at the 1947 rate, in about seventy-five years (from 1951, the year his book was published) the total population would more than double and that about 60 percent of the children would be descended from "Group One" (women with zero to seven years of schooling); 22 percent from "Group Two" (women with schooling from eight grades to three years of high school); with only 18 percent from "Group Three" (high school graduates and some college work). [16]

This prognosis was foreboding when made a quarter-century ago, but is even more ominous today. In the past decade there has been a marked decline in child-bearing by Groups Two and Three, with a corresponding increase in Group One, our poorest and least-informed segment of women, due to the failure of our public health clinics to help these women with their fertility problems.

Professor Cook's concern is shared by Nobel Prize physicist William B. Shockley of Stanford University, who told a Nobel symposium audience some time ago that overbreeding among "the lower classes" is one of the three great threats to mankind. (He named nuclear war and overpopulation as the other two). He advocates legalized abortion and sterilization of the mentally retarded to check the population explosion.

Shockley said he was concerned with the genetic degeneration of the human race because the "less gifted" members of society were multiplying through extra large families and illegitimate births.

Family Planning Is Color Blind

As noted above, with little over 11 percent of the country's population, blacks provide 45.8 percent of the AFDC beneficiaries. Because of this situation, many black activists oppose family planning, or any form of population control, regarding it as a form of "black genocide." A successful program in the predominantly black Homewood-Brushton district of Pittsburgh proves that indigent Negro women are just as anxious as poor white women to improve their lot. With threats of violence, black militants forced the Homewood-Brushton birth control clinic to close for four months in the latter part of 1968 and early 1969, and threatened to close such clinics in all the city's poverty areas. Valiant and intelligent Negros fought the militants tooth and nail, and eventually won the battle. "No militant black power leader is going to tell a woman when to have a baby," said Clarence Huff, the Democratic ward leader in the largely black Homewood-Brushton district of 30,000 residents. [17]

Commenting on the charge by black militants that population control is "a white plot to commit genocide against the blacks," Dr. Paul Ehrlich, Stanford University biologist, says, "Like most racist plots. . . this one is incompetent, because if the blacks actually listened and had smaller families, it would mean more black power. Fathers would be more likely to stay with their families, the kids would get better education, better nutrition and so on."[18]

While, as noted above, there has been a drop in the United States' fertility rate during the past decade, this simply means that we have won a skirmish, not the war. In fact, there is every reason to fear another "baby boom" in the next decade or so. In the United States in 1960 there were approximately 11 million women aged 20-29 (the peak child-bearing age); in 1970 there were approximately 15 million, and a decade later there will be 20 million women in this age group. This virtual doubling of the highest fertility category means that the fertility rate for this particular age group will have to be cut in half if they are to produce the same number of babies in 1980 as this age group did in 1960. With such sharp increases in women at the peak of child-bearing years, a declining fertility is hardly possible, even if there were a sharp drop in the birth rate at each age. [19]

As we have seen, war, hunger, illiteracy, political instability, religious pressures—all are directly related to runaway population growth. The Japanese entered World War II largely because of their exploding population: 72 million in 1940. After losing the war and some of their off-shore islands in 1945, that nation was in a desperate position. Millions of soldiers were coming home with no jobs in sight. By 1950 eight-three million Japanese faced the problem of precarious survival under conditions of almost hopeless privation. Every square mile of arable land had to support 3,640 people — six to the acre. This was twelve times the population density of the United States, three times that of Germany, Italy, or India. Obviously their most pressing problem was overpopulation.

The United States spent over a billion dollars in the fiscal year 1948-1949 to feed the Japanese and to inaugurate the most intensive public health program ever undertaken anywhere on earth. These heroic measures had a dramatic affect, cut the death rate from a wartime high of 29 per thousand to 11.4 in 1948 — *but nothing was done by the Occupation to lower the birth rate.* Between 1945 and 1948 it went up steadily until in 1948 it reached the highest point in the island's history—34.8 per thousand.[20] In 1948 births exceeded deaths by nearly two million. In the five years following the war Japan added eleven million to her population.[21]

In an effort to help, the Occupation invited Dr. Edward Ackerman of Harvard to conduct a comprehensive study of Japan's problems and come up with the answers. This eminent sociologist and his staff spent two years surveying the situation and arrived at the obvious conclusion: prompt measures had to be taken to cut the excessive birth rate. Dr. Ackerman's report brought a stinging protest from the Catholic Women's Club of Tokyo, consisting of wives of the American occupation forces. General Douglas MacArthur, the intrepid Supreme Commander surrendered without firing a shot. He wrote the ladies a long, profuse apology and reprimanded the officer responsible for issuing the report, which was immediately suppressed. Copies of the report already distributed were recalled; it has not been published elsewhere, nor is it available in any library in the United States. Furthermore, MacArthur saw to it that not one dime was contributed by the United States to help the hard-pressed Japanese solve their most serious problem.[22]

The Catholic Women's Club also protested when the Birth Control Institute of Tokyo first invited Margaret Sanger to Japan, hoping to get the benefit of her long experience in organizing and publicizing the work of the institute. MacArthur refused to give her an entry permit.[23]

In May 1948 the Japanese Diet, or parliament, decided to meet the crisis head on by legalizing abortions for women "whose health might be impaired from the physical or economic viewpoint," but within a few years the new law was amended to provide unlimited abortion at the woman's request. From 246,000 in 1949 reported abortions rose to a peak of 1,128,000 in 1958, then tapered off slightly to about 955,000 in the following years. This program produced the most dramatic results in demographic history—cutting the birth rate of 34.3 per thousand in 1947 to 16.9 by 1961.

Although these Spartan measures cut her birth rate in half in little over a decade, Japan still had 102 million people, half as many as the United States but living on one-twenty-fifth as much land. So the long-range problem was far from solved.

After a few years the Japanese government itself became increasingly concerned with their dependence on abortion, partly because of the outside world's repugnace to such a drastic method, but chiefly because so many women were becoming pregnant again in six months or so. In such an overpopulated country where few couples, especially in the rural districts, even had a private bedroom, using contraceptive measures is most difficult. Desperate for a solution, the government backed Dr. Yoshio Koya, director of the National Institute of Public Health, in a drastic attempt to introduce and popularize modern contraceptive methods.

Koya set up a clinic and lecture program, distributed posters and leaflets, obtained the services of trained doctors and midwives. He purposely selected the most difficult groups—rural villages that set great store on large families; people on public relief, coal miners, farmers, and fishermen, all noted for their high records of fertility. The results were striking. *In the coal-mining and rural areas the abortion rate dropped two-thirds below the original level.* In the national program, use of contraceptives proved 67 percent greater in areas receiving intensive education by health officers than in those receiving none. Of course, Japan is still a long way from solving her problem of population control, but polls sponsored by the Mainichi newspapers proved that although abortion remained a dominant factor in family limitation, the contraceptive campaign had produced lasting results. Seventy percent of all couples now approved contraception. In slightly more than a decade, contraceptive practice had more than doubled.[24]

PART THREE

In their effort to ban "artificial"—that is, *effective* — contraception, the Roman heirarchy claims that it violates "the natural law," that any attempt to control human fertility is an impermissible "meddling with life." They don't seem to realize that effective "meddling with death" by science and technology has made a balance of births and deaths imperative today. If science and technology had not "violated the natural law" by stamping out the mass killers—epidemic diseases—we wouldn't need fertility control.

12

When Is a "Myth" Not a Myth?

During the 1960s and early part of the 1970s there was a flood of books on the world population problem, calling attention to serious food shortages throughout the Third World, and predicting the starvation of millions in the early future. Several of these books were written by internationally recognized demographers, biologists and economists, and all were meticulously documented; yet there were many "authorities" who shut their eyes to all this unpleasant information.

Egged on by the initial success of the "green revolution" and some evidence that family planning programs in the Third World were inching ahead, a number of skeptical observers declared an end to the world food crisis.

In 1972, five years after William and Paul Paddock startled the world with their widely read *Famine—1975!*, a professor of political economy at Massachusetts Institution of Technology wrote:

> The prospect of a world famine crisis in the foreseeable short run period, such as the next three decades, the notion of a world famine, arising from food scarcity and overwhelming us by 2000 A.D., seems to me altogether fanciful.[1]

151

A year or two later the roof fell on these skeptics. The complacent world got a double whammy: the Arab oil boycott, along with undeniable evidence of mass starvation in the Sahel. Soon afterwards there were similar reports from Bangladesh, parts of India, and other countries of the Third World. The oil boycott underscored the dependence of modern agriculture on oil-derived fertilizers, the Sahel disaster proved that the Paddocks, Paul Ehrlich, Georg Borgstrom, and other leading scientists were not—as characterized by some shortsighted critics—"ignorant alarmists"; and the 1974 World Population Conference in Budapest made it clear that optimistic reports of success with family planning programs in the Third World were vastly exaggerated, that *Famine—1975!* was an idea whose time had come. *Once again food scarcity was on the world agenda.*

Here was a baffling situation the likes of which our world had never faced before. Amid all the conflicting reports, naturally there were conflicting opinions on ways and means of solving the monumental problem. While not denying that a serious crisis existed, there were those who held it was not a problem of inadequate food production so much as an inadequate and unjust system of food *distribution*; that the solution was a radical, long-range economic and political reform. At the other extreme were those who, admitting political inequities and poor distribution, believed that the gist of the problem was a world population growth that continues to outrun the possibility of adequate food production.

In this chapter we comment briefly on facts, figures, and fallacies advanced by influential problem solvers in the recent past. An interesting approach will be found in *Diet for a Small Planet,* by Frances Moore Lappé, a brilliant maverick who didn't dream her book—primarily a thesis on meatless protein and how to get it—would interest a national publisher, but who, like Lord Byron, awoke one day to find herself famous.[2]

While no one can quarrel with the main thesis of her book—a meatless solution to the vital need for protein and what the resulting saving in grain would mean to the Third World—the plan she proposes is putting the cart before the horse, the very thing she accuses family planning advocates of doing.

Ms. Lappé says the first fallacy "is the notion that the world food problem has been caused by rapid population growth and that, therefore, the answer to the food crisis must lie in slowing that population growth." She then goes on to say that "a secure food supply is a necessary precondition *before* a society, or a couple, would be motivated to limit its reproduction, for without the most basic security need—*food*—can there be any other?" She doesn't explain how, with the Third World breeding like rabbits, it would be possible to supply that "basic security need" for all those rapidly increasing billions.

In spite of the fallacies, there are some valuable observations in Lappe's book: "If our forage crops and grazing land were used optimally, we could reduce the grain we feed our livestock by 50 percent without reducing our meat output at all." — "Another recent study estimates that currently enough rough forage (corn and sorghum stalks) is unused to feed 12 to 30 million head of beef annually." (p. 21). She also points out that one out of ten cropped acres in the world is planted with nonnutritional cash crops, such as cotton, rubber, tobacco, coffee, tea, jute, and the like; that "as a result of the fixation on nonfood crops for export (and profit for multinational corporations and big landowners) the position of subsistence farmers and the local markets has worsened in much of the poor world." (p. 27). She then goes on to say, "More and more imported food is necessary. The irony is that a poor country has to give up much of what it has earned from its cash crop in order to pay for imported food!" (The imported protein in the shape of canned meat, milk, and fish costs about 11 times more than the exported protein in the shape of peanuts and oilseed cakes).

With the exceptions noted, we think this best-selling book is basically sound and recommend it heartily.

The success of *Diet for a Small Planet* led Frances Moore Lappe to write—in collaboration with Joseph Collins—*Food First*, a book devoted entirely to the world population problem. Here is a book that has much valid information, one that would pay any student of the problem to read, yet it is badly flawed by a Utopian dream.

Never mind the millions in the Third World who are starving as you read these lines, "the scarcity of food in the Third World is a *myth*," or so the book implies in its title, *FOOD FIRST—Beyond the Myth of Scarcity*.[3]

In order to make family planning programs work throughout the Third World, all we have to do, say the authors, is to make sure that its four billion inhabitants are well fed; set up a social security system in all these countries, so that parents won't have to beget a whole flock of children in order to provide security for their old age; force the developing world's dictators to expropriate the vast holdings of the super-rich landlords so the masses will all have a small plot to cultivate and thus feed themselves!

While it is true, as the authors say, that food is the number one priority of the world population enigma, still by no means is it the *only* problem, as they imply. *Accommodating this world's surging billions is almost as difficult as feeding them.* Even if everybody could eat like kings, we'd still be in deep trouble. With an additional four billion people crowding this crowded planet in another three or four decades—as some authorities predict—this world would be in for eight billion year-round headaches. With all our rivers, lakes, seas and the oceans, along with the air, polluted by chemical, manufacturing, and human wastes as they are today, can anyone imagine what life on this planet would be like with *twice as many* polluters? With crime, unemployment, the housing and energy shortages what they are today, can anyone imagine what life would be like with twice as many men, women, and children compouding these problems? Stepped on, pushed around, harrassed, and harried day after day, 365 days a year, millions—instead of starving—would end up in the booby hatch, or like lemmings, would swim out to sea in order to find surcease from the intolerable barbs of their intolerable lives.

There is much, however, to commend in *Food First,* especially the authors' exposé of greedy, multinational corporations which appropriate to themselves the bulk of the best crop lands in much of the Third World, to produce for export cash crops like cotton, tobacco, rubber, coffee, tea, and jute; also their practice of encouraging the world's poorest women to forego natural, wholesome breast-feeding and further impoverish themselves by purchasing infant feeding formulae despite the lack of sanitary facilities and refrigeration which makes this a dangerous product for them to use.[4] ("Bottle Babies," a film exposing this repulsive practice, is available through the National Council of Churches in New York).

It is amazing that authors as smart as Lappé and Collins could mix such a vast amount of common sense with so much impractical, wishful thinking. They must be dreaming of that never, never land which Sir Thomas More called Utopia.

Not by Bread Alone

In *This Hungry World,* Ray Vicker, a veteran journalist who has personally observed the nutrition problem all over the Third World, takes sharp issue with the authors of *Food First* and others who say that food scarcity is a "myth." He says, "There are so many hungry people in the world that it is doubtful that we could feed them satisfactorily even if the United States decided to give away all its food."[5]

In 1958, when Prime Minister Nehru was at the height of his power, Vicker asked him, "What do you think should be done about the overpopulation of your country?"

There was a moment of silence; then the prime minister's mouth opened slightly in astonishment, "Overpopulation!" he exploded. "That is a myth which has been created by you people in the Western world!" Overpopulation didn't exist for Nehru, said Vicker, even though people were dying of starvation in the streets.[6]

As many world watchers have observed—and as the authors of *Food First* and other proponents of the "myth" theory don't seem to consider—the problem of accomodating the world's surplus population, we repeat, is just about as serious as feeding them. Vicker says:

> One study by the government of India, for instance, showed that to accommodate the country's annual population increase (about 13 million people) requires an additional 12,500 schools, 400,000 teachers, 2.5 million houses, and 4 million jobs each year. This in a country which already is experiencing difficulty in providing for the needs of its population without the increase.[7]

In his most recent book, Lester R. Brown, internationally known demographer and head of the Worldwatch Institute, says:

> Population analysts have devised dramatic means to alert humankind to the consequences of continuing rapid population growth. Concerned demographers have calculated the time remaining until we reach standing room only. Biologists have calculated the number of centuries that population growth at current rates would take to yield a human mass greater than that of the earth itself.[8]

Good Old Uncle Sap

In commenting on the 1974 World Food Conference in Rome, Ray Vicker tells how Agricultural Secretary Butz, angered at three Democratic senators who gave the world the wrong impression about the generosity of the American people, took the floor to correct that impression. He presented figures to show that American aid accounted for 84 percent of all food aid to developing countries in the eight years from 1965 to 1972; 46 percent of all aid since 1972 (Canada, second largest donor, contributed 13 percent); one-third of all the food given to Bangladesh since its independence; over $25 billion worth of food aid over the years; $27 billion of food aid to India over a five-year stretch in the 1960s; about half a million tons of food for Sahel relief in the two preceding years; 400 agricultural technicians scattered around the world offering assistance of different kinds; and 1200 foreign agricultural technicians in training in the United States. Moreover Butz affirmed American willingness to join with other donors in a conference-suggested program for giving 10 million tons of grain annually over a three-year period to needy nations.

"It was a sterling performance which many publications on the European side of the Atlantic ignored," says Vicker. "THE U.S.A. STILL SAYS NO, " headlined one Italian paper the next day. The Paris-based *International Herald-Tribune* ran an Associated Press story headlined, "U.S. REJECTS BID TO BOOST FOOD AID." Pickets on the steps of the convention hall were carrying placards which read: "TODAY'S HUNGRY TOMORROW'S DEAD, " and "FORD AWAITS, MILLIONS STARVE."[9]

Teach the Third World to Fish

An old Chinese proverb says, "If you give me a fish I'll eat it today; *teach* me to fish and I'll eat indefinitely."

Certainly we should extend aid to the Third World—as we have done so generously in the past—but such aid should be designed to help these countries help themselves. We should step up creative research in all areas and give the underdeveloped countries all the technical assistance possible. As the world's largest food exporter, the United States has tremendous power, but we must use this power intelligently. It would be the height of folly to surrender control of our harvests to an international body, as some of our impulsive do-gooders have been urging. With the United Nations more or less dominated by Third World countries, it doesn't take much imagination to predict the outcome of such an arrangement. There is much we can do to help in this distressing situation, but the United States is no Atlas. Powerful as this nation is, we can't carry the entire Third World on our shoulders.

13

Worldwide Need for Population Control

In the *Smithsonian Magazine* for July 1976, Dr. Georg Borgstrom, professor of food science, nutrition and geography at Michigan State University, has an illuminating article entitled, The Numbers Force Us into A World Like None in History." He ends the article with a full-page illustration of a sperm penetrating a human ovum, with this caption: "Here, with the sperm penetrating a human ovum, is where the problem might be said to start."

This is a graphic way of saying the start of the world population problem — and its solution — lies in the bedrooms of the world.

The United Nations Demographic Yearbook announced in January of 1977 that the world population had reached 4 billion and predicted that the population would double by the year 2011 if the increase continued at the current worldwide rate of 1.9 a year.

In the fall of 1976—shortly before the U.N.'s 1975 yearbook was published—a report by the Worldwatch Research Institute, based in Washington and funded in part by the U.N., said falling birth rates and *"unforeseen deaths from hunger"* have slowed global population growth to the point where a doubling of the world population by 2011 is no longer anticipated.

Paced by two of the world's four most populous countries, China and the United States, population growth had decreased in several countries both rich and poor, reversing for the first time in history a trend of gradually accelerating growth, the Worldwatch study adds.

Dr. Lester Brown, an agricultural economist who heads the institute, said in the report, released October 28, 1976, that the decline in population growth reflects more than anything else the widening availability of family-planning services, *including both contraception and abortion,* and a growing desire to use them. By early 1976, 68 percent of the world's people lived in countries where abortions were legal, up from 38 percent in 1971, a gain of about 60 percent in five years.

But in some of the poorest countries, like India and Bangladesh, according to the report, *"food shortages pushed up the death rates, resulting in millions of additional and avoidable deaths over the past five years."*

While this decline in the world's population growth is most encouraging, it is only a candle glow, not by any means "the light at the end of the tunnel." The fact that this decline was due in large part to *"millions of additional deaths" from starvation* should alert us to the fact that the rapid growth of the world population is still the most serious problem this world faces, or is ever likely to face. In *The Hungry Planet,* Professor Georg Borgstrom, eminent agronomist, says:

> Most people are unable to see our almost terrifying inclination to confuse means with goals. . . The prevailing escapism is of such dimensions that it is bordering on insanity. . . The sooner we accept and adjust to reality, the better our chance to save at least part of the values which western civilization has accumulated over a period of two or three thousand years. If we continue as hitherto, we are heading for inevitable disaster.[1]

Forty or fifty years ago alert scientists began calling attention to our frightfully overcrowded world, so the failure of the general public to become concerned and the gross indifference on the part of so many scientists and political leaders is truly shocking. A Gallup poll in 1963 revealed that almost 70 percent of Americans had heard about the population "explosion," but only one in four regarded it as something to worry about. A year later a Harris survey of our country's chief problems disclosed general concern for peace, civil rights, juvenile delinquency, and similar troubles, but no one mentioned the population problem.[2] It is difficult to pinpoint the major factors that account for this apathy, but in my opinion the chief ones are these: (1) The feeling on the part of most editors that anyone who rates as an "expert" in one particular field—economy, sociology, history and the like—is *ipso facto* an expert in all branches of knowledge, so they often publish a lot of expert nonsense; (2) The padlocked minds of many pseudo-experts, so strongly biased by orthodox thinking or religious training that it is impossible for any new ideas to disturb the tenor of their ways; (3) The typical editor's "nose for news," the knowledge that most readers eschew realistic presentations of bad news, while they lap up optimistic nonsense. If, for example, a truly competent expert on agronomy, mass nutrition, and population problems presents a factual account of the situation, showing that the world is headed for starvation, his audience is limited; but let some publicity seeker come out with a tub-thumping article saying the scientists are all wrong—spewing the kind of palaver the public wants to heai and believe—too many editors will rise to the bait like starving fish.

In the preceding chapter we dealt with the "food scarcity is a myth" school of thought and observers who felt that if we just ignored the problem it would go away. No doubt millions of starving and half-starved people in Asia, Africa, and Latin America would like to ask these dissenters to name another problem that is more serious than the one described by Dr. Raymond Ewell, vice president for research, State University of New York at Buffalo, former advisor to the government of India:

> During (recent years) we have heard an increasing amount of talk and publicity on many problems associated with our increasing population in the United States—increased crime, juvenile delinquency, water pollution, air pollution, urban deterioration, noise, dirt, waste disposal, racial friction, and others. . . But even these problems, which seem important to us in the United States, fade into relative insignificance compared to the food problem faced by many countries. The very real threat of mass starvation within the next ten to fifteen years hangs over the 2.5 billion human beings of Asia, Africa, and Latin America. This is the biggest, most fundamental and most nearly insoluble problem that has ever faced the human race. . . Such a famine will be of massive proportions affecting hundreds of millions, possibly even billions, of persons. *If this happens, as now appears probable, it will be the most colossal catastrophe in history.*[3] (Emphasis added).

159

The first informed forecasts on the world population glut were based on an attempted worldwide census in 1950. Ten years later, when the second worldwide census was taken, most of the earlier predictions had to be scrapped because the new data showed a faster rate of growth than demographers had previously thought possible.

Thirty-five or forty years ago one-third of the world's people lived in the impoverished areas of Asia, Africa, and Latin America. In 1975, according to U.N. population studies, 2.67 billion people, *more than 70 percent of the world's population,* lived in these developing nations.[4] (U. S. Census estimates 75 percent).

Eyewitness Accounts of Hunger

Those who think famine conditions in the Third World are a "smoke screen" should read *Born to Hunger,* the story of a trip through hungry nations of Africa, Asia, and Latin America by the British journalist, Arthur Hopcraft. He tells of appalling conditions in Tanzia, Kenya, Brazil, India, and other underdeveloped countries. Typical of all the countries Hopcraft visited is Colombia, where "infant deaths average 260 a day, 100 of them due to malnutrition"; where such deaths account for 72 percent of total mortality, but where "such deaths are not the worst problem since the consequences to some of the survivors were mental and physical inadequacies which crippled them for the rest of their lives."[5]

Just one month after issuing his encyclical banning birth control, Pope Paul arrived in Bogata, the troubled capital of that troubled country. Under the date line August 20, 1968, Vatican City, George Weller of the *Chicago Daily News* Service wrote:

> Pope Paul VI has received disturbing news of one important feature of his three-day visit to Colombia. The ragged urchins of Bogata, who might by their presence have visually challenged his encyclical on birth control, are being swept from the streets.
>
> The gamins are orphans, too poor to own even the rubana, that poncho which serves as blanket and overcoat for the half-Indian peons. They steal and beg in the chill rains of Bogata's 8,660 foot height.
>
> The apostolic administrator, the Rev. Munoz Duque, tried to move some 5,000 of these homeless urchins out of the alleys and into some kind of orphanage before Paul arrived.

In the same article, Weller said the Camillist Fathers were demanding that the gamins be left free, not snatched out of sight of the pope. "Only in this way," said a Camillist priest, "can Paul see the real face of the Latin social problem in the cities."[6] It isn't clear whether Paul was spared this distressing sight or not; all we know is that his visit didn't shake Paul's conviction that a just and merciful God is pleased with the slaughter of the innocents, pleased to watch them starve, slowly and painfully, while He damns us for taking simple measures to keep such innocents from being born.

Disclosures by Arthur Hopcraft and other authors with eyewitness accounts of conditions in the hungry world prove that the facts are there for any who care to investigate. Obviously a great many dissenters have an axe to grind and simply "don't want to be convinced by the facts." It would be hard to find a neater summary of the situation than Professor Borgstrom's:

> An overwhelming number of scientists, technologists, and educators from various continents travel around the globe preaching, completely contrary to fact, about our unlimited resources and all the technological magic we can master in areas like irrigation, fertilization, and genetics. In lieu of this reassuring gospel they ought to make mankind aware of its real predicament, familiarize it with all the limiting factors of our existence, recognize the indisputable fact that man needs water and very specified carbon molecules to survive, that in the dictionary of Nature there exists no such concept as *limitless,* and that we have gone far beyond the feeding resources of our globe. We need to declare the Great War for Human Survival—but it is getting late. Time is running out on us. It is five minutes to twelve.[7]

The following statement by Buckminster Fuller is typical of what Dr. Borgstrom means: "Humanity's mastery of vast, inanimate, inexhaustible energy resources and accelerated doing more with less of sea, air and space technology has proven Malthus to be wrong. Comprehensive physical and economic success for humanity may now be accomplished in one-fourth of a century."[8]

Buckminister Fuller may be tops in the field of design, but what he doesn't know about the world population problem would fill volumes.

161

Another eminent purveyor of nonsense is Nobel Prize winner and Harvard professor, George Wald. Writing in *The Progressive* (1975) Dr. Wald says that by doing away with feeding grain to live stock, "It would be altogether possible to feed the present world population. In fact, some of the demographers who tell us not to worry too much about the population explosion, estimate that with careful management we could feed as many as forty billion people on earth."

Many scientists concentrate so intently on their specialty that their brain becomes muscle-bound and often the most brilliant scientist is as naive as a child when he enters an alien field. Instead of analyzing the statement of "some demographers" that our earth could feed as many as forty billion people, Dr. Wald swallows this fallacy hook, line, and blinker. As I have said more than once, the problem isn't merely *feeding* the countless billions that are now crowding our planet, it is *accommodating* them. At the rate the world population is now growing, in another hundred years nobody will have room enough to lie down. If such overcrowding doesn't drive everyone mad, bodily wastes alone would just about pollute every living soul off the face of the earth.

Countering such fallacies as those expressed by Buckminister Fuller and George Wald, Richard A. Falk, a recognized authority on the population problem, says:

> A more conventional and convenient view of the future arises from assumptions of *automatic adjustment processes.* Something will turn up, a technological solution can be found, action will be taken when the situation becomes really dangerous. . .
>
> Neither *exponential-mindedness* nor the prospect of *automatic adjustment* seems to locate the situation quite accurately in *political space-time.* Every recorded civilization has been blind to the threats directed at its ascendancy. Who could have believed in the fall of Rome when the Empire was at its height? Or in the collapse of the great civilizations of Egypt, China, Greece, Latin America when they had gained ascendancy? The blindness of man to the causes of his own downfall is a persistent strain of historical experience. Because of the scope of the crisis and the technology of warfare there appears to be more likelihood that the downfall will imperil the entire world, not just a civilization, and that the earth processes of recovery and continuation will be

more difficult than anything so far experienced in the history of the planet.[9] [*Original emphasis*]

One realist who leaves no doubt about the problem is Paul Ehrlich, biological scientist at Stanford University. In the prologue to *The Population Bomb,* he says:

> The battle to feed all humanity is over. In the 1970s and 1980s hundreds of millions of people will starve to death in spite of any crash programs embarked upon now. At this late date nothing can prevent a substantial increase in the world death rate, although many lives could be saved through dramatic programs to "stretch" the carrying capacity of the earth by increasing food production and providing for more equitable distribution of whatever food is available.[10]

According to the latest estimate of the World Health Organization, at least two-thirds of the world's people are undernourished. In view of this situation one might ask the Colin Clarks and other "scientists" who claim we could feed many times the world's present population, "If we can't feed billions now on this earth, how will we be able to feed many times the present population of the world?"

The world population problem, which has a thousand facets and involves theology, ethics, and philosophy, as well as virtually every science known to man—biology, sociology, agronomy, ecology, demography, psychology, and others—is too complex to treat within the confines of one chapter or of several chapters. I can only touch on some of the chief factors and comment briefly on the most common and fatuous "solutions" offered by the many "experts" who have given the situation only superficial study. I wish I could be more optimistic, but in dealing with the most serious problem the world has ever faced, I feel I must "tell it like it is," or at least as I see it after intensive study from all angles.

The Life You Save May Be Your Doom

Paradoxical as it may seem, modern Science and Technology themselves are the hero villains in this looming tragedy. For thousands of years, so long as the great killers—malaria, smallpox, cholera, yellow fever, children's diseases—were on the job, births and deaths were so nearly balanced that the world population growth was almost too gradual to be noticed. All through the Middle Ages a family with ten or twelve children would be lucky if three or four lived to adulthood. By drastically stamping out the great killer diseases of the underdeveloped countries in the past few decades, with no drop in the birth rates, science and technology brought about the imbalance that is now rapidly shoving the world to disaster.

In their effort to ban "artificial"—that is, *effective*— contraception, the Roman hierarchy claims that it "violates the natural law," that any attempt to control human fertility is an impermissible "meddling with life." They don't seem to realize that effective "meddling with death" by science and technology has made a balance of births and deaths imperative today. If science and technology had not "violated the natural law" by stamping out these mass killers, we wouldn't need fertility control.

As eminent biologist Robert Cook says in *Human Fertility,* "the doctrine of 'naturalness' could be cited to support the thesis that a high death rate is the 'natural way' to prevent runaway population increases," but few opponents of population control "would be willing to carry the principle of 'naturalness' that far."

In totting up the questionable "gains" made in world population, the time to start is about a hundred and fifty years after Columbus discovered America—1650. At that time it is generally conceded that the world population reached its first half-billion—that is, 500,000,000 people. The annual rate of growth was a tiny one-tenth of one percent, a rate at which the population would take about 700 years to double. It took about a million years for the population to reach this half-billion in 1650, *but only two hundred years to double this number* and reach our first billion—about the year 1850. By this time the more advanced nations began to take a serious interest in periodic censuses, so the figures—at least for the developed world—from then on were much more accurate. By 1925, only 75 years later, the world population had doubled once more, so then there were two billion of us. Less than four decades later, in 1962, we added another billion, bringing the total to three billion. By the mid-70s we reached the four billion mark, and in spite of the recent slow-down in the world population growth, as noted above, observers predict a total of about seven billion by the end of this century.

When we deal with such astronomical figures—3 billion, 4 billion, 7 billion, and the like—it is simply impossible for the human mind to comprehend them. Stupefying as such figures are, even more startling is the rate of growth. Malthus didn't have all the answers when he first pointed out the population problem nearly two hundred years ago (1798), but his major thesis proved to be substantially correct. He said the world population grows in geometic progression (1-2-4-8-16-32-64, etc), while the world's resources lag along at an arithmetical drag (1-2-3-4-5-6-7, etc.) As a banker would say, without strict control *population grows like compound interest.* (Due to the opening up of new lands and the introduction of better agricultural methods in the nineteenth and early part of the twentieth century, food production for a time actually outstripped population needs and thus seemed to refute Malthus's prognosis. In recent years, however, the increase in the world's population has far outstripped the increase in food production, so now we find that Malthus wasn't far off at that.)

More about the soaring birth rates in a moment, but first a word about the sponsors of the death-dealers' death blow. One of the most recent and typical examples is Sri Lanka (formerly called Ceylon), where a few decades ago malaria was a grave problem. The actual death rate from this malady itself was relatively small —about two per thousand— but malaria was so common and weakened its victims' resistance to such an extent that great numbers died from other diseases, as also happens when people are grossly undernourished for long periods of time. The introduction of DDT in 1946 brought prompt control over the mosquitoes that carry malaria. As a result Sri Lanka's death rate was cut in half in five years. The island's death rate in 1945 was 22 per thousand. In the first year (1946-1947) the death rate dropped 34 percent, plunging to 10 per thousand in 1954. Since then it has dropped to 8.

In most of the underdeveloped countries the victory over malaria, smallpox, yellow fever, cholera and other infectious diseases has resulted in similar plunges in the death rates. Between 1940 and 1950 the death rate in Puerto Rico fell 46 percent, 43 percent in Formosa, and 23 percent in Jamaica. In eighteen underdeveloped countries the average drop in the death rate in the half-decade from 1945-1950 was 26 percent.[11]

The effectiveness of modern medicine and methods—pesticides, mass inoculations, antibiotics that are easily administered, and control of infections—has brought about the incredibly rapid and drastic reduction of death rates in the hungry world as shown in this table:

FALLING DEATH RATES AROUND THE WORLD [12]

	1935	1950	1965	1980
Entire World	25	19	16	12.7
Asia	33	23	20	13
Africa	33	27	23	18
Latin America	22	19	12	8.2

In contrast to these dramatic declines in death rates, most countries of the Third World have shown a small but gradual rise in the birth rate! The chief factor, which presages a sharper rise in the future, is the youthfulness of the present population. Says Ehrlich:

> One of the most ominous facts of the current situation is that over 40 percent of the population of the underdeveloped world is made up of people *under 15 years old.* As that mass of young people moves into its reproductive years during the next decade, we're going to see the greatest baby boom of all time. Those youngsters are the reason for all the ominous predictions for the year 2000. They are the gunpowder for the Population Explosion. [13]

World Population Doubles and Redoubles

Now that we have grasped the chief factor in our population explosion—*death control*—it will be much easier to size up the only antidote — *birth control.* Obviously a country's population will continue to grow as long as births exceed deaths, provided no substantial emigration is occurring. The birth rate is the number of births per thousand people per year in the population. The death rate is the number of deaths per thousand people per year. If the birth rate is 30 per thousand per year and the death rate is 10 per thousand per year, the rate of increase is 20 per thousand per year. Reduced to a percentage (rate per hundred people), the rate of 20 per thousand becomes 2 percent. At this rate the doubling time will be 35 years.

Now if you simply added 20 people per 1000 per year to the population, it would take fifty years to add a second thousand people (20 times 50 equals 1000). But the doubling time is actually much less, *since populations grow at compound interest rates.*

Just as dollars earned as *interest* go to work immediately to produce more capital and more interest, so year by year the children added to the population will soon be producing more children. *It is this growth at compound interest that doubles populations so much more rapidly than seems possible.*

At a rate of 1 percent increase annually it will take a country about seventy years to double its population, in the absence of any substantial emigration or immigration, or a radical change in birth rate. So to find the approximate time it will take a country to double its population just divide seventy by the percentage of increase.

Annual percentage of population increase	Approximate years for population to double
1.0	70
1.5	46.7
2.0	35
2.5	24
3.0	23.3
3.5	20
4.0	17.5

TABLE 1

Estimated Population (in millions) and Growth Rates for Thirty-four Countries

Country	1965	1978	Annual Rate of Population Increase	Number of Years to Double
Algeria	11.92	18.5	3.3	21.2
Argentina	22.18	26.4	1.3	53.8
Bangladesh	60.48	78.5	2.4	29.1
Bolivia	4.33	5.14	2.7	26.0

Country	1965	1978	Annual Rate of Population increase	Number of Years to Double
Brazil	81.01	115.4	2.8	25.0
China	710.32	933.03	1.4	50.0
Colombia	18.04	25.6	2.7	25.1
Domican Republic	3.51	5.12	3.0	23.3
Ecuador	5.15	7.8	3.4	20.6
Egypt	29.39	39.6	2.1	33.3
Haiti	3.91	4.8	1.8	38.8
Honduras	2.18	3.4	3.6	19.4
India	482.53	638.4	2.1	33.3
Indonesia	. . .	145.1	2.4	29.1
Iran	24.81	35.2	2.2	31.8
Iraq	8.05	12.3	3.5	20.0
Israel	2.56	3.7	2.2	31.8
Japan	98.88	114.9	1.0	70.0
Kenya	9.53	14.8	3.5	20.0
Mexico	41.28	67.4	3.1	22.5
Nigeria	48.68	72.2	3.6	19.9
Pakistan	50.19	76.7	3.0	23.3
Paraguay	2.03	2.89	3.0	23.3
Peru	11.65	16.8	2.8	25.0
Philippines	31.77	46.3	3.3	21.2
Puerto Rico	2.58	3.3	2.1	33.3
South Africa	19.61	27.7	2.8	25.0
Syrian Arab Rep'c	5.33	8.0	3.2	21.9
Thailand	31.03	45.0	2.3	34.3
Turkey (in Asia)	. . .	43.2	2.3	34.3
United States	194.3	222.0	0.6	116.6
Venezuela	8.71	13.1	3.0	23.3
Zaire	17.57	27.7	3.7	18.9
Zambia	3.7	5.5	3.2	21.9

Source: United Nations Demographic Yearbook, 1978 (latest available). It gives the following estimates of the world population (in millions): 1950—2,513; 1960—3,027; 1965—3,344; 1970—3,678; 1976—4,044; 1978—4,258. Annual population increase for the entire world (1970-1978)—1.8.

The U.N. Demographic Yearbook for 1976 gives the estimated population of the above countries *as of 1965*. The 1978 yearbook gives the population "as of the latest census," but doesn't indicate when the latest census was taken. It could have been a few years ago, or a decade or more. In view of this uncertainty I have quoted the estimated population of these countries as given in the 1976 issue, i.e., *as of 1965*, and also the 1978 estimate.

The countries listed in this table were selected more or less at random, chiefly those where the population problem is most pressing. Omitted were several of the most important countries of Europe: Great Britain, France, Spain, Italy, Portugal, Belgium, the Scandinavian and Eastern European countries, because the annual increase in those countries is relatively small.

The U.N. Demographic Yearbook for 1978 estimates that it would take 36.8 years for the population of the entire world to double (about A.D. 2014). As noted above, however, there has been a slowdown in population growth since this yearbook was published.

Where the 1978 issue of the U.N. Yearbook does not give an estimate of the current annual rate of increase, we have taken the one given in the 1976 edition. (Because of the tremendous task involved in compiling each issue of the United Nations Demographic Yearbook there is nearly a two-year lag between the date of issue and the calendar year.)

In the fifteen years from 1960 to 1975 the world's total population, as estimated by the United Nations, has risen from roughly three billion to roughly four billion. Five-sixths of this increase, an estimated 836 million, accrued to the less developed regions, while in the more developed regions the gain was about 157 million. As a result of faster growth the less developed regions comprise a growing proportion of the world's total population, 71.6 percent in 1975 compared with 67.4 percent in 1960.[14]

As we see from Table 1, population growth in most of the underdeveloped countries ranges from 2 to 3.7 percent a year. About 2.67 billion people who live in the underdeveloped countries have only about one-sixth of the world's income. For more than a billion people the incomes range from $100 to $250 a year. Slightly less than a billion have to make out on even smaller incomes, less than $100 a year.

Adding to the misery of these underprivileged peoples is their "rising expectations." Gradually over the years they have been finding out what life is like in our advanced countries. Pictures in magazines, films, public television, word-of-mouth accounts of wonders brought back by native diplomats and United Nations representatives have opened their eyes to the miracles worked by western technology—automobiles, airplanes, tractors, electric refrigerators, air conditioning, and television sets. As they contrast their mode of life with ours their tensions become more convulsive. Every day at least 200,000 more competitors are added to the world population, the great majority being in Asia, where the average family income is less than $150 a year.

Double Trouble for a Troubled World

By focusing our attention on the time it takes a country to double its population we readily get a clear picture of the situation. For example, say Country X has a 3 percent rate of increase, which means that its population will double in about 23.3 years. This tells us that Country X has a time limit of 23.3 years to double its food supply in order to maintain its current level of nutrition, to say nothing of doubling the number of houses, schools, roads, highways, transportation and sanitation facilities, and so on. Suppose Country X, like Holland, is already bursting at the seams. Assuming that you double the food supply—which agronomists say is impossible for any countries of the Third World—where would you find room for twice as many people, twice as many houses, schools, sanitation facilities, and so on?

Suppose the population of the United States should double in the next generation. Can you imagine the Los Angeles "can of worms" twice as large and complex as it is? Twice as many tourists swarming like locusts into Yellowstone or the Great Smoky Mountains National Parks? Twice as many nitwits littering the resort areas of California, Arizona, and Florida? Twice as many cars choking the roads around Chicago and the currently overcrowded Eastern Seaboard?

The number of outboard motorboats went up from 5.8 million in 1960 to 7.6 million in 1977; hunting licenses from roughly 12.6 million in 1950 to 25.3 million in 1975, while fishing licenses more than doubled, from a bit over 15 million to 34.7 million in 1976.[15]

Current statistics show that we are rapidly turning "the home of the brave" into an anthill. In 1950 there were 33.3 million visitors to our National Park Service lands. Twenty-seven years later, 1977, there were nearly eight times as many—262.6 million. The parks' growing popularity has led in many cases to the kind of congestion

170

one finds on urban freeways. Campsites are usually crowded to capacity. Mule trips from the rim of the Grand Canyon to its floor must be booked months in advance; so must boat trips down the Colorado. As this is written, there are well over 300 million people visiting the National Parklands every year.[16]

The following excerpts from one issue of the *Memphis Commercial Appeal* give some idea of what life in these United States will be like if we add another hundred million litterbugs by the end of the century: "What this shortage of beach produces is massive overcrowding. On Long Island's beaches in New York, for example, annual attendance is estimated at 70 million people. . . . One of the hardest things to do this summer was to survey the American camping scene without a certain sense of despair and an awful premonition of things to come. Partly, of course, it was a problem of numbers. . . . The despoilers of our environment are everywhere, from below sea level in Death Valley to the highest reaches of Mt. Everest. . . Not long ago an anti-litter expert estimated that Americans dump more than 40 million tons of trash annually on our roads, beaches, parks, and other public areas. If piled one-foot high, he said, that much litter would cover a highway between New York and San Francisco, or about 3000 miles. . . . Litterbugs not only despoil the environment, they also hurt the taxpayer. It cost more than 21.5 million dollars to clean the 752.2 million acres of federal parks, forests, and lands during the fiscal year 1971. State and local communities are forced to pay out millions more of your dollars."[17]

Jokers like the British economist Colin Clark, who claims that at the American level of food consumption, the world could feed 47 *billion people—157 billion* at the subsistence level—don't tell us how we could retain a modicum of sanity with fellow-lemmings standing on our feet and bumping into us every time somebody turned around! With only 6 or 7 billion people predicted little past the year 2000, I daresay millions of us will then be ready to start swimming out to sea—to find relief in that never-never-land—as our brother lemmings do when overcrowding gets to be more than they can stand!'[18]

14

We Are All in the Same Boat

Our 1972 sales of grain to Soviet Russia brought home to us the interdependence of all nations. Had we not sold this grain many Russians would have gone hungry; but what did this and similar sales do to our own food supplies? As a result the cost of poultry and stock feed went up to such an extent that it was hardly possible for producers to raise poultry, hogs, and cattle at a profit. More than any one thing, that sale—the largest exportation of grain in history—was responsible for the sharp rise in food prices that has plagued our crowded planet ever since.

As one of the many ways to verify the failure of the Third World's food production to keep up with the exploding demand, the Paddock brothers, authors of *Famine—1975!*, point to the reduced yields per acre, verifying that argicultural production in the Third World has been declining not only on a per capita basis but also on a basis of yield per acre. *Land was put into production that simply lacked the qualities needed to maintain production. They were tilling land that should never have been farmed.* [1]

Everyone who reads is familiar with the depressing news of the past few years—millions dying of starvation, tragedies predicted for the more or less distant future—but which have already occurred. These stories corroborate the forecasts of the Paddock brothers, Paul Ehrlich, Georg Borgstrom, and other realists who

172

have been trying for years to warn our national leaders and the general public of the worldwide catastrophe we are facing, not in future decades *but today*.

"Deaths Stalk Millions in Sahara Drought". . . "Drought Bedevils Brazil's Sertas". . . "Everybody's Hungry in India" — so have been the headlines in recent years. Perhaps these tragedies can best be summed up with a few quotations from a special section in *Time* magazine headed "The World Food Crisis":

> Nearly half a billion people are suffering from some form of hunger; 10,000 of them die of starvation each week in Africa, Asia, and Latin America. There are all too familiar severe food shortages in the sub-Saharan countries of Chad, Gambia, Mali, Mauritania, Senegal, Upper Volta, and Niger; also in Ethiopia, northern Brazil, India, and Bangladesh. India alone needs 8 to 10 million tons of food this year from outside sources, or else as many as 30 million people might starve. . .
>
> Even the beggars of Calcutta are better off than the estimated 15 million people now starving in West Bengal. . . In Bangladesh, there are barely rations to provide even gruel for the starving in Dacca's crowded refugee camps.[2]

Under the heading "Drought Horrors Grow," a UPI dispatch dated June 5, 1975 said:

> The worst drought in Africa's history has killed at least 20,000 persons and possibly twice that number in parts of Ethiopia and Somalia on the horn of Africa, relief officials said Thursday.
>
> Nearly one million persons in the two countries are on the edge of starvation and about four million have been affected to some degree by the drought, which has swept eastward across the continent in the past few years, officials say.[3]

In *The Picture of Health,* Erik Eckholm estimates that in the *Fourth* World, "thirteen million children aged five and under die each year—about thirty-five thousand a day, so many that the power of the living to comprehend the deep, daily tragedy has grown dull."[4]

Technology vs. Mother Nature

In a country like the United States that worships only one god—*Technology*—and where mass production miracles are common as sin, it is hard not only for the bewildered "man in the street" but also for well-informed scientists, technicians, educators, and editors to visualize a production problem that can't be mastered readily by our unlimited capital and our unlimited know-how. If, for instance, the demand for trucks, motor cars, tractors, or airplanes should be doubled overnight, virtually overnight the demand would be met. Now that the exploding population of the world demands a doubling of the world's food supply, why can't the almighty god Technology repeat, on a worldwide basis, the miracle of the loaves and fishes? Wishful thinkers like Colin Clark, Buckminster Fuller, and their disciples say it is easy to provide enough food for the burgeoning population. All you have to do is cut down millions of trees all over the world and put these forest lands into cultivation. They don't tell you what happened in China when the Chinese did just that three thousand years ago—a mistake that produced the Gobi desert and has kept that nation fighting soil erosion, devastating floods and famine, or near-famine, ever since. [5]

They don't tell you how, a hundred years ago, Japan made the same mistake. Fortunately for the Japanese, their deforestation was on a limited scale and when the rulers discovered the devastating results they stopped further cuttings and did what they could to repair the damage. [6]

On the continent of Europe, the British Isles, Mexico, New Zealand, North and South America—virtually all over the world the story is pretty much the same: mass deforestation resulting in frightful soil erosion, destructive flooding, and dangerous stortages of water. [7]

Nowhere on earth has the vandalizing of forests been so devastating as in Brazil during the past decade. Norman Lewis, who tells Brazil's story in a recent issue of the *London Observer* magazine, rates the eventual outcome as "possibly the greatest ecological disaster in history."

In an area larger than Europe, expanding over half of Brazil, one-third of all the world's trees grow in the tropical forests' five million square kilometers, a little over three million square miles. In the past six decades about one-fourth of the Amazon Basin and Mato Grosso forests have been destroyed, partly for firewoood, partly for croplands. In the past decade alone 11 million hectares of trees—better than 27 million acres—have been cleared. If this incredible vandalism isn't stopped, it will be just a matter of time before the entire forest is destroyed, only to turn into a desert as large as Sahara's 3 million square miles.

Lured on by a literal *ignis fatuus* that seemed to offer mass employment for its unemployed masses, the Brazilian government practically gave away the forest in tens-of-thousand-acre plots to foreign "developers" who were to replace the forests with colossal ranches. To clear the forests gradually and make use of the lumber would take much too long. Great fires—many of them ignited by napalm bombing—raged all over Amazonia, consuming trees by the hundred million, and roasting between 5,000 and 20,000 vertebrate animals per square kilometer. Fauna and flora be damned—this was the cheapest way to clear the land! With the land virtually a gift and wages about one-tenth of those paid in Europe and the United States, the profits made by these "developers" were super-spectacular.

The government's early enthusiasm for the colossal ranches began to wane when it discovered that, like the trees they replaced, they seemed to live on themselves and did little to reduce its burdensome "balance of payments," and even less to reduce unemployment. Reason: when the ranch became a going concern it took only one man to look after 1,000 head of cattle.

The Brazilian government put on the brakes when it realized the folly of this giveaway, but when it was discovered that two barrels of petroleum substitute could be made from a ton of wood, a new, more ominous threat arose. The Amazon forest is now estimated to contain 415 billion feet of timber, so it's anybody's guess how much of this forest will be left by the year 2000.

Scientists who have studied the Brazilian situation for years differ in their prognoses, but since the Amazon forest provides one-half of the world's annual production of free oxygen all agree that a continuation of such destruction will upset global climatic patterns, could result in heightened world temperatures, the melting of polar ice caps and sufficient rise in ocean levels to bring about the inundation of hundreds of coastal cities throughout the world—in any event, environmental suicide.[8]

Professor Borgstrom gives us a good picture of the partnership between trees and agriculture. Forests not only protect the soil but also shield adjacent agricultural regions from high winds and their erosive results. By catching the rainfall the forest slows down the runoff and forces the soil to absorb more water. Forest areas also retain rain water for gradual release at a slower rate. Borgstrom notes that in many parts of the world, reforestation is a prerequisite for dependable agriculture.[9]

Those of us who are old enough to remember the Mid-West's great "dust bowls" of the 1930s will readily understand what Professor Borgstrom is talking about. He admits that a great deal of tree cutting has been necessary; what he deplores is the permanent denudation and massive topsoil destruction that has been too prevalent in the past. "The forest is no longer limitless," he says. "Current speculations about how to feed the future billions from forest wastes, or even through direct forest culture, neglect the obvious fact that presently accessible forests are desperately required for a whole range of other needs."[10]

Commenting on this problem, *Time* magazine says:

> During the past decade. . . India, Pakistan and Bangladesh cleared Himalayan foothills to make more room for crops. Without the forests, which act as great sponges that sop up and hold rainfall, the water rapidly ran off the slopes. The accelerated runoff caused disastrous floods over the past year. In cleared jungles in Mexico, Guatemala and Brazil, heavy rains quickly leached the nutrients from the thin layer of topsoil, rendering the land infertile within a year or two. (The trees had both anchored and nourished the soil.) In other cleared jungles, the sun burned out the soil's valuable organic content.[11]

In his informative new book *The Twenty-ninth Day*, Lester R. Brown points out many other disturbing factors in the worldwide decimation of forests: the need for firewood in the poorer countries, lumber, newsprint and paper products of every kind. In his landmark work on land degradation, *Losing Ground*, Erik Eckhorn notes that Western Europe has "achieved a reasonable balance between the economical need for forests and other land uses, but it is a balance maintained in part by large imports of wood and wood products," mainly from Scandinavia, the Soviet Union, and tropical Africa.[12]

In most of the world little is being done to reverse the trend to misuse land; only North America, Scandinavia, and the Soviet Union appear to have both relatively satisfactory forest-management programs and sufficient forest resources to cover domestic needs.

I have gone into some detail on the worldwide problem of deforestation because this is the most compelling refutation of those escapists who tell us we can feed many more hungry billions. With one-third of the earth's land mass now taken up by deserts, it is sheer madness to augment these deserts by more deforestation. Robert C. Cook, an internationally known biologist and geographer, estimates the total land area of the earth at about 52 million square miles, but says that only two to five percent can be rated as crop land, on which food can be grown efficiently. He points out that in terms of arable acres the present population of the earth is near the point of actual shortage. "On the basis of an extensive agriculture such as practiced in the United States," Cook explains, "the world as a whole has already passed the optimum relationship of population to usable land."[13]

Although Brazil tripled its cultivated acreage in the past half-century there has been a very limited increase in food production. The cropland is of such poor quality that experts say it would require fifty times as much fertilizer as is now used to bring about a substantial increase in productivity.[14]

India provides another good example of the difficulty of adding enough farm land to keep up with the world's exploding population. Some years ago, with scores of mammoth bulldozers, Indians eradicated 15 million acres of Kan's grass (closely related to sugar cane). Within two years this vast acreage—equal to one-third of the wheatlands of America—was cleared and planted. But this terrific increase in production wasn't enough to feed the 10 to 12 million new people India adds each year to her population.[15]

Oil Revolution vs. Green Revolution

A few years ago mankind's greatest hope was the so-called "green revolution"—the development, after years of experimentation, of ultra high-yielding strains of wheat and rice. With extensive irrigation and generous application of fertilizer, pesticides, and herbicides, some of the new varieties quadrupled production on the same amount of acreage. However, shortage of water for irrigation was a major problem, but even more serious was the vulnerability of these new, high-yield grains to insects and plant diseases. This extreme vulnerability was due to the fact that all these new strains were developed from the same genetic bases, so when the blight struck they didn't have the resistance possessed by strains developed from several different genetic bases.

Long before the energy crisis of 1973, everything needed by these revolutionary strains for revolutionary high produciton—fertilizers, pesticides, herbicides, and irrigation—was in short supply. Since petroleum is the chief source for most fertilizers, quadrupling the price of petroleum by the oil-rich nations in 1973 raised the price of fertilizer out of sight and took most of the steam out of the "green revolution."

On top of this disappointment, the underdeveloped world was also to discover the fallacy of the old adage "There's enough fish in the sea to feed the whole world." Enterprising "fish-farmers" with ponds, lakes, and bays throughout the world have added materially to world nutrition, especially the vitally needed proteins,[16] but so far as the ocean is concerned, recent experience refutes the old saying. With 500 to 600-foot floating "fish factories," with nets that catch 250 tons of tuna at one casting, with facilities for freezing this catch until its tanks are loaded with more than 1000 tons of tuna, the United States, Russia, Peru, and other mass-fishing countries are on the verge of depleting the world's fisheries as increasing demands have denuded its forests. A good summary of this situation appeared in *Life* magazine: "The world is on its way to running out of fish. The endless riches of the sea that were supposed to mean salvation for the world's multiplying population turn out to be far from endless. They are being plundered by over-fishing so great that some stocks may be on an irreversible voyage to extinction."[17]

Along with over-fishing there is a constantly increasing problem of pollution. Once a major source of human food, especially protein, the oceans—along with many of our rivers and lakes—have degenerated into sterile waste receptacles, passive recipients of incredible amount of industrial, agricultural, and human wastes. Oil, chemical and radioactive wastes, pesticides, detergents, all manner of pollutants are routinely dumped into the sea. The menace of hydrocarbon pollution, the result of offshore drilling, is getting worse every day. Over ten thousand oil spills in U.S. navigable waters were reported by the U.S. Coast Guard in 1975 alone.[18]

In July of 1976, a gigantic fish kill spreading over a thousand square miles was found off the New Jersey coast. Microbiologist Pat Yanaton reported that the ocean "was completely dead—starfish, eels, lobsters, all sizes of crab—everything was dead." Apparently, decomposing sewage sludge from New York and other adjourning municipalities was responsible.[19]

Such disasters are not surprising. An article in the *Marine Pollution Bulletin* in 1973 reported that concentrations of chromium, copper, lead, nickel, and zinc were "10 to 100 times greater near waste disposal areas" than in other waters in the Atlantic Ocean off New York. Robert S. Dyer, an oceanographer with the U.S. Environmental Protection Agency, reported finding traces of plutonium off both the Atlantic and Pacific Coasts of the United States. The plutonium had leaked from some of the 114,500 barrels of radioactive waste materials dumped into the oceans by the United States government between 1946 and 1970.[20]

Fish have virtually disappeared from some of the more polluted rivers and coastal zones of the industrial countries. The once-rich oyster beds of Raritan Bay, New Jersey, have been all but obliterated. The shrimp harvest of Galveston Bay shrank by more than half between 1962 and 1966. The shad catch in Chesapeake Bay, estimated at fourteen million pounds in 1890, has averaged only three million pounds in recent years.[21]

Fortunately a new discovery in the marine world provides a silver lining for some of these dark clouds. An article in the November 21, 1974 issue of the *Christian Science Monitor* says that Krill, a shrimp-like shellfish eaten chiefly by whales could supply the world with a new source of protein. Within the foreseeable future it could become one of the world's major economic foods, according to various experts in Japan.

"Krill is available in huge quantities and is the biggest source of animal protein left in the world today," said Kyo Yui, executive manager of the Japan Marine Resources Research Center. Scientists speculate that a catch of 50 million to 100 million tons annually can be expected within a few years. "This would be the equivalent of the present worldwide fish catch," they added.

Another ray of hope is the "winged bean" described in the April 17, 1978 issue of *Time*, under the heading "Miracle Plant." Technically known as *psophocarpus tetragonolobus,* it gets its nontechnical name because of four winglike flanges on its pod. It is now regarded as a great green hope among the experts who worry about new food sources for the underdeveloped world. Noel Vietmeyer, a staff director of the National Academy of Science, is most enthusiastic about the possibilities of this "miracle plant." He says:

> It's a veritable supermarket. From top to bottom it is edible. The leaves are like spinach, the stems like asparagus, and you can eat the flowers and tubers too. And after they are steamed or boiled, the seeds and pods taste like good mushrooms.

From a long range standpoint there are even greater advantages. As a legume, the winged bean converts its own nitrogen from the atmosphere, thanks to a happy symbiosis with guest *Rhizobium* bacteria in the plant's potato-like tubers. Consequently, it needs no fertilizer and even enriches the soil in which it grows. Any parts choosy humans do not want to eat can be fed to cattle. As horticulturist Jack Kelly of the University of Florida's Institute of Food and Agriculture Sciences puts it, "It's like the butcher's pig. Everything's useful but the oink."

Another important discovery that may bring about a radical improvement in food production has been announced by Dr. Stanley Ries of Michigan State University: a substance extracted from alfalfa, the common hay that farmers feed their cattle. Dr. Ries says his experiments indicate that when this substance is sprayed over growing crops, it can increase their yields from 8 to 63 percent. "Here is a nature compound that may increase food production all over the world," Dr. Ries recently told a seminar sponsored by the Council for the Advancement of Science Writing at Rockefeller University.

The "magic" substance to which Ries referred is known to scientists as triacontanol, an alcohol that is produced naturally in many plants. It is present in such things as honey and beeswax, salad greens, carrots, potatoes, and apples. He found that tomatoes grown in soil mixed with chopped alfalfa gave twice the yield he got in similar plots which had been treated with an amount of synthetic nitrogen equal to that naturally present in the alfalfa.

Such yields—like 10 tons of tomatoes an acre above normal—convinced Ries there was something in the alfalfa other than the nitrogen that was pushing up production. Only minute amounts were needed to bring about the yield increases. "Most of us probably ate more triacontanol for dinner last night than it takes to treat an acre," Ries told the science writers. Since this substance works better in higher temperatures, it holds great promise for many areas of the underdeveloped world.[22]

What may prove to be the most promising development of all is the "beefalo," a cross between cow and buffalo, which offers many advantages over our current meat-producing cattle. Because the new-fangled "beefalo" thrives on grass and doesn't require expensive grain to fatten, this amazing hybrid may eventually knock the props out from under bleeding hearts like Dr. Wald, who think we should deny ourselves meat in order to fatten up the Third World with massive gifts of grain and thus accelerate the population growth of the developing nations at the expense of our own.

An article in the *Christian Science Monitor* gives the essential facts about this promising new hybrid. A purebred beefalo is three-eights buffalo, three-eights Charolais (a French-bred cow) and one-quarter Hereford. The beefalo grows to more than 1000 pounds in nine months, compared to twenty-four months for cattle. Tender, succulent beefalo meat is 19 to 20 percent protein compared to 10 or 11 percent for beef. "It takes 20 pounds of grain to add one pound to cattle," says D. C. Basolo, the man who developed this new hybrid. "Beefalo thrive on grass and roughage (weeds and cactus). This means all that grain can go straight into hungry people's mouths."

Mr. Basolo believes beefalo will be this country's main meat staple within a few years. He recently sold a prime beefalo bull for $2.5 million to a breeding company in Calgary, Canada. When their herd of 5,000 builds up enough—probably within a few years—they plan to market beefaloburger, beefalo stew meat, roast beefalo, and beefalo steaks, along with by-products from beefalo hides.[23]

The Prohibitive Cost of Irrigation

Trying to cover all the fallacies that uninformed optimists have dreamed up for coping with the population explosion would carry us too far afield, but there are two more I must touch on briefly: irrigation and emigration to other planets. The latter is hardly worthy of comment. If we assume that any of the other planets are habitable for earth-beings, how can we assume that they aren't just as crowded as the earth? Or, if we could bridge the multi-lightyear gap, could we assume that "the little green men" would welcome our hardy adventurers? On this score Dr. Ehrlich produces figures proving that even if we could accomplish the impossible and that Americans were willing to reduce their living standards to eighteen percent of our present levels, *We could export to other planets only one day's increase of our population each year!*

The prospects for irrigation are almost as hopeless. In its issue of May 22, 1972, *Awake* says:

> The United Nations' Food and Agricultural Organization reports that the human family will run short of water within a century because of the swiftly increasing demands of industry and an exploding world population. Some areas listed as already affected by chronic

water shortages are the following: Spain, southern Italy, the Dalmatian Coast, Greece, the Anatolian Plateau, all Arab states except Syria, most of Iran, Pakistan, western India, Japan, Korea, the western and southern belts of Australia and New Zealand, the Northwest and Southwest African coasts, the American Southwest, Panama, Northern Mexico, central Chile, and parts of Peru.

At a United Nations Conference on Water held early in April of 1977 at Mar del Plata, Argentina, Syrian delegate Saub Kaule warned that the day is not distant when a drop of water will cost more than a drop of oil.

Spacecraft pictures of the earth show that the planet has an abundance of water, but the trouble is that very little of it is directly usable by man. Fully 97.3 percent of the world's 1.4 billion cubic kilometers (8.7 million cubic miles) of water is ocean and thus unfit for drinking or agriculture. Of the 2.7 percent of water that is fresh, more than three-quarters is locked up either in glaciers or polar ice. Of all the world's fresh water, only .36 percent in rivers, lakes and swamps is easily accessible and available for human use. The form and location of this usable water can be altered by human activity, and its quality can be improved, *but the total always remains the same.*

The demand on this limited supply has been increasing in recent years at an ominous rate as more and more people use water not only for drinking and cooking but to bathe, flush toilets, wash cars, water lawns, and to air condition homes and office buildings.

The amount of water used directly for human consumption does not compare with the quantity required for agriculture, which accounts for at least 80 percent of all water used by mankind. *Between 30 and 40 percent of the world's food production is now dependent on irrigation.* As the world population grows and the demand for food increases, additional irrigation will be needed to cultivate marginal farm land for necessary crops. Industry is also using ever increasing amounts of water to generate electricity, to cool nuclear reactors, and to manufacture chemicals and metals. As a result, many lakes and streams have been so badly polluted by agriculture and industry, as well as by wastes from increasing numbers of humans, that they require costly treatment to be usable. Furthermore, drinking water taken from contaminated sources, despite purification measures, has caused widespread disease. The World Health Organization estimates that as much as 80 percent of all the world's disease is due to unclean water.

Droughts that have plagued the western United States and many areas of the underdeveloped world in recent years are too well known to detail here, but they bring home to us the realization of just how limited global water supplies really are.

Assuming that sufficient water could be found, *Time* magazine tells us that the costs for further extensive irrigation would be prohibitive:

> To irrigate 57 million extra acres of farm land (a 25 percent increase over the present irrigated acreage) would cost $3.5 billion annually for the next eleven years. To provide an FOA-requested agricultural development fund for the LDCs (Less Developed Countries) would run another $5 billion annually. To expand fertilizer production to meet estimated demand would cost $8 billion each year until 1980 and $12 billion yearly after that. Most staggering is the price of bringing new land under cultivation. An approximate 10 percent increase in the world's arable land—adding 400 million acres—would cost at least $400 billion and might run $1 trillion or more. [24]

A Nation of Rip Van Winkles

As we have pointed out before no country in the history of the world has been so generous as the United States has been in helping less fortunate nations during the past quarter-century. In 1966 we shipped one-fourth of our entire wheat crop to India—virtually a gift—a neighborly act that not only solved our surplus wheat problem but literally kept millions of India's citizens from starving. Yet it has been a game of "put and take." Desperately hard up for foreign exchange, all the underdeveloped countries have been forced to sell us food stuffs, especially fish which is their chief source of desperately needed protein, along with raw materials, metals and mineral products which, in many cases, they could use to better advantage themselves. The U.S. has one-sixth of the world's population, yet we consume at least one-half of the entire world's nonfood raw materials, and demographer William Vogt says, "If our population and economy continue to grow at its present rate, it is estimated that by 1980 we should use 83 percent of these raw materials!" [25]

Lolling in the lap of luxury—two cars in every garage, super-jets galore, air conditioners and TV sets running out of our

183

ears; bewitched by the highest standard of living in world history, every couple with as many children as they want, and often more; possessed by mountains of possessions—it is only natural here in America for us to think that we can go on forever living on Cloud Nine, only natural that we must pinch ourselves to awaken long enough to give a moment's thought to the two billion unfortunates in the Third World who don't know what a full stomach feels like —to the millions who are literally starving as you read these lines.

Birth control is fine for the other fellow—for the starving billions in the hungry world—but why should we, the richest nation in the world, worry about it? Why shouldn't we go on having as many children as we want, or at least, as many as we can afford? What has our affluence to do with the other world's starving billions?

Aside from any ethical or charitable considerations, we are on the verge of polluting and crowding ourselves off the face of the earth—as every thinking person knows. With a hundred million cars and trucks choking and polluting our nation's roads, with new superhighways gobbling up much of our best farmlands at approximately forty acres per mile, with new houses, new motels, new airports, new amusement, shopping and recreation areas year by year taking a greater toll of our limited farmlands—we can't stand pat and let the other countries do all the trimming. With our vanishing farmlands and our increasing population, it won't be long before we are reduced to limited rations ourselves, to say nothing of being jostled, like lemmings, into mass insanity. Because our life expectancy is about double that of our undernourished cousins, each of us enjoys about twice as many consuming years, so our annual addition of more than four million babies gives both the hungry nations and us something to think about. As Dr. Ehrlich says, "Affluence and effluence go hand in hand. . . Each American child puts far more strain on the world environment than each Asian child. We've got to put our own house in order before we start telling Asians and Africans what to do." [26]

In a *Reader's Digest* article, Nathaniel P. Reed, assistant secretary of the interior says:

> We are the world's greatest extractor, greatest producer, greatest refiner, greatest consumer and greatest discarder. Last year alone, we discarded 40 million tons of paper, 200 million tires, 76 billion containers, 38 billion bottles, 78 billion cans, 7 million junked cars.

The 220 million people in the United States use more energy than the combined 500 million people in other leading industrial nations, including Germany, Great Britain, Japan, and the Soviet Union. By one estimate, the United States wastes 25 percent of the energy it produces. In effect, the American people squander as much energy as 107 million Japanese consume. How much longer will the rest of the world permit one neighbor to live so lavishly?[27]

15

"We Breed—You Feed!"

In spite of the generous aid from many countries and the heroic efforts to defuse the population bomb by an army of Good Samaritans, no informed person can be too happy over the results to date. As noted above, the growth rate has been reduced perceptibly in China and to some extent in India and a few other Third World countries, but the fact remains that this crowded planet is still sitting on a powder keg.

Throughout most of the Latin American countries politicians feel compelled to ignore the population problem because of Catholic opposition to fertility control. In Canada, Asia, and Africa, all the world international organizations have been subjected to Catholic pressure. As far back as 1951, India asked for technical aid from the United Nations to promote its national family planning program. The UN World Health Organization (WHO) sent a special mission on that occasion to experiment with the rhythm method, which was a flat failure; but until the mid-sixties Catholic-controlled nations banned even this sort of U.N. action. In 1961, during the U.N. General Assembly's debate on birth control, Argentina's ambassador declared that his government was "categorically opposed" to approval of birth control principles by the U.N.; later the Vatican praised his statement as a "noble document." [1]

The United Nations involvement with population issues dates back to 1946 with the establishment of the Population Commission. As has just been noted, there was some foot dragging during the following two decades, but as the organization expanded, so did its interest in the population problem. In 1954 the first World Population Conference was held in Rome; the second in 1965 in Belgrade. In 1966 the heads of state of twelve countries presented a declaration on population to the U.N., and the following year eighteen additional countries signed the declaration. In that year (1966) the General Assembly, in a landmark resolution, requested the U.N. system to provide technical assistance, when requested by governments, in population and family planning. This led to the first real breakthrough the following year, when the General Assembly authorized the establishment of a U.N. Fund for Population Activities (UNFPA). This was set up as a trust fund for the Secretary-General, the overall management of which was entrusted in 1969 to the administrator of the United Nations Development Program (UNDP). "By a decision of December 18, 1972, the General Assembly placed UNFPA under the authority of the General Assembly and designated the Governing Council of UNDP as its governing body, taking into account the responsibilities and policy functions of the Economic and Social Council."[2]

The UNFPA began operations in 1970, becoming the nerve center for all population programs within the U.N. system, and being financed by voluntary contributions from over sixty governments. The budget is now well over $100 million, just under half of which comes from the United States. The Fund is now assisting more than 500 projects in seventy-eight countries.

Compared with the problems faced by the U.N. in this undertaking, the Twelve Labors of Hercules was a breeze. Because of the great diversity in demographic, religious, social, economic, and political considerations, no world population agency can provide a unitary solution. Any action that is taken must be on a voluntary basis. All the U.N. can do is offer such financial and administrative aid as is available, along with recommendations that are sufficiently specific and differentiated to meet the divergent problems in the various member nations.

Mexico Takes a Second Look

Some Latin American countries—notably Brazil and until recently, Mexico—haven't gone in for population control because their leaders thought they needed an even larger population "to take their rightful place in the world." In an article headed "A Continent Resists Birth Control," James Nelson Goodsell, Latin American correspondent for the *Christian Science Monitor,* tells us that in most Latin American countries "good family planning" means eight, ten or twelve children. "The more the merrier"— and the greater the degree of "security." Ignorance and backwardness make contraception difficult. Moreover, it is generally the wife who worries about birth control, "since Latin America's traditional 'machismo,' which translated means manliness or male virility, prevents the man in Latin societies from engaging in birth control." Mr. Goodsell thus concludes his article: "In the time it has taken to read this article (average speed about eight minutes), the population of Latin America has grown about 100 persons. No other statistic can illustrate so vividly the impact of Latin America's population dilemma."[3]

Recently, however, there has been a relaxation of Mexico's intransigent position on population control, both on the part of the government and the Roman church. In another *Monitor* article, "Mexico Today," Mr. Goodsell tells us that Mexico's government officials and business leaders are taking a second look at the population problem, are beginning to realize that "too many Mexicans" is the cause of much of that country's difficulties. With nearly half its citizens under seventeen years of age the population has been growing so fast that, if not checked, it will double in twenty years. Only twenty-four years ago the population was 25 million; in 1973 it was 52 million. Mexican leaders have begun to realize that if they don't take drastic steps to slow down this growth, their population will be over 100 million by the end of this century. At long last President Echeverria's government began a national family-planning program, a major and significant change in attitude.[4]

Writing in the *National Catholic Reporter*, Father Wilfred Wilhelm says, "Faced with an annual population growth of over 3 percent, a 40 percent illegitimacy, and a 20 percent abortion rate, and strapped with unjust socio-economic structures, the Mexican government has embarked on a nationwide family planning program in a country that is at least nominally 85 percent Catholic."

The Mexican Catholic hierarchy's approval was conditioned on the government's fulfilling its promises to respect the freedom of the spouses. "The substance of these statements (government's planning program), so respectful of human dignity and freedom," wrote Father Wilhelm, "is fully in keeping with the teaching of Vatican II as confirmed by the encyclical *Populorum Proggessio.*" The hierarchy's conditional approval hasn't undermined Pope Paul's position, says Wilhelm; just "blunted the sharp edge of *Humanae Vitae.*" In reaching their decisions, the bishops "will weigh all factors that go to make up a proper conscience."[5]

Some time ago the Roman Catholic bishops of Colombia, South America, also "blunted the sharp edge of *Humanae Vitae*" by encouraging effective birth control among women of that country. A more detailed discussion of the situation in Latin American countries would take us too far afield, but these are most promising developments which students of the world population problem will watch most hopefully.

India Cuts the Gordian Knot

It is not only in Roman Catholic lands that religion conflicts with family planning. In India the people regard sex as a part of their religion and to many of them the mere mention of birth control sounds too much like sex control. Moreover, for religious reasons every Hindu must have at least one son, better still, two or three. "Children are valuable: at the age of four or five they can start selling newspapers or doing tiny jobs."[6]

There is still another problem: the Moslems of India are often against birth control because they want to correct a situation in which they are outnumbered by the Hindus. In Sri Lanka (formerly Ceylon) the Moslems are trying to catch up with the Tamils![7]

An even greater obstacle in India is the high rate of illiteracy—76 percent—but the biggest problem of all is the teeming population. About a third the size of the United States, India is jampacked with nearly three times as many people, a population which is growing at the rate of 12 to 13 million a year. Three-fourths of the subcontinent's 650 million people live in more than half a million villages, speak fifteen major languages, and nearly a third of them have an annual income of less than $200. The great majority, children and adults, are grossly undernourished, if not actually starving. The food crisis is chronic. The World Bank recently estimated that India would have to import 10 million tons of grain annually for at least five more years before she could ease her dependence on foreign sources. The 1976 harvest was better than average, but in the preceding year her food production fell short of the target by 12 million tons.

In a country such as India, trying to control the population is like bailing out a 500,000 ton tanker with a teacup. Even though they realize it would take tens of thousands of technicians and billions of non-existing dollars to clip the wings of India's hard-working stork, until recently the authorities were hoping to accomplish the impossible by conventional methods. Shocked by the realization that the current birth rate would rocket their population to a *billion* by the year 2000, the government finally concluded that compulsory sterilization was the only answer to their problem.

In March of 1976 the state of Maharashtra, whose capital is Bombay, introduced the world's first compulsory sterilization law, under which two million Indian couples with three or more children were threatened with fines and jail terms if they refused to comply.[8]

About the same time the federal government announced a nationwide program under which couples with two children who would not agree to sterilization for one spouse would lose their rights to a wide range of government benefits, from public housing to government jobs and loans. Couples who did comply would be given preferential treatment in employment, housing, and free medical treatment in government hospitals.[9]

In a speech she made shortly after the program was initiated, Prime Minister Gandhi said her government aimed to reduce the growth rate from 2 percent to 1.4 percent by 1980. She recommended a strong program of incentives and "disincentives," raising the legal marriage age from 15 to 18 for girls and from 18 to 21 for young men, as well as imposing compulsory sterilization on all couples who already had two or more children. She said she preferred to use persuasion but warned, "We don't have all the time in the world."

While Mme. Gandhi was somewhat reluctant to decree compulsory sterilization, she was egged on by her son Sanjay and other activists, and it wasn't long before the situation got out of hand. No one took the time and effort to explain to the rural and urban illiterate masses the real effects of the operation; most of them thought it would result in impotence and naturally they were terror-stricken.

To millions of ordinary people, sterilization was the cutting edge of the government's restriction of liberties. With a target of 4.3 million sterilizations, the campaign produced 7.8 million between April 1976 and January 1977, when Mrs. Gandhi called for national elections. To help insure the program's success, the government censors prohibited newspapers from publishing any criticism of family planning. The program was pressed by the government bureaucracy from Delhi to the district level, and quickly became the pet project of Indira's zealous son Sanjay.

Officially there was no coercion, but the elaborate system of disincentives amounted to the same thing. Government employees had to produce two or more candidates for sterilization. When proffered incentives did not enable local officials to meet their quotas, they turned to harsher means. In Katauli, several young men without children were ordered sterilized. After a police attack on the Muslim village of Uttawar, 800 vasectomies were performed. Across North India, villagers often slept in the fields to avoid sterilization teams, or hid in their houses during the day.

In the city of Muzaffarnagar vasectomy camps handled between 1,200 and 1,800 cases a day. Each operation took five to ten minutes, and there was often no follow-up when the patient suffered postoperative bleeding, infection, or even tetanus. The state quota for Uttar Pradesh had been set at 400,000, but the chief minister raised it to 1.5 million, presumably to please Sanjay. Some 700,000 operations were actually performed, a phenominal increase over the previous year's total of 129,000.

Without any doubt it was Prime Minister Gandhi's compulsory sterilization campaign and the brutal way it was executed that caused her to lose the election.[10]

If the Indian government had made a serious attempt to enlighten the public and had relied more on persuasion than brute force, the outcome might have been different. However, with the situation as it is in India, no one can deny that forceful measures of one kind or another are indicated. In January of 1978 President Neelam Sanjiva Reddy called for a family planning law that would penalize families with more than two or three children. "With 650 million people—going to be a billion by the year 2000," Reddy asked, "how are you going to feed them, clothe them, educate them?"

A Roman Holiday

To those who are really familiar with the population problem, both the World Population Conference in Bucharest (August 19-31, 1974) and the World Food Conference in Rome ten weeks later were bitter disappointments. Proponents of a radical approach didn't expect much progress, yet they were hardly prepared for the complete rejection of effective family planning methods by most of the Third World countries. To the leaders of these nations the solution was simple enough. Just let *us* go on breeding like rabbits, and the "affluent nations"—the United States and a few prosperous countries of the West—set up "food banks" to feed the booming populations!

The selection of delegates for both conferences was typical of our bungling bureaucracy. Instead of picking qualified scientists who had at least some of the answers, we sent uninformed officials and hack politicians who knew less about the problems than most teenagers.

Virtually nothing was accomplished at Bucharest, and the Rome conference was even less fruitful. Secretary of State Kissinger, who set up the conference, made a few opening remarks and then dashed off to more important meetings. As *Time* magazine noted, "Out of deference to the sensibilities of both Catholic Rome and the Third World delegates, Kissinger decided not to bear down hard on the issue of population control." [11]

Every time he spoke, Caspar Weinberger, secretary of HEW, highlighted his ignorance of the situation, and Senators Hubert Humphrey, George McGovern, and Richard Clark all made impassioned pleas on TV for America to "do something decent"— let millions of Americans go on existing on starvation diets while we shipped millions of tons of our grain to the Third World millions who are too busy raising children to worry about raising foodstuff. No doubt the senators efforts were wildly applauded by their constituents, farmers in the grain belt, if by no one else. *None of them mentioned the colossal aid the United States has given these hungry nations in the past few decades.*

As might be expected, Pope Paul enlivened the food conference by lashing out at birth control. In an Associated Press dispatch of November 9, 1974, he assailed "the rich nations," accusing them of imposing birth control on the poor "to keep them poor." Before an audience of 2000 delegates at the Vatican the pope said, "It is inadmissible that those who have control of the wealth and resources of mankind should try to solve the problem of hunger by forbidding the poor to be born." He attacked what he called the rich nations' "irrational and one-sided campaign against the demographic growth," and said hunger is not man's "inevitable destiny." The pope said the rich nations don't give enough in food aid and also attempt to "impose a restrictive demographic policy on nations to insure that they will not claim their just share of the earth's goods." [12] Strange talk coming from an institution that has long been opposed to communism!

192

A delegate from Thailand was better informed and more objective. "Population control will help ease the food crisis," he said.

Two other World Population Conferences were held in 1976, but little was said about them in the press. Opening a Habitat Conference on Human Settlements in Vancouver, B.C., early in June of 1976—the largest U.N. conference ever held, according to UPI—Secretary-General Kurt Waldheim "challenged delegates to set a minimum standard of decent housing for all and to promote 'social changes' necessary to achieve the goal."

Waldheim didn't say who was supposed to pick up the quadrillion dollar tab for all this largess, but it is likely he was looking in the direction of rich old Uncle Sam. If we can spend billions sending a man to the moon, etc., etc., etc.

The Twelve-day conference was attended by nearly 5,000 delegates and observers from about 140 countries and a handful of national liberal movements. U.N. urban specialists predicted that in the next twenty-five years urban areas that already hold some 700 million people will absorb another 1.8 billion—most of them poor and unskilled.

Providing "decent housing" for 700 million people is easier said than done. It is hard to imagine what a hopeless situation the world will face twenty-five years from now.

The 1976 World Food Conference, also in June of that year, was held in Ames, Iowa. The conference, keynoted by Clifton Wharton, Jr., president of Michigan State University, brought together more than 650 scientists and professionals from sixty countries to analyze the world food situation. In his opening address, Wharton warned that "millions of people could die of starvation before a solution is found to excessive population."

Sartaj Aziz, deputy executive director of the U.N. World Food Council and a former official of the government of Pakistan, told participants that the United States—as the world's leading industrial nation—"must bear prime responsibility for averting future food crises."

It would be impossible to find a better example of the "we breed, you feed" mentality than that statement by Aziz. In a dispatch dated at Karachi, Pakistan, William Borders of the *New York Times News Service* says:

> After an intensive program of education at a cost of more than $50 million, Pakistan is scarcely any closer to solving its population problem now than it was 10 years

ago, according to an official survey.

The comprehensive survey indicates that only 6 percent of the fertile couples in the country are practicing any method of birth control, despite propaganda and an inundation of contraceptives.

With 75 million people living in a poor arid land that is only twice the size of California, Pakistan has one of the world's gravest population problems, as it officially recognized in the middle 1960s. . .

According to the fertility survey, which was based on interviews with 5,000 carefully selected women around the country, Pakistan's birthrate is 40.5 per 1,000 of population. . . At the present rate of growth, Pakistan's population will double by the time a child born today reaches his 23rd birthday. . .[13]

In a plea before the United Nations on June 25, 1965 to "seek the answers to the population explosion"—the "most profound challenge to the future of all the world"—President Johnson said, "Let us act on the fact that five dollars invested in population control is worth a hundred dollars invested in economic growth." No doubt encouraged by the approval of family planning by a large segment of the Catholic world, President Johnson took "a long leap forward" with his promotion of birth control through his Office of Economic Opportunity program, which provided millions in aid for Catholic schools and other institutions. Much to Mr. Johnson's surprise, the hierarchy immediately rapped his knuckles with a strong denunciation of his plan—at least the birth control part.

"Far from seeking to provide information in response to requests from the needy," the bishops charged, "government activities increasingly seek aggressively to persuade and even coerce the underprivileged to practice birth control." In Pennsylvania, while pressing hard for tax aid to parochial schools, the Catholic bishops were lobbying forcefully against government-sponsored family planning clinics.[14]

How to Enrich Human Life

Anything approaching a detailed report of the United Nations' campaign for worldwide population control would require not another chapter but another book. Perhaps the best single-volume study of the problem is *Family-Planning Programs: An Interna-*

tional Survey, edited by Bernard Berelson, with an introduction by John D. Rockefeller III. In his prologue Mr. Rockefeller makes some salient observations that few people have considered heretofore:

> Men of influence must be shown that the true objective of population stabilization is the enrichment of human life, not its restriction. When this affirmative fact is fully understood, most of the sensitivity that now hampers action on family planning will be eliminated. When the leaders are secure in the conviction that population stabilization is an enriching force, the negatives which now haunt them will swiftly disappear. To my mind, population stabilization is not a brake upon human development, but rather a release that, by assuring greater opportunity to each person, frees man to attain his individual dignity and to reach his full potential.[15]

Based on personal observation and reflection, recent travels and years of interest and concern in the population field, Mr. Rockfeller thus sums up the results of the United Nations' campaign to date: "Let us assume that 100 represents the optimum effort required if sufficient progress toward population stabilization is to be made soon enough to avoid immense human suffering and tragedy. In my opinion, our current rating on that scale is 20."[16]

For those who wish detailed information on this situation I recommend the May and July-August 1974 issues of the *UNESCO Courier.* Dedicated to "The World Population Year," both issues are devoted entirely to this subject and contain a mass of information that could hardly be found in any other medium.

I have said it more than once and I shall repeat here: Some important members of the Roman hierarchy, a large segment of the clergy, and a great majority of enlightened Catholic laymen were as strongly opposed to Paul's position on family planning as most non-Catholics. Their attitude was shown most graphically by this excerpt from a letter that Stanford University's Roman Catholic biologist, John H. Thomas, wrote to San Francisco's Archbishop Joseph T. McGucken—a letter which sums up the new look in Catholic attitudes better than anything I could say:

The Church must affirm that the birth rate must soon be brought in line with the death rate—i. e., the growth rate of zero. This is the responsibility of all people regardless of race or religion. The Church must recognize and state that all means of birth control are licit. . .
[it] must put concern for people, their welfare, and their happiness above its concern for doctrine, dogma, and canon law. . . It is time that the Church stop being like a reluctant little child, always needing to be dragged into the present.[17]

Lifeboat Ethics—Pro and Con

Writing in *Psychology Today* just before the World Food Conference in Rome (November 1974), Dr. Garrett Hardin, a University of California (Santa Barbara) biologist, presents a convincing case against an increase in our massive food aid to those countries of the Third World which stand pat on their right to reproduce as fast as they wish while the "affluent" nations "pick up the tab." To most of these nations, Hardin says, the problem is simple. Just redistribute the world's wealth, let the United States lower its own food consumption to feed booming populations among the "have nots." Thus the less provident and less able will multiply at the expense of the abler and more provident and bring eventual ruin to all.

Hardin pictures a situation that brings home to us most graphically our current dilemma. A group of fifty people representing "the affluent world" is in a lifeboat that has a full capacity of sixty. Swimming in the water outside are a hundred others, begging to be taken aboard. At most we might admit ten of these unfortunates, but which ten would we choose? And what would we say to the ninety we exclude? If we took more than ten aboard we would lose our "safety factor" and thus endanger the lives of all. But some insist that we must live up to "the Christian ideal," so we take all hundred aboard. With 150 people in a boat designed at most for sixty the boat swamps and everyone drowns. So we have complete justice and complete catastrophe!

Hardin is realistic in pointing out that impoverishing ourselves to feed a stubborn, misinformed world is not the answer; that once we accept the philanthropic burden of sharing our food without regard to national boundaries the load would increase year after year to our mutual destruction.

In this process, says Hardin, given the great imbalance in the birth rates in the two kinds of nations, the United States and similar food-contributing nations would be subsidizing their own decline while building up the nations that are unwilling to cut back on their birth rate. In other words, he says, we would be deliberately committing national suicide. On the other hand, if the "affluent" nations refuse to share their wealth, they will force the underdeveloped world to stabilize its own growth. That will come about either through the belated efforts of its own leaders, or by the natural results of famine. [18]

On the question of bailing out the Third World, Alan Berg, food and nutrition expert on the staff of the World Bank and director of the successful U.S. famine relief program in India during the mid-1960s, is a bit more sympathetic. Writing in the *New York Times* magazine he admits the situation is pretty grim, but he says we should do all that is humanly possible to help.

Berg tells about the disastrous affects of the 1972 Russian grain deal, and our following year's drastic cut in production, which was largely responsible for bringing the world stock levels to their lowest point in twenty years. This action, along with the oil boycott, brought drastic rises in the price of wheat, corn, and rice, together with a four-fold increase in the price of petroleum-based fertilizer. He says, "The International Monetary Fund estimates that the low-income countries import bill for food and fertilizer alone has gone up from $6.4 billion to $15.6 billion," nearly two-and-a-half times as much.

After admitting there are critical food shortages, especially in parts of Africa and South Asia, Berg continues:

> The crises that have developed in these areas, however, do not mean that starvation is global, nor are they necessarily a prelude to wider starvation. . . The prospects for increasing food production to meet projected needs, furthermore, are far from grim. Discussions of lifeboats and triage give the impression of a steady downhill movement over the past 20 years. But in most disadvantaged countries, progress has been substantial. [19]

In Berg's opinion, all of these interrelated problems—food production and distribution, nutrition, and population control—must ultimately be dealt with by the poor nations themselves. Meeting this challenge will require a great sense of commitment on their parts, a shifting of priorities, a redeployment of resources and basic structural alterations, such as land and tenancy reforms and income distribution. In many instances, in order to reach all these goals, basic political reforms will be necessary.

In the final analysis, Berg says, helping the Third World to deal with these monumental problems is a moral issue, and he concludes, "We have no choice but to try."

The Third World Must Help Itself

Though this plea from a man of Berg's stature and experience is not to be taken lightly, most of us would feel a great deal more sympathetic towards these underdeveloped nations if their spokesmen showed a little better understanding of the difficulties faced by the industrial world in its efforts to help. Instead of approaching the problem in a conciliatory spirit, day by day as more of the Third, Fourth and Fifth World countries are admitted to the U.N. they become more arrogant in their demands. A couple of years ago Tanzania's Julius Nyerere told a meeting of the Commonwealth Society in London: "I am saying it is not right that the vast majority of the world's people should be forced into the position of beggars, without dignity. We demand change, and the only question is whether it comes by dialogue or confrontation."

Another attempt by the underdeveloped nations to force increased aid from "the world's rich nations" was the May 1979 session of the U.N. Conference on Trade and Development in Manila. According to an AP dispatch "representatives of 156 nations" assembled in the city "to debate the best way to divide the world's dwindling resources." A bloc of 80 poor nations called for $25 billion in new aid from rich nations.

The AP dispatch predicted that the long standing animosity between the "have" and "have not" nations would be sure to surface at that Conference, whose theme was the need for a profound change in the world's economic system. As predicted, the debate centered on how fast and how much the system would change.

In the U.N. General Assembly, where the underdeveloped nations constitute a solid and virtually unbeatable bloc on any given issue, there is simply no limit to their *demands* for massive and painful sacrifices by the "rich" on behalf of the poor. So one-sided have the assembly's actions become that Daniel Moynihan, when he was the United States ambassador to the United Nations, denounced the assembly as a "tyranny by the majority," and characterized their actions as "the politics of resentment and the economics of envy."

Some time ago, in an editorial that will benefit anyone to read, *Time* magazine dealt with this problem at length. While deploring the glaring contrast between the opulent life of the industrialized nations and the poverty, misery, and despair that blanket about three-fourths of the world's population—where each year an estimated billion human beings suffer in some degree from malnutrition and perhaps half a million die of starvation, or disease induced by starvation each year—the editors point out that during the past fifteen years nonmilitary gifts to the developing countries from the industrialized world totaled about $57 billion, plus concessional loans comprising some $84 billion. During the 1960s the United States contributed more than half of that assistance.

Foreign aid, *Time's* editors contend, has often been more effective than most of the poor nations are willing to admit. Scattered through the developing countries are new dams, low-rent public housing, irrigation systems, power plants, and canals. These projects have contributed significantly to the impressive 5.5 percent annual GNP increase logged by the developing nations as a group during the 1960s, and nearly 6 percent annual rise from 1970 to 1974. Naturally some of these nations have developed more rapidly than the others. In most of the underdeveloped countries, programs that have achieved planned rates of growth have failed to raise living standards because the gains have been offset by population growth. [20]

Our Billions Intensify Food Crisis

On our openhanded congressmen who insist on increasing our food aid to the Third World, a recent report by the General Accounting Office (GAO) will have the impact of an atom bomb: *The billions we have pumped overseas to aid the starving nations have had little affect; in fact, they have in many areas contributed to the critical world food shortage!*

After throwing the spotlight on twenty-one years of our Third World food-aid policy, costing an incredible $27 billion, that's the shocking conclusion of a report by the GAO, watchdog of Uncle Sam's bank account. [21]

To their surprise, a team of fifteen GAO investigators found that in every one of the eight developing countries they examined, our generous food dollars have encouraged famine-stricken nations to put off mounting their own food producing programs.

In most of these countries the GAO investigators found that food prices have been kept so low that local farmers can't afford to harvest their crops. Here are a few of the shocking situations covered by the GAO report:

> In Peru, the government ignored a 100 percent increase in the cost of fertilizer and pesticides and kept potato prices at rock-bottom. So a critical shortage arose because growers refused to plant potatoes—driving the black market price to three times that of the controlled price for potatoes. Now only the rich can afford them.
>
> In Kenya, farmers refused to invest in fertilizers and modern equipment to increase yields because government controlled farm prices were so low they faced bankruptcy.
>
> In India, the government refused to permit farming areas with a crop surplus to bail out famine zones—with the result that unwanted food rotted in one location while people starved in another.
>
> In every case the government looked to the United States for food. [22]

Other examples of many countries that face the same problem are Poland and Burma. In its issue of March 13, 1978, *Time* says, "Although 85 percent of Poland's farm land remains in private hands, (food) output is poor because low official prices provide no incentive for the farmer to work harder."

In the same essay on "Socialism" *Time* says, "No Third World country has fared worse under socialism than Burma. Its 16 years on the 'Burmese Way to Socialism' have turned what was once the lush rice bowl of Asia into an international pauper. Government policies have led the peasant to produce only what his family needs. As a result, rice output fell from 1.9 million tons in 1962 to 530,000 tons in 1976."

Obviously it would be wrong to conclude, simply because the world food crisis still exists, that our billions for Third World aid were misspent. At the same time we must ask ourselves if we aren't giving these countries too strong a crutch to lean on. Certainly we should be most wary about sending them more and bigger crutches.

Aside from encouraging the famine-stricken nations to depend too much on our aid, there is another problem that "experts" in this field seldom mention. Most likely they ignore it because, on the surface, it does seem utterly heartless; nevertheless it is a problem we simply have to face. If the rapidly growing populations of the hungry nations are fed today, they will continue to multiply until no amount of assistance could possibly save them. *In essence, those we save momentarily will surely continue to reproduce their kind at an alarming rate, so that for every miserable life we prolong today there will be four or five of his descendents facing starvation a generation hence.*

As the population of these hungry nations expands year by year, the available food supply contracts at even a greater pace. Our hearts are wrung by reports of millions starving in Country X, *but how much worse will it be twenty, thirty, forty years from now when there will be two or three times as many victims?*

It stands to reason that foreign help alone cannot solve the Third World's economic problems. "No nation, no matter how rich, can develop another country," says Egypt's Ismail Sabry Abdullah. As he points out, there are some things the developing world must do for itself: stress agricultural development; *limit population growth;* reform education; encourage entrepreneurs; reject prestige projects (like India's atomic bomb); encourage foreign investments.

As *Time's* editors have made it clear, it is unrealistic for the developing nations to expect the industrialized world voluntarily to dismantle its existing economic order and slash the living standards of its citizens. If there is to be useful dialogue on economic justice, the developing countries must come to understand the limits of what the First World can and will do.

In his long service as ambassador to India, Daniel Moynihan got a first-hand knowledge of poverty, observing that in Calcutta nearly a third of the stored grain is devoured by mice and other pests. In an article that appeared in *Commentary* magazine our erstwhile ambassador to the United Nations said, "The Third World must feed itself. . . and this will not be done by suggesting that Americans eat too much!"

Some time ago Alice Widener, nationally known columnist, summed up the problem most graphically:

> Clamoring for food aid from the United States, leaders of the Third World countries and our homegrown giveaway lobbyists are demanding that we Americans change our eating habits. Nobody in the United Nations or our Congress has the courage to say that no matter how much food we give to hungry nations, they will go on starving unless they change their sexual and religious habits. [23]

Enough has been said about the problem of increased aid to the Third, Fourth and Fifth worlds, but I should like to mention just one more fact. Our food surpluses were wiped out long ago, so about all we could give now would be increased *financial* help. Assuming we did just that, what assurance would we have that, for every dollar we sent, so much as a dime in benefits would trickle down to the poverty-stricken masses? Wouldn't we be compounding the mistake we made in Vietnam, when most of our financial aid stuck to the fingers of the big time politicians?

Conclusion

Any realist sizing up the multitudinous problems confronting this planet is bound to conclude that the population situation is going to get a lot worse before it can get even a little better.

In a report labeled "World Populations Trends: Signs of Hope, Signs of Stress," Lester Brown, director of the Worldwatch Institute, takes issue with the United Nations' prediction that the world population will more than double, from the present 4 billion to somewhere between 10 and 16 billion, before it begins to level off. Brown says it's going to level off much sooner, because the earth's food support systems can't take the strain, and starvation will cause a rise in death rates "if governments don't move swiftly on the family planning front." He says that the global population growth rate peaked in the early 1970s and is now subsiding. The total population increased by 69 million in 1970, but is now increasing by "only" 64 million a year. Brown says sooner or later governments are going to realize that their only real choice is not "*whether* population growth will slow, but *how*."

The "how" to slow the population growth in many countries is through deterioration of food-producing systems — overfishing, overgrazing, land erosion, and deforestation. As pointed out above, the worldwide fish catch peaked at 70 million tons in 1970 and declined since then because of depleted stocks. The seventies have shown us, continues Lester Brown, that "land-based food systems can also give way under intense pressures," such as catastrophic droughts or floods.

Whereas in the 1950s and 1960s rich nations could come to the aid of a country that had a bad crop year, surplus food stocks have shrunk to perilously low levels, and bad years will mean increasingly frequent and widespread famines and consequent deaths by starvation. On the optimistic side, most of the reduction in the population growth rates has come through reduction of birth rates. This global reduction has been concentrated in Western Europe, North America, and East Asia—the latter chiefly through the success of family planning in the People's Republic of

202

China, where a sharp drop in the birth rate, from 32 to 19 per thousand, occurred over a five-year period.

Other nations, especially in Latin America and Africa, show little progress, but there have been a few breakthroughs. Although Mexico is still producing more babies than Canada and the United States combined, it has backed off from its pronatalist policy, as mentioned above, and so far has set up 600 family planning clinics. *Other countries are liberalizing their abortion laws. At the beginning of 1971 only 38 percent of the world population lived in countries where legal abortion was available; now the figure stands at 68 percent.* [24]

To summarize, after an extensive review of evidence and opinion, the following conclusions are clear: whether we consider one individual, one family, or one world, the countless problems pertaining to contraception and abortion are interrelated. Complications that confront the individual and the family are no different from those that confront the world—except in degree. Further, without controls the worldwide runaway birth rate will surely lead to overpopulation and its catastropic consequences. Hence, the quality of life on earth is at stake. In closing, lest future generations be condemned to a life that is not worth living, I feel constrained to repeat what I said at the start: *the only solution of the greatest problem of all lies in universal birth control.*

APPENDIX

Environmental Control vs. Birth Control

In the 1980 Congressional elections the anti-abortionists were elated over the defeat of pro-choice Senators Culver of Iowa, Bayh of Indiana, Church of Idaho, McGovern of South Dakota, Nelson of Wisconsin and other legislators they wished to drive out of public life. On the surface it did look like a decisive victory for the anti's, but a thorough analysis of those election campaigns shows that the question of abortion was not the chief factor in the defeat of these liberals. Of course, the anti-abortion campaign did play a big part, but the main factor in the defeat of these liberal lawmakers was their position on environmental controls.

The opponents of these pro-choice Senators—Grassley of Iowa, Quayle of Indiana, Symms of Idaho, Abdnor of South Dakota and Kasten of Wisconsin were backed to the hilt by the "Filthy Five" and other monumental "scofflaws," notorious polluters of air and water, opponents of all environmental laws designed to protect the general public. None of these big corporations—dubbed "the Filthy Five" by Environmental ACTION—the Weyerhaeuser Company (annual sales $4.4 billion), Dow Chemical Company (annual sales $9.2 billion), Republic Steel Corporation (annual sales $3.98 billion), Occidental Petroleum (annual sales $9.5 billion), Amoco Oil Company, Standard Oil of Indiana (annual sales $18:6 billion)— gave a hoot about abortion or anti-abortion. They were out to "get" these liberal Senators because of their support of Environmental Laws.

These five corporations contributed $1,031,190 to elect their *friends to Congress.*

Here is the score card of the five anti-environmental Senators who defeated their pro-environmental opponents, the amounts contributed to each by the Filthy Five and their voting records on Environmental Laws:

Charles Grassley got $20,275 in campaign funds from the Filthy Five, voted against Environmental Laws 75 percent of the time. (His opponent, John Culver's rating on pro-Environmental Laws was 91 percent). Don Quayle received $17,500 from the Filthy Five, voted against Environmental Laws 70 percent of the time. (His opponent, Birch Bayh voted in favor of Environmental Laws 69 percent of the time). Steven Symms received $17,000 from the Filthy Five and voted against Environmental Laws 92 percent of the time. (His opponent, Frank Church wasn't a dedicated environmentalist, but he voted for Environmental Laws 55 percent of the time). James Abdnor got $13,600 from the Filthy Five and voted against Environmental Laws 80 percent of the time. (His opponent, George McGovern voted for the Environment 74 percent of the time). Bob Kasten got $10,500 from the Big Five Polluters to defeat Gaylord Nelson, who voted the "Environmental Ticket" 86 percent. (For more detailed information see *Environmental ACTION,* May 1981 issue, pp. 10-16).

Since a Supreme Court ruling in 1976 held that Political Action Committees could raise and spend as much as they wished to oppose or support a candidate, so long as there are no ties to the candidate's campaign operations, there was nothing illegal in the contributions made to their anti-environmental friends by the Filthy Five, but it certainly wasn't a contribution to good citizenship.

The National Independent Conservative Political Action Committee (generally referred to as NICPAC), and similar groups from every corner of the land, contributed more than $4 million dollars in "hate funds" to help defeat the above named senators and other liberals. The opposition to these liberals was due in part to their support of the pro-choice position but chiefly to their support of liberal legislation in general. Even if we make due allowance for the affect of the millions spent in the 1980 campaigns by the various hate groups, it is very doubtful if the anti-abortionists could have won without these tremendous contributions made by the Filthy Five and other anti-environmental groups.

Some years ago, in commenting on the green light given by the Supreme Court to Political Action Committees, Terry Dolen, organizer and director of NICPAC, said: "A group like ours could lie through the teeth and the candidate it helps stays clean."

In April of 1981, twenty months before the 1982 Congressional elections, the NICPAC started a vicious campaign against Maryland Senator Paul Sarbanes. The victim, an honor graduate of Princeton, a Rhodes scholar who got his law degree at Harvard *cum laude,* is one of the most competent members of the Senate. As the spoilers' campaign began he had not yet announced his intention to run in 1982, nor had any opponent taken the field.

Why did "Nick-Pack" start its campaign against Sarbanes so far in advance of the next Congressional election? The reason is obvious. This ultra-rightist group knew that every member of Congress lives within range of Maryland television channels. Its real objective was to scare into line every member of Congress who might be thinking of voting against that group's philosophy.

205

So far this scare tactic seems to work. Only weeks after the campaign against Sarbanes got under way the Senate approved by a vote of 52-43 the strongest anti-abortion provision that Congress ever has seriously considered Already approved by the House, this provision—sponsored by the ubiquitous Jesse Helms—prohibits the use of federal funds for any abortion except when the woman's life is in danger.

In the 1980 Congressional campaigns, NICPAC and other unscrupulous groups spent millions, played their "license to lie" to the hilt and got away with murder, defeating a number of the most competent members of Congress. I daresay it will be a different story in the future, however, since liberation groups, goaded to their wits end by the administration's undeclared war on women, each month are adding new members by the thousands and are now building up a substantial war chest, determined to expose such fraudulent tactics in the next go-round.

Reproduced with the permission of Bill Garner
and the Memphis Commercial Appeal

REFERENCES

Introduction

1. *New York Times* News Service Dispatch, March 5, 1978. (See also *Newsweek*, June 5, 1978, "Abortion Under Attack.")
2. *Time*, Jan. 29, 1979, pp. 62-63.
3. *America*, (Editorial), Dec. 27, 1975. *The Commonweal*, (Editorials) Jan. 2, 1976 and Feb. 27, 1976. (See also: Planned Parenthood *Washington Memo*, Dec. 15, 1975.)
4. *Eleven Million Teenagers: What Can Be done About the Epidemic of Adolescent Pregnancies in the U.S.* A publication of the Allan Guttmacher Institute, the Research and Development Division of Planned Parenthood Federation of America, 515 Madison Avenue, New York, N.Y., 10022.
5. *A Woman's Choice*, Samuel J. Barr, M.D., with Dan Abelow, (New York: Rawson Associates, 1977), p. 247.
6. *Ibid*, p. 171.
7. *Science*, Nov. 12, 1976, p. 704.
8. *Time*, July 16, 1965. (In his "Confessions," St. Augustine tells how he prayed, while a young man still enjoying the favors of his concubine, "Lord, give me chastity; but not yet!" No doubt he wrote "the marriage chamber is a brothel," in his old age after the Lord answered his prayer.)
9. *New York Times*, Jan. 21, 1980: "Abortion Foes, at Conference, Plan Strategy of Political Activism."
10. *Time*, Feb. 4, 1980: "Stars of the Cathode Church; TV-Radio Preaching; A Controversial Billion-dollar Industry." The article continues: "This new outlet of religion is controlled almost totally by the Evangelical-Fundamentalist-Pentecostal wing of Protestantism. They own more than 1,400 radio stations and 35 TV stations. In his 1979 book, *The Electric Church*, Ben Armstrong, Executive Director of National Religious Broadcasts (NRB), claims that each week at least 14 million Americans watch a religious TV show and 115 million listen to a radio gospel program, vastly more than go to church."

Chapter 1

1. *Washington Star-News*, Jan. 23, 1973.
2. *New York Times*, Jan. 23, 1973.
3. *Planned Parenthood Washington Memo*, Dec. 15, 1975.
4. *Church and State* magazine, October, 1977.
5. *Time*, Aug. 1, 1977, p. 49.
6. *Abortion and the Poor*, a publication of the Alan Guttmacher Institute, New York, 1976, pp. 31-32.

Chapter 2

1. *Memphis Commercial Appeal*, July 3, 1980.

Chapter 3

1. *Time*, July 4, 1977, p. 7.
2. *UPI* Dispatch, Feb. 18, 1978.
3. *Newsweek*, June 5, 1978, pp. 37-47.
4. *Newsweek*, March 3, 1978, p. 3.
5. *Planned Parenthood, Washington Memo*, Nov. 11, 1977.
6. *A Woman's Choice*, Samuel J. Barr, M. D., with Dan Abelow (New York, Rawson, 1977), p. 247.

Chapter 4

1. *Time*, Feb. 1, 1971, p. 54.
2. Allan F. Guttmacher, M. D., "Why I Favor Legalized Abortion," *Reader's Digest*, November, 1973, pp. 143-144.
3. John A. O'Brien, Ed., *Family Planning in an Exploding Population.* (New York: Hawthorne, 1968), p. 215.
4. On 29 November 1974 the French National Assembly, after a prolonged and vicious debate, voted to legalize abortion on demand at fixed prices during the first ten weeks of pregnancy. The Assembly thus ended fifty-four years of total prohibition of abortion in France, overturning a law which provided stiff fines and prison sentences for any person performing an abortion and any woman who underwent an abortion.
5. Statistics on the number of abortions in Italy vary greatly. The minister of health estimates about 800,000 a year. A 1968 convention of Italian gynocologists said up to 3 million. The World Health Organization's estimate is 1.5 million.
6. *Who Shall Live?* A Report Prepared for the American Friends Service Committee, (New York: Hill & Wang, 1970), p. 24.
7. Paul and Anne Ehrlich. *Population-Resources-Environment: Issues In Human Ecology.* (San Francisco: Freeman, 1970), pp. 223-224.
8. Philip Appleman, *The Silent Explosion.* (Boston: Beacon Pr, 1965), p. 74.
9. Lawrence Lader, *Abortion.* (New York: Bobbs, 1966), p. 7.
10. *Ibid.*, p. 151.
11. *Ibid.*, pp. 160-161.
12. Quoted by Rev. Patrick A. Finney in *Moral Problems in Hospital Practice*, 2nd Ed., (St. Louis: Herder, 1922), p. 47.
13. The latest figures from the Vatican show that in 1975 more than 4,000 priests out of a total of 405,000 left the priesthood. *Memphis Commercial Appeal*, Feb. 13, 1978.
14. *Time*, Feb. 21, 1972.
15. William C. McCready and Andrew M. Greeley, "The End of American Catholicism," *America*, Oct. 28, 1972, pp. 334-338.
16. *Time*, Jan. 13, 1975.
17. *New York Times* Special News Service dispatch, published in the *Memphis Commercial Appeal*, Oct. 27, 1977.

18. *11 Million Teenagers: What Can Be Done About the Epidemic of Adolescent Pregnancies in the United States*; a publication of the Alan F. Guttmacher Institute, pp. 58-59.
19. "General Statistics on A.F.D.C. - Fiscal Year 1977-78—given to the author by Congressman Harold Ford in a letter dated Feb. 8. 1979.
20. "Statistical Data on Public Assistance Programs," published by the Committee on Finance, U.S. Senate, February 1980.
21. Under the heading "Shortcut Vasectomies," the following item appeared in the February 1978 issue of *Moneysworth Magazine*: "A Chicago medical team is experimenting with a vasectomy procedure which involves no surgery and may prove to be reversible. Instead of severing the vas deferens, the tube through which sperm travels from the testicles, the doctors have injected certain chemical agents into it, causing a build-up of scar tissue which effectively blocks the passage of sperm. The new technique takes only about ten minutes. The team believes that a reversal procedure, as yet unperfected, could be performed just as quickly."

Chapter 5

1. Ellen Weber, "Incest—Sexual Abuse Begins at Home,"*Ms. Magazine*, April 1977, pp. 64-66.
2. Naomi Feigelson Chase, *A Child Is Being Beaten*. (New York: H R & W, 1975), p. 101.
3. Dr. Phillip J. Resnick, "Child Murder by Parents: A Psychiatric Review of Filicide, "*American Journal of Psychiatry*, Vol. 126-#3, 1969, pp. 325-334

Chapter 6

1. Lawrence Lader, *Abortion*, (New York: Bobbs, 1966), pp. 148-149. Note: Not to be confused with Lader's second book on the subject, *Abortion II*.
2. Paul R. and Anne H. Ehrlich, *Population-Resources-Environment: Issues in Human Ecology*. (San Francisco: Freeman, 1970), p.225.
3. *Modern Medicine*, April 24, 1967, p. 216.
4. *Memphis Commercial Appeal*, Nov. 15, 1968.
5. Samuel J. Barr, M. D., director of the EPOC clinic, which averages 4,000 abortions a year, says "abortions performed during the first trimester of pregnancy are six times safer than childbirth." (See *A Woman's Choice*, p.291.)
6. In countries where restrictive laws are actually enforced, women have not been deterred from seeking abortions, but rather they have resorted to various methods of self-induced abortion and abortion by untrained illegal practitioners. The limited impact of restrictive laws on the demand for abortion is suggested by the Romanian experience. Following passage of a more restrictive abortion law in 1966, abortion-related deaths rose seven-fold over a decade, and illegal abortions reached the level of legal abortions. (See "POPULATION: World Abortion Trends," #9, April, 1979.)

7. Lawrence Lader, *Abortion II: Making the Revolution*. (Boston: Beacon Pr., 1973), pp. 209-211. (Another who has done yeoman service in this field is Bill Baird. See "Abortion," *Coronet Magazine*, June 1969, pp. 9-16.)

8. Edgar R. Chasteen, *The Case for Compulsory Birth Control*. (Englewood Cliffs, N. J., Prentice-Hall, 1972), p. 150.

9. In "A Scientist's Case for Abortion," *Redbook*, May 1967, Dr. Garrett Hardin says, "The work of Hertig, Rock and Adams has revealed that at least 38 percent of all zygots produced are spontaneously aborted."

10. Lader, *Abortion*, pp. 148-149.

11. *New Times Magazine*, Jan. 23, 1978.

12. *Memphis Commercial Appeal*, Oct. 8, 1972.

13. "The New York Abortion Story," a booklet published by Planned Parenthood Federation of America in 1972. Also "Facts and Figures on Legal Aboriton," published by the same organization.

14. *Family Planning Perspectives*, Vol. 7, No. 2; March-April, 1975, p. 59.

15. *New York Times*, Jan. 30, 1973.

16. *Time*, Sept. 4, 1972.

17. Roy Larson, *Chicago Sun-Times*; reprinted in the *Memphis Commercial Appeal*, Nov. 17, 1973.

18. Amitai Etzioni, "Stimulous Response: Doctors Know More Than They're Telling You About Genetic Defects," Psychology Today, Nov. 1973.

19. UPI Dispatch, Oct. 22, 1975.

20. In fairness to the March of Dimes I must say that in a letter replying to my protest, the president of that organization said they had not "cut off" funding for amniocentesis; that their original grant was for a limited time and since that time period had expired, no further funding was in order.

21. Following is a list of eighty-two organizations that have spoken out in support of legal abortion:

American Association of University Women
American Baptist Churches
American Civil Liberties Union
American College Health Association
American College of Obstetricians and Gynecologists
American College of Nurse-Midwives
American Ethical Union
American Ethical Union, National Women's Conference
American Friends Service Committee, Inc.
American Home Economics Association
American Humanist Association
American Jewish Congress
American Lutheran Church
American Medical Association
American Medical Women's Association, Inc.

American Protestant Hospital Association
American Psychiatric Association
American Psychoanalytic Association
American Psychological Association
American Public Health Association
American Veterans' Committee
Americans for Democratic Action
Americans United for Separation of Church and State
Association of Planned Parenthood Physicians
B'Nai B'rith Women
Baptist Joint Committee on Public Affairs
Catholics for a Free Choice
Center for Law and Social Policy
Center for Women Policy Studies
Central Conference of American Rabbis
Child Welfare League of America
Church of the Brethren
Church Women United
Community Service Society
Environmental Action
Environmental Policy Center
Federation of Protestant Welfare Agencies, Inc.
Friends of the Earth
Friends Committee on National Legislation
Group for the Advancement of Psychiatry
League of Women Voters
Lutheran Church in America
Medical Committee for Human Rights
National Abortion Rights Action League
National Association of Laity (Catholic)
National Association of Social Workers
National Association of Women Deans, Administrators and
    Counselors
National Association of Women Deans, Administrators and
    Counselors - Intercollegiate
National Association of Women Students
National Commission on the Observance of International Women's
    Year, 1975.
National Council of Churches
National Council of Jewish Women
National Council of Family Relations
National Education Association (NEA)
National Emergency Civil Liberties Committee
National Federation of Temple Sisterhoods
National Organization for Women
National Women's Political Caucus
Physicians' Forum
Planned Parenthood Federation of America, Inc.
Presbyterian Church in the U.S.A.

The Reformed Church in America
Religious Coalition for Abortion Rights
Reorganized Church of Jesus Christ of Latter Day Saints
Sierra Club
Lutheran Baptist Convention
Union of American Hebrew Congregations
Unitarian-Universalist Association and Unitarian-Universalist
  Women's Federation
United Auto Workers
United Church of Christ
United Methodist Church
United Methodist Church, Women's Division
United Presbyterian Church, U.S.A.
Urban League
Women of the Episcopal Church
Women's Equity Action League
Women's League for Conservative Judaism
Women's Legal Defense Fund
Women's Lobby
Women's Circle
Young Women's Christian Association of the U.S.A.
Zero Population Growth

Chapter 7

1. Marion K. Sanders, "Enemies of Abortion," *Harper's Magazine*, March 1974, pp. 26-30.
2. J. C. Willke, M. D., and Barbara Willke, *Handbook on Abortion*, (Cincinnati: Hayes Publishing Co., Rev. Ed., 1975.
3. Father Robert E. Drinan, "The State of the Abortion Question," *Commonweal*, April 17, 1970.
4. Daniel Callahan, *Abortion: Law, Choice and Morality*. (New York: Macmillan, 1970). pp. 4-5.
5. *Ibid.*, pp. 381-382.
6. *Ibid.*, p. 440.
7. *Ibid.*, pp. 486-487.
8. *Ibid.*, p. 506.
9. Garrett Hardin, *Mandatory Motherhood: The True Meaning of "Right-To-Life."* (Boston: Beacon Pr. 1972). p. 7.
10. *Ibid.*, p. 103.
11. Arlene Carmen and Howard Moody, *Abortion: Counseling and Social Change*. (Valley Forge, Pa.: Judson Pr., 1973), pp. 114-115.
12. Garrett Hardin, "Semantic Aspects of Abortion," ETC, 24:3. Quoted in *A General Guide to Abortion*, p. 38.
13. R. Bruce Sloan, M. D., and Diana Frank Horvits, *A General Guide To Abortion*. (Chicago: Nelson-Hall, 1973), pp. 11-12.
14. Israel R. Margolies, "A Reform Rabbi's View" in Robert E. Hall, Ed., *Abortion In a Changing World*. (Columbia Univ. Pr., 1970), quoted in *A General Guide To Abortion*, p. 13.

15. David M. Feldman, *Birth Control in Jewish Law*. (New York New York Univ. Pr., 1968, p. 81. (Also London: Un. of London Pr.)
16. *Ibid.*, p. 83.
17. Joint Statement of the Council of Churches of the city of New York; New York Association of Reform Rabbis; New York Federation of Reform Synagogues; and the New York State Council of Churches: New York City, May 6, 1971. Quoted in *A General Guide To Abortion*, pp. 15-16.
18. *Memphis Commercial Appeal*, April 4, 1976.
19. On 18 May 1978 the law was approved in the Italian Senate by a vote of 160 to 148. It permits state-subsidized abortion on demand in the first 90 days of pregnancy for any woman over 18 who says childbirth would endanger her physical or mental health. A medical certificate is required after more than 90 days, and girls under 18 must have the approval of a parent or guardian.
20. *Planned Parenthood Washington Memo*, Dec. 26, 1975.
21. Samuel J. Barr. M. D., with Dan Abelow, *A Woman's Choice*. (New York: Rawson Associates Publishers, Inc., 1977), pp. 234-235.
22. *Ibid.*, p. 247.
23. *Ibid.*, p. 253.
24. *Ibid.*

Chapter 8

1. Federal Reports: 86 - 2nd, p. 737.
2. *Time*, July 16, 1965.
3. John T. Noonan, Jr., *Contraception: The History of Its Treatment by Theologians and canonists*. (Cambridge: Harvard Univ. Pr., 1965), p. 258.
4. *Ibid.*, pp. 260-261.
5. G. Egner, *Contraception vs. tradition*, (New York: Herder, 1967), p. 11. On the degree of resistance that a wife should put up if her husband tried to use a condom, Egner gives the position of the early Church: "For the wife to admit him would be joining in this unnatural act and so itself a great sin. She must, says the Penitentiary, put up a positive physical resistance 'as a maiden would to her ravisher.' Only the fear of death or grave physical injury can justify her (purely passive) submission; quarrels, domestic strife and the rest are not sufficient reasons for tolerating the abuse."
6. Noonan, *Contraception*, p. 273.
7. *Ibid.*, p. 303.
8. *Ibid.*, p. 307.
9. *Ibid.*, p. 308.
10. *Ibid.*, p. 309.
11. *Ibid.*
12. *Ibid.*, p. 383.
13. *Ibid.*. p. 388.

14. Quoted by Noonan in *Contraception*, pp. 406-409.
15. Noonan, *Contraception*, p. 427.
16. *Ibid.*, p. 432.
17. *Ibid.*, pp. 445-446.
18. Daniel Callahan, Ed., *The Catholic Case for Contraception.* (London: Macmillan, 1969), p. 132. (paperback edition).
19. Sidney Cornelia Callahan, *Beyond Birth Control.* (New York: Sheed, 1968).
20. *Time*, Aug. 10, 1968, pp. 61-62.

Chapter 9

1. *Time*, Feb. 7, 1977, p. 65.
2. Andrew M. Greeley, William C. McCready and Kathleen McCourt, *Catholic Schools in a Declining Church.* (New York: Sheed, 1976). See also *Time*, April 5, 1976, p. 56.
3. *Look*, Oct. 19, 1971.
4. John Cogley, *Catholic America.* (New York: D. Pr., 1973), p. 132.
5. *Time*, Aug. 21, 1968.
6. Michael de la Bedoyere, Ed., *Objections to Roman Catholicism.* (Philadelphia: Lippincott, 1965), pp. 44-45.
7. *Christian Century*, Aug. 14, 1968.
8. Charles Davis, *A Question of Conscience.* (New York: Harper-Row, 1967), pp. 102-103.
9. John T. Noonan, Jr., *Contraception: The History of Its Treatment by Theologians and Canonists.* (Cambridge: Harvard Univ. Press, 1965), pp. 275-276. (Author's note: In taking this position: "The bigger the population, the bigger the population in heaven," the Church ignores the estimates of most theologians-statisticians that a relatively small percentage of souls go to heaven; by far the greater number go to hell.)
10. William Peterson, *Population*, 2nd Ed., (New York: Macmillan, 1969), fn., p. 493.
11. *America*, Spet. 30, 1967.
12. Noonan, *Contraception*, pp. 34-35.
13. *Ibid.*, p. 47, et sec. Some authorities claim that Onan was punished for engaging in contraception by *coitus interruptous*, but modern exegetes hold that his punishment was due to breaking the law designed to perpetuate the name of his brother.
14. Charles E. Curran, Robert E. Hunt, et al., Eds. *Dissent In and For the Church.* (New York: Sheed, 1969), pp. 4-6.
15. Andrew M. Greeley, *Priests in the United States.* (New York: Doubleday, 1972), pp. 65-71.
16. *Planned Parenthood-World Population Washington Memo*, Nov. 14, 1975, p. 4.

Chapter 10

1. Daniel Callahan, Ed., *The Catholic Case for Contraception.* (London: Macmillan, 1969). pp. x-xi. (paperback edition)
2. *Ibid.,* pp. 130-131.
3. *Ibid.,* p. 131.
4. *Ibid.,* p. 140.
5. Hans Küng, "The Pope's Unsolvable Problem," *Look,* Dec 13, 1966.
6. Callahan, Ed., *Catholic Case,* pp. 228; 232-233.
7. *Ibid.,* p. 230.
8. UPI Dispatch, Dec. 30, 1968.
9. *Ibid.*
10. *New York Times,* July 30, 1968.
11. Charles E. Curran, Robert E. Hunt, et al., Eds. *Dissent In and For the Church.* (New York: Sheed, 1969), pp. 198-201.
12. *Washington Post,* July 31, 1968.
13. *Awake Magazine,* Sept. 22, 1969.
14. *Science,* Jan 5, 1973. Quoted in *America,* July 21, 1973, p. 31.

Chapter 11

1. Joseph J. Tydings, *Born To Starve* (New York: Morrow, 1970). "At 10:56 P.M. on July 24, 1969, as perhaps a billion earth men and women listened and watched, Neil Armstrong became the first human to set foot on another heavenly body . . . During the eight-day mission of Apollo II, the population of the world increased by more than one and on-half million human beings—a rate of 192,000 more people a day, 76 million a year. Over this eight-day period, an estimated 100,000 human beings starved to death—most of them children." (From the introduction to *Born to Starve.*)
2. *Life,* May 19, 1972.
3. Alejandro Portes, "Labor Functions of Illegal Aliens," *Society,* Sept/Oct. 1977.
4. The statistics in this section on immigration are taken in part from an article by Leslie Aldridge Westoff, entitled "The Mother of Exiles May Have Too Many," in the Memphis *Commercial Appeal,* Sept. 23, 1973.
5. John Rock, M.D., *The Time Has Come,* (New York: Knopf, 1961), p. 24.
6. Quoted by Paul R. Ehrlich in *The Population Bomb.* (New York: Ballantine, Rev. Ed., 1971, p. 136. (Dr. Thomas is a biologist associated with Dr. Ehrlich at Stanford University.)
7. Quoted by Leslie Aldridge Westoff in *From Now To Zero,* (Boston:Little, 1971), p. 185. (Westoff also quotes a New York cab driver: "They never should have told the pope about the pill!")
8. John A. O'Brien, Ed., *Family Planning in an Exploding Population.* (New York: Hawthorn, 1968), quoted in *Christian Century,* Vol. LXXX, p. 1050.

9. O'Brien, Ed., *Family Planning*, pp. 88-89.
10. Figures furnished me by Congressman Harold Ford, Tennessee, in a letter dated Feb. 8, 1979.
11. UPI Dispatch, July 21, 1975.
12. Julius Horwitz, "The Grim State of Welfare," *Look*, March 16, 1963, pp. 69-80.
13. O'Brien, Ed., *Family Planning*, p. 96.
14. Pope Pius XI, *Casti Connubi*, 1930.
15. O'Brien, Ed., *Family Planning*, pp. 38-39.
16. Robert C. Cook, *Human Fertility: The Modern Dilemma*. (New York: Sloane 1951). pp. 246-247. This book by a nationally known biologist, is a gold mine of information on the influence of heredity and environment and similar problems. It is a book of sound scholarship, and though it was published a quarter-century ago, is still as authentic as the day it was published.
17. AP Dispatch, March 27, 1969.
18. Paul R. Ehrlich, "Ecology's Angry Lobbyist," *Look* Magazine, April 21, 1970.
19. Paul and Anne Ehrlich, *Population-Resources-Environment: Issues in Human Ecology*. (San Francisco: Freeman, 1970), pp. 32-33.
20. Cook, *Human Fertility*, pp. 280-282.
21. Lawrence Lader, *Abortion*. (New York: Bobbs, 1966), p. 132.
22. Cook, *Human Fertility*, pp. 285-287.
23. *Ibid.*, p. 286.
24. Lader, *Abortion*, pp. 132-133.

Chapter 12

1. Quoted in *Lifeboat Ethics*, George R. Lucas, Jr., and Thomas W. Ogletree, Eds., (New York: Harper Forum Books, 1976).
2. Frances Moore Lappé, *Diet for a Small Planet*, (New York: Ballantine, 1975).
3. Frances Moore Lappé and Joseph Collins, *FOOD FIRST—Beyond the Myth of Scarcity*, (Boston: H-M, 1977.)
4. On this disgraceful practice, see *Christian Science Monitor*, Nov. 19, 1974, "Tradition vs. 'Progress': Feeding the Third World Babies."
5. Ray Vicker, *This Hungry World*, (New York: Scribner, 1975)
6. *Ibid.*, pp. 36-38.
7. *Ibid.*, p. 42.
8. Lester R. Brown, *The Twenty-ninth Day*, (New York: Norton), p. 72.
9. Vicker, *This Hungry World*, pp. 115-116.

Chapter 13

1. Georg Borgstrom, *The Hungry Planet*. (New York: Macmillan, 1965), pp. 454-455.
2. *Life*, May 19, 1972.

3. John A. O'Brien, Ed., *Family Planning in an Exploding Population*. (New York: Hawthorne, 1968), pp. 55-56. See Raymond Ewell, "Birth Control the Only Answer," (Chapter 6 in *Family Planning*).
4. Concise Report on the World Population Situation in 1970-1974. *U.N. Population Studies #56*, 1974, p. 5.
5. Arthur Hopcraft, *Born to Hunger*. (Boston: H-M, 1968), pp. 183-185.
6. *Memphis Commercial Appeal*, Aug. 21, 1968.
7. Borgstrom, *Hungry Planet*, p. 454.
8. R. Buckminster Fuller, *Comprehensive Design Strategy, World Resources Inventory, Phase II*. (Carbondale, Ill.: University of Southern Illinois Press, 1967), p. 48.
9. Richard A. Falk, *This Endangered Planet*. (New York: Random House, 1971), pp. 212-213.
10. Paul Ehrlich, *The Population Bomb*. (New York: Ballantine, 1971), Rev. Ed. p. xi.
11. *Ibid.*, p. 12.
12. *U.N. Population Reference Bureau*, Dec. 1965.
13. Ehrlich, *Population Bomb*, p. 12.
14. *U.N. Concise Report on World Population*, 1970-1975. 1974.
15. *Statistical Abstract of the U.S., 1974 and 1978*.
16. *Time*, July 4, 1977. "Bumper To Bumper In The Wilderness."
17. *Memphis Commercial Appeal*, July 23, 1972.
18. In her charming and informatvie book *Wild Heritage*, Sally Carrighar says that experiments with lemmings, snowshoe hares, and other small animals show that overcrowding often causes enlarged adrenal glands and fatal heart attacks; that zoo animals are afflicted the same way when crowded together in groups for the entertainment of visitors. Her experience has convinced her that lemmings, instead of committing mass suicide because of food, "take the easy way out to sea" because of irritation due to overcrowding. Her book gives the crowded human race something to think about!

Chapter 14

1. William and Paul Paddock, *Famine — 1975!* (Boston: Little, 1967).
2. *Time*, Nov. 17, 1974.
3. UPI Dispatch, June 5, 1975.
4. Eric Eckholm, *The Picture of Health: Environmental Sources of Disease*. (New York: Norton, 1977).
5. Georg Borgstrom, *Too Many: A Study of the Earth's Biological Limitations*. (New York: Macmillan, 1969), p. 2.
6. *Ibid.*, p. 1.
7. *Ibid.*, pp. 405-407.
8. Norman Lewis, "Not Seeing the Forest for Debris," *London Observer*, reprinted in Memphis *Commercial Appeal*, May 6, 1979.

9. Borgstrom, *Too Many*, p. 9.
10. *Ibid.*, pp. 15-16.
11. *Time*, Nov. 11, 1974.
12. Lester R. Brown, *The Twenty-Ninth Day*. (New York: Norton, 1978). pp. 23-27.
13. Robert C. Cook, *Human Fertility*. (New York: Sloane, 1951). pp. 61-62.
14. Georg Borgstrom, *The Hungry Planet*. (New York: Macmillan, 1965), pp. 306 and 333.
15. *Ibid.*, p. 130.
16. In *Race Against Famine* (Philadelphia: Macrae Smith, 1968), Melvin A. Benarde tells how fish production at the local level can be dramatically increased. In Africa, China, Japan, the Philippines, India, and Israel, small-scale "fish farming" has brought gratifying results. He says that "growing fish in the back yard" can provide higher yields of protein per acre than any known agricultural crop.
17. *Life*, Dec. 3, 1971.
18. "Symposium Weighs Effects of Oceanic Oil Pollution," *BioScience*, October, 1976.
19. "Huge Fish Kill Found in Ocean," *New York Times*, July 8, 1976.
20. Lester R. Brown, *The Twenty-ninth Day*, (New York: Norton, 1978), pp. 51-53.
21. *Ibid.*
22. *Memphis Commercial Appeal*, Nov. 20, 1977.
23. *Christian Science Monitor*, Nov. 15, 1974. See also *Catholic Digest* April, 1976, pp. 101-106, and *Mid-South Magazine*, Nov. 24, 1974.
24. "The World Food Crisis," *Time*, Nov. 11, 1974.   ☐
25. William Vogt, *People: Challange to Survival*, (New York; Sloane, 1960), pp. 79-80.
26. *Look*, April 21, 1970.
27. Nathaniel P. Reed, "Spacecraft Earth Is Overcrowded," *Reader's Digest*, Dec. 1974.

Chapter 15

1. *Christian Century*, Vol LXXXVIII (1961), pp. 1196-1197.
2. *United Nations Year Book*, 1972, p. 249.
3. James Nelson Goodsell, "A Continent Resists Birth Control, *Christian Science Monitor*, Dec. 30, 1970.
4. James Nelson Goodsell, "Mexico Today," *Christian Science Monitor*, July 31, 1973.
5. *National Catholic Reporter*, Aug. 17, 1973.
6. Arthur Hopcraft, *Born to Hunger*. (Boston: H M, 1968), p. 223.
7. *Ibid.*, p. 226.
8. UPI Dispatch, March 31, 1976.
9. *Time*, March 8, 1976.
10. *Time*, April 4, 1977.
11. *Time*, Nov. 18, 1974.

12. *Ibid.*
13. *Memphis Commercial Appeal*, Jan. 2, 1977.
14. W. V. D'Antonia, "Birth Control and Coercion," *The Commonweal*, Dec. 2, 1966, quoted by Louise Young, ed., in *Populations In Perspective*. (New York: Oxford Un. Pr., 1968), p. 414, ff.
15. Bernard Berelson, Ed., *Family Planning Programs: An International Survey*. (New York: Basic, 1968).
16. *Ibid.*, p. 11
17. Paul and Anne Ehrlich, *Population-Resources-Environment: Issues in Human Ecology*. (San Francisco: Freeman, 1970), pp. 261-262.
18. Garrett Hardin, "Lifeboat Ethics: The Case Against Helping the Poor," *Psychology Today*, Sept. 1974, pp. 38-43 and 123-126.
19. Alan Berg, "The Trouble With Triage," *New York Times Magazine*, June 15, 1975, pp. 26-35.
20. *Time*, Dec. 22, 1975, Special Report: "Poor vs. Rich: A New Global Conflict," pp. 34-42.
21. *National Enquirer*, March 23, 1976.
22. *Ibid.*
23. Alice Widner, "Hungry Nations Must Change Life-Styles," *Memphis Commercial Appeal*, Dec. 4, 1974.
24. *Science*, Nov. 12, 1976, "World Population Trends," p. 704.

INDEX

A Woman's Choice (Barr), 2, 33, 34

Abortion (Lader), 43, 72

Abortion: Law, Choice, Morality (Callahan), 90. 91

Abortion II - Making the Revolution (Lader), 74

Abdnor, Senator James, 204, 205

abortion
  fanaticism of opponents, 1, 4, 5
  high incidence among Catholic women, 2
  gaining approval throughout world, 3
  defection from Roman church largely due to this controversy, 46, 47
  history of, · 68-71
  revolutionary changes in attitude, 74
  studies on after-effects of, 76, 77
  legalized in New York. 79
  affects of legalization in N. Y. 76-78
  legalized by U. S. Supreme Court, 79
  new techniques developed by science. 80, 81
  National Observer survey shows nation's approval. 92
  intransigence of "Right-to-Lifers" pointed out by sociologists, 92, 93
  Garrett Hardin tells why abortion is needed, 93
  legalized in Catholic Italy, 98 99
  abortion rights, call to concern by 200 national leaders, 84, 85

AFDC Program (Aid to Families of Dependent Children)
  big increase in payments due to Hyde Amendment, 19, 21
  half of AFDC payments go to teenagers, 22
  tremendous costs of, 56

America (Jesuit Magazine) opposes hierarchy stand on abortion, 11

American Association for Advancement of Science criticizes Paul VI for banning contraception. 128, 129

American Public Health Ass'n approves sex education for children, 54

amniocentesis, safe technique for testing genetic abnormalities before birth, 81, 83

Amoco Oil Company. 204

Anthony Comstock: Roundman of the Lord, (Heywood Broun) (Margaret Leech), 71

anti-abortionists
  vandalism by, 29, 31
  Constitutional Amendment banning abortion opposed by majority of Catholics, 11-13
  "Right-to-Lifers" change their opposition when need for abortion comes home to them, 100

assassins, spawned by unwanted births, 65-69

Augustine, Saint: "marriage chamber is a brothel," 3

Barr, Dr. Samuel J. criticizes anti-abortionists 33, 34

Bayh, Senator Birch, 204, 205

Berg, Alan: "developing world must solve own problems," 197. 198

Beyond Birth Control (Callahan), 112

Birth Control and Catholic Doctrine (Sulloway), 104

Blackmun, Justice Harry A., one of four justices to dissent on Supreme Court decision upholding Hyde Amendment, 26

Borgstom, Dr. Georg:
  "solution to world population problem lies in bedrooms of world," 157
  describes appalling conditions in Third World, 161

Born To Hunger (Hopcraft), 160

Boyle, Patrick Cardinal, opposes legalized abortion, 8

Brazil. hotbed of illegal abortion, 42

Brennan, Justice William J., Jr., dissenting opinion in Hyde Amendment case, 18, 25

INDEX

Brooke, Senator Edward, opposes Hyde Amendment, vii, 15, 16, 19

Brown, Lester R., worldwide deforestation promotes disaster, 176
why world population will level off sooner than most observers predict, 202

Califano, Joseph A., Jr., stops Medicaid payments for abortion, 16

Callahan, Dr. Daniel approves sex education for teenagers, 52 53; opposes "Pastoral Plan," 90, 91

Callahan, Sidney Cornelia, strongly critical of rhythm method, 112

Carter, President Jimmy, opposes legal abortion, 53

Carter, Rosalyn, approves legal abortion, 53

Casti Connubii encyclical (Pius XI), 110, 111

Catholics favoring legalized abortion, 79, 80

Catholic Theological Society of America favors contraception, 44, 45

Catholics United for the Faith castigates contraception, 3, 5

child abuse
statistics on, 60-62
self-perpetuating, 61

childbearing rates among adolescents, 49, 50

children, sexual abuse of, 60, 61

Chile, nearly one-third of pregnancies end in abortion, 42, 43

China, sharp drop in birthrate over recent five year period, 203

Christianity's debt to Judaism, 93-96

Church, Senator Frank, 204, 205

Commonweal magazine, favors legalized abortion, 12

Committee for the Survival of a Free Congress, opposes legalized abortion, 3

Comstock, Anthony, rabid reformer, 70, 71

Comstock Law, 5, 70

Constitutional Amendment to outlaw abortion favored by hierarchy, 10-12

Constitutional Amendment to outlaw abortion, states favoring, 35

contraception
1930 Lambeth Conference, affect on, 72, 109, 110
regarded as homicide by Church Fathers, 105, 107
changes in attitude by Catholics, 107, 108
by entire world, 108-110
banned by Pius XI in 1930 encyclical
Casti Connubii, 110, 111
Pius XII opens door a trifle with approval of rhyhm method, 111

Robert C. Cook says world is running out of arable land, 177

Cooke, Terence Cardinal, dissents from Supreme Court's decision on abortion, 8

criminals spawned by unwanted births, 65-67

Culver, Senator John, 204, 205

custodial institutions, abuse of children in, 64-65

deforestation, affects of, 174-176

Diet for a Small Planet (Lappe), 152

Dolan, Terry, founder and director of NICPAC, 205

Dooling, Judge John F.:
suspends operation of Hyde Amendment, 16
his restraining order overturned by Supreme Court, 16
holds Hyde Amendment unconstitutional in test case, *McRae vs. Califano,* 23-24
reversed by Supreme Court in 5-4 decision, 24-25
Justices Brennan, Blackmun, Marshall and Stevens strongly dissent, 25-26

222

INDEX

Dornan, Congressman Robert, fails in attempt to outlaw contraception, 34, 35

Dow Chemical Company, 204

Drinan, Father Robert F., S.J., speaks for liberal element of his church, 89, 90

East, Senator John, iv

Ehrlich, Dr. Paul R., paints gloomy picture of starving millions in Third World, 163

Says illegal abortion rampant in Latin America, 42, 43

Ethics of Feticide (O'Malley), 46

Ewell, Dr. Raymond, says world population most serious problem ever faced by human race, 159

Falk, Richard A., says food shortage imperils world, 159-163

Family Planning in an Exploding Population (Ed. by O'Brien) 42

Famine—1975! (Paul and William Paddock) 152

fertility control,
difficulties in India, 189
Indian government decrees compulsory sterilization, 190, 191

"Filthy Five," corporations so-called by Environmental Action, 204, 205

Food First; Beyond the Myth of Scarcity (Lappe-Collins), 153

food production, affects of pollution on, 178, 179

food, important new sources of, 179, 181

German measles epidemic of 1963, 75

Gibson, Melisha, four-year-old child beaten to death by stepfather, 59-60

Global 2000 Report confirms author's documentation, vi

Grassley, Senator Charles, 204, 205

Greeley, Father Andrew M., blames hierarchy for mass exodus from church, 46, 47

"Green Revolution," reason for failure, 177

Guttmacher, Dr. Allan says objective of pro-choice advocates is to eliminate the need for abortion, 41, 42

Guttmacher, Alan Institute
first national survey of affects of Hyde Amendment, 36, 37
proposes massive program for family planning, 53-55

Handbook on Abortion (Dr. J. C. and Barbara Willke) 87

Hardin, Dr. Garrett:

importance of child being wanted, 58

properly performed abortion not dangerous, 74

sociological advantages of legalized abortion, 93

"life-boat ethics," 196, 197

Harper's Magazine article, "Enemies of Abortion," by Marion K. Sanders, 87, 88

Catholic League for Religious Rights protests article, 97

Helms, Senator Jesse, seeks to ban abortion through Constitutional Amendment, 35

Hierarchy, Roman Catholic
opposes legal abortion, 1, 2

declares "Holy War" against abortion, 10-12

drafts parochial school children for anti-abortion demonstrations, 32, 33

opposes fertility control of any kind, 186

Hopcraft, Arthur, describes Third World's appalling conditions, 160

Human Fertility (Cook) 177

Humanae Vitae, Pope Paul's encyclical banning birth control, see Pope Paul VI)

Hungry Planet (Borgstrom) 158-161

Hyde, Congressman Henry J., (R-IL) iv; introduces Hyde Amendment, 14

223

Hyde Amendment
  bitter struggle in Senate, 15;
  opposition to, 21; cost to taxpayers, 19, 36; costs to society,
  38, 39; sociological affects of,
  36-39

India
  problems of fertility control, 189
  introduces first compulsory sterilization program, 191; reasons for failure of, 191

Innocent III, Pope (1198-1216)
  lights fires of Inquisition that
  destroys Languedoc, 4
  irrigation, limitations of 181,
  183

Italy
  repeals laws restricting contraception, 4
  great number of abortions before
  repeal, 42
  legalizes and subsidizes abortion,
  98, 99

Japan
  swamped by population explosion, 147; General Douglas
  MacArthur, leader of Occupation Forces, surrenders to
  Catholic opposition, refuses
  to help Japan control fertility, 147, 148; refuses entry
  permit to Margaret Sanger,
  advocate of contraception,
  148
Japanese Diet attacks problem by
  legalizing abortion, 148; massive contraception program
  produces lasting results, 149

Kasten, Senator Bob, 204, 205
Kennedy, President John F., promotes family planning program, 132
Konner, Dr. Melvin J., tells about
  epidemic of teenage pregnancy, 48, 49
Krol, John Cardinal, opposes legal
  abortion, 8

Lader, Lawrence, on abortion,
  43, 72

Lambeth Conference of 1930
  makes contraception morally
  acceptable, 72, 109, 110
Latin America resists fertility control, 187, 188; Mexico relaxes
  opposition, 188, 190
"license to lie" 205, 206

McGovern, Senator George,
  204, 205
McRae vs. Califano, test case for
  Hyde Amendment, 23
Maddox, Ronald, sentenced to 99
  years for killing four-year-old
  step-daughter, 59, 60
Mandatory Motherhood (Hardin)
  58
Marshall, Justice Thurgood, warns
  against restrictive laws on contraception and abortion, 22;
  criticizes majority ruling on
  Hyde Amendment, 25, 26, 38
Mitchell, Congressman Parren J.,
  tells why blacks oppose Hyde
  Amendment, 37, 39
Moral Majority, promotes funda-
  mentalists' control of politics,
  4

NARAL (National Abortion
  Rights Action League) de-
  feats anti-abortion candidates,
  19, 21; activation of Hyde
  Amendment brings big increase in membership, 21
National Catholic Reporter rejects
  "Pastoral Plan," 11, 12
National Council of Catholic Bishops (NCCB) announces "Par-
  toral Plan," 11, 12
National Family Planning forum
  backs increased family services, 54, 55; projects cumulative savings under program,
  55, 57
Nelson, Senator Gaylord, 204, 205
New York City
  near bankrutpcy largely due to
  generous welfare program,
  142; typical example, 143
New York State, affects of 1970
  law legalizing abortion, 77, 78

Nixon, President Richard M., attacks legalized abortion and dissemination of contraceptive information, 133

O'Brien, Father John A., criticizes hierarchy's policy on contraception, 42
Occidental Petroleum, 204
O'Malley, Dr. Austin, expresses medieval position of Roman church on abortion, 46

Pakistan, efforts at birth control fail, 193, 194
Pastoral Plan for Pro-Life Activities launched by hierarchy, 10-14
  opposed by all three of America's leading Catholic magazines: *America, National Catholic Reporter, The Commonweal,* 10-12
Protestant-Jewish protest, 96, 97
  largely to blame for mass exodus of Catholics from their church, 101
Pediatric Bill of Rights, 51, 52
Planned Parenthood
  strives to eliminate *need* for abortion, 29.
  attacks on by "pro-lifers," 31, cuts abortions in Corpus Christi, 43
  promotes alternatives to abortion, 53, 54
polls on abortion, 13
Pope Paul VI
  bans birth control with encyclical
  Humanae Vitae, 40, 41
  opposition to *Humanae Vitae* by leading Catholic theologians, 116, 118
  encyclical opposed by many Catholic authors, 120, 126
  Father Greeley says that encyclical is responsible for massive loss in Catholic membership and financial support, 117
  severely criticized by *National Catholic Reporter,* 125, 126
  also criticized by majority report of Papal Birth Control Commission, 126
  defended by minority report of Commission, 127
  criticized by American Association for Advancement of Science, 128, 129
  denounced by Catholic physicians, 130
  ignored by majority of Catholic women, 130, 131
Pope Pius XI bans contraception in 1930 encyclical, *Casti Connubii,* 110, 111
Pope Pius XII authorizes rhythm method of birth control, 111
Poplis, George, convicted of murdering his three-year-old stepdaughter, 60
Population Bomb (Ehrlich), 163
Population-Resources-Environment (Paul and Anne Ehrlich), 42, 43
population problem
  in 1977 world population reaches four billion, 157; slight decline in birth rate of a few countries in latter 1970s, 158; only solution lies in universal birth control, 203
pregnancy among teenagers, 47, 52

Quayle, Senator Don, 204, 205

Reagan, President Ronald, iv
Religions Coalition for Abortion Rights opposes Pastoral Plan, 99
rhythm method, scientists warn against, 112, 113

Sanger, Margaret; Pioneer of Birth Control (Lader-Meltzer) 104
Sanger, Margaret, chiefly responsible for sane attitude toward contraception in U. S. and many foreign countries, 105
Sarbanes, Senator Paul, 205, 206
sex education, importance of, 2; endorsed by Dr. Daniel Callahan, 52

sexual abuse of children, 60, 61

Simon, Roger, says Supreme Court decision upholding Hyde Amendment means "all the justice that money can buy," 26, 27

sociological effects of Hyde Amendment, 36, 39

South America, illegal abortions in, 42, 43

Standard Oil of Indiana, 204

Stokes, Congressman Louis tells why Black Caucus opposes Hyde Amendment, 14, 15

Symms, Senator Steven, 204, 205

teenagers, sexual activity among, 49, 51
  pregnancy and childbearing among, 49, 51
  rate of illigitmate births among, 50, 51

Tennessee Volunteers for Life, 45

Third World
  Arthur Hopcraft tells of appalling conditions in, 160
  billions in aid have had little effect, 199
  shocking situations in Peru, Kenya and India, 200
  similar failures in Poland and Burma, 200
  greedy corporations force costly, dangerous feeding formulas on poverty-stricken mothers of Third World, 154

This Hungry World (Vicker), 154, 155

Thomas, John H. criticizes hierachy's opposition to birth control, 195, 196

Title X of Public Health Service Act, 54, 55

Twenty-ninth Day (Brown) 176

United Nations, finally engages in global birth control, 187

U. S. Catholic Conference (USCC) announces Pastoral Plan for Pro-Life Activities, 11

United States Coalition for Life opposes family planning services, 4, 5

United States
  temporary decline in birth rate, 134, 135
  illegal immigration swells population growth, 135, 137
  problems caused by refugees, 137, 139
  Catholic bishops oppose any curbs on fertility, 140, 141
  frightful cost of AFDC program, 141, 142

U. S. Supreme Court
  legalize abortion, 7
  reverses Judge Dooley's first decision on Hyde Amendment, 16
  by 5-4 upholds Hyde Amendment, 23, 25
  1976 decision gives green light to Political Action Committees, 205

unwanted births, chief factor in child abuse, 62

Vatican position on birth control announced by Pius XI in encyclical Casti Connubii, 2

Vicker, Roy, points out problem of accommodating surplus world population, 154, 155

Weyerhaeuser Company, 204

Willke, Dr. J. C. and wife Barbara, authors of Handbook on Abortion.
  rabid anti-abortionists, 87, 88
  grossly exaggerate dangers of abortion, 87, 88
  nation's strongest proponents of anti-abortion position, 89

women's rights, supporters of, 103, 104

World Food Conference in Rome (1974) 155, 156
  American aid underrated, 156
  Conference bitter disappointment, 191, 192

World Food Conference of 1976 (Ames, Iowa) accomplishes little, 193

World Population Conference of 1976 (Vancouver, B. C.) challenges delegates to set "minimum standards of decent housing for all the world," 193; up to press time, no takers. 193

World Population Problem
most serious to face human race, 159
population growth proceeds at geometrical rate. 165
problem due chiefly to falling death rates, rising birth rates, 165, 166

table showing population growth rates for underdeveloped countries, 167-169

food shortage not only problem, 170, 171

in 1971 legal abortion was available to only 38 percent of world population. in 1981 it was 68 percent, 203

Zero Population Growth organization backs increased family services, 54

University Club of Chicago

76 EAST MONROE STREET
CHICAGO, ILLINOIS 60603

(312) 726-2840

April 15, 1981

Mr. A_____ F_____
_____ W. Madison Street
Chicago, Ill. 60602

Dear Mr._____:

Several of your fellow members have expressed
an interest in the book, "You Can Stop Arthritis"
that you so kindly donated to the library last
year. The book proved most popular, but unfortunately, as I explained to you recently, has disappeared from the library. Under the circumstances
would it be possible to get an additional copy?

I would greatly appreciate your efforts in our
behalf.

Sincerely yours

Jane Hanrahan, Libn.

YOU CAN STOP

ARTHRITIS

(By the same Author)

As you can see from the letter reproduced on the opposite page, a member of the exclusive University Club of Chicago found this book too tempting to resist.

No one should judge him too harshly, for after all, "Self-preservation is the first law of Nature." Furthermore, according to our leading psychologists, "there's a bit of larceny in *all* of us!"

"A delightful book," says the Dean of one of America's leading medical schools, "far ahead of its time."

"Beyond a doubt," says *Bestways Magazine,* "the author's regime worked wonders for him. An octogenarian happily approaching his ninetieth birthday, he's 'healthy as a playful pup and spry as a cricket.' "

If you are tempted to beg, borrow or steal a copy of this book, we say *"Don't!"* After all, it's only $2.50 at your favorite book store. (If you prefer to order direct from the publisher, please add 75c for postage/handling).

Tennessee Residents
Please Add 6% Sales Tax

ISBN# 0-965680-0-X

VITA PRESS

2143 Poplar Avenue - Memphis, TN - 38104

WALDO ZIMMERMANN was born in the last decade of the last century—December of 1892 to be exact. He is a graduate of Vanderbilt University School of Law (LL.B. '15). Not finding the practice of great interest, he gave up the Law to enter the field of advertising, spending most of his business life as a copywriter and account executive in major advertising agencies of Chicago and New York, and as Director of Advertising for a Chicago pharmaceutical house. Upon his retirement in the later 1950s he returned to his home town, Memphis, and engaged in free lance writing.

Born and reared a Catholic, his interest in religion, though chiefly academic, was too universal to be confined to any particular creed. Over a period of many years he has been engrossed in the study of religious history, the world's great religions, the peaks and valleys of the Enlightenment and the travail of religious freedom. There's no way to pinpoint his "religion," but perhaps it can best be described as a combination of Agnosticism and Pantheistic Humanism.

During most of his life the author has had conservative leanings, but in recent years the extreme "one issue" conservatives have forced a radical change in his position. To those who don't agree with his views as expressed in this book he can only say—along with the embattled Luther—*"Here I stand. I can do no other!"*